Heidegger's Philosophy of Art

This book, the first comprehensive study in English of Heidegger's philosophy of art, starts in the mid-1930s with Heidegger's discussion of the Greek temple and his Hegelian declaration that a great artwork gathers together an entire culture in affirmative celebration of its foundational 'truth', and that, by this criterion, art in modernity is 'dead'. His subsequent work on Hölderlin, whom he later identified as the decisive influence on his mature philosophy, led him into a passionate engagement with the art of Rilke, Cézanne, Klee and Zen Buddhism, liberating him not only from the overly restrictive conception of art of the mid-1930s but also from the disastrous politics of the period. Drawing on material hitherto unknown in the anglophone world, Young establishes a new account of Heidegger's philosophy of art and shows that his famous essay 'The Origin of the Work of Art' is its beginning, not its end.

JULIAN YOUNG is Honorary Research Fellow in Philosophy at the University of Auckland. His previous publications include *Willing and Unwilling: A Study in the Philosophy of Arthur Schopenhauer* (1987), *Nietzsche's Philosophy of Art* (1992), and *Heidegger, Philosophy, Nazism* (1997).

Heidegger's Philosophy of Art

Julian Young

University of Auckland

CAMBRIDGE
UNIVERSITY PRESS

PUBLISHED BY THE PRESS SYNDICATE OF THE UNIVERSITY OF CAMBRIDGE
The Pitt Building, Trumpington Street, Cambridge, United Kingdom

CAMBRIDGE UNIVERSITY PRESS
The Edinburgh Building, Cambridge CB2 2RU, UK
40 West 20th Street, New York NY 10011–4211, USA
477 Williamstown Road, Port Melbourne, VIC 3207, Australia
Ruiz de Alarcón 13, 28014 Madrid, Spain
Dock House, The Waterfront, Cape Town 8001, South Africa

http://www.cambridge.org

First published 2001
First paperback edition 2004

Typeface Times New Roman 10.25/13.5 pt   *System* QuarkXPress™   [SE]

A catalogue record for this book is available from the British Library

ISBN 0 521 79176 6 hardback
ISBN 0 521 61622 0 paperback

For Becky and Tori

Contents

List of illustrations   *page* ix
Acknowledgments   xi
List of abbreviations   xii

Introduction   1

1   'The Origin of the Work of Art'   5
    Hegel and the 'death of art'   6
    Heidegger's endorsement of Hegel   7
    'Aesthetics' and the death of art   8
    'Aesthetics' and 'enlightenment'   12
    Heidegger's rejection of Hegel   14
    The question: what is art?   15
    Expanding the concept of art   16
    Art as the 'opening up of world'   19
    What is a 'world'?   21
    Ontology and ethics   25
    What is 'opening up'?   29
    What is 'earth'?   38
    'Earth' in the artwork   41
    Difficulties in the account of 'earth' in the artwork   46
    Great art is communal   50
    The artwork creates a people   52
    The artwork preserves a people   57
    Clarity and the priority of poetry   60
    Heidegger's self-criticisms   61

2   Hölderlin: the early texts   69
    'The Essence of Poetry'   72
    'The absence and arrival of the gods'   73
    Poetry, thought and politics   76
    Not poet but thinker   78
    Graecocentricism   80

3   Hölderlin: the later texts   84
     The festival   84
     The modern poet's exclusion from 'the highest essence of art'   89
     What are poets for in 'needy times'? The modern paradigm   94
     The Apollonian and the Dionysian   96
     The epic and the lyric   100
     Is Hölderlin a poet for 'needy times'?   101
     Poetry and prose   102
     The *Ereignis*   105
     From the sublime to the holy   108
     From Nikeism to waiting   111
     Knowledge or faith?   115

4   Modern art   120
     Anti-metaphysical art   123
     Another 'turn'   124
     What is dwelling?   128
     Supernaturalism   134
     Naturalism   140
     Rilke   143
     East Asian art   147
     Cézanne   150
     Klee   158
     Cubism   162
     Abstract art   166
     Music   168
     A *philosophy* of art?   171

Index   175

Illustrations

1 Temple of Hera II (so-called Temple of Neptune),   *page* 20
  Paestum. Reproduced by permission of Scala/Art Resource,
  NY
2 Paul Cézanne, *The Gardener Vallier*, c. 1906. Reproduced by   151
  permission of the Tate Gallery, London
3 Paul Cézanne, *Mont Sainte-Victoire seen from the Colline des*   156
  Larves, 1904–6. Reproduced by permission of Kunsthaus, Zürich
4 Paul Klee, *Saint from a Window*, 1940. Reproduced by   160
  permission of the Paul-Klee-Stiftung, Kunstmuseum, Bern

Acknowledgments

I should like to express my thanks to Friedrich Voit, Thomas Rohkrämer, Jeff Malpas, Christoph Jamme, Günter Seubold, Herman van Erp, Charles Guignon, Armin von Ungern-Sternberg and Rebecca Young (the elder) who in various ways have made this a better book than it would otherwise have been. Also to my Auckland students, in particular, Hannah Slade, Sean Sturm, Karl Stevens and Jonathan Oosterman, for the sympathetic yet searching examination to which, on a weekly basis, they subjected both Heidegger's and my own ideas. My greatest debt is to Hubert Dreyfus, who twice went through versions of the manuscript with a fine scalpel. (Notwithstanding, there remains a great deal with which he would certainly disagree.)

Abbreviations

Primary works

BT *Being and Time*, tr. J. Macquarrie and T. Robinson (Oxford: Blackwell, 1962). References are to the pagination of the 7th German edition of *Sein und Zeit* given by Macquarrie and Robinson in the margins

BP *The Basic Problems of Phenomenology*, tr. A. Hofstadter (Bloomington: Indiana University Press, 1988)

BW *Martin Heidegger: Basic Writings*, ed. D. F. Krell (San Francisco: Harper and Row, 1977)

D *Denkerfahrungen 1910–1976* (Frankfurt-on-Main: Klostermann, 1983)

DK 'Denken und Kunst' in *Japan und Heidegger – Gedenkschrift der Stadt Messkirch zum hundertsten Geburtstag Martin Heideggers* (Sigmarinen: J. Thorbecke, 1989), pp. 211–15

DT *Discourse on Thinking*, tr. J. M. Anderson and E. H. Freund (San Francisco: Harper and Row, 1966)

GA *Martin Heidegger: Gesamtausgabe*, ed. F.-W. von Herrmann (Frankfurt-on-Main: Klostermann, 1977 and onwards). Numerals refer to volume numbers from this collected work

HE 'Hölderlin and the Essence of Poetry' in *Existence and Being*, ed. W. Brock (London: Vision, 1949), pp. 291–315

ID *Identität und Differenz* (Pfullingen: Neske, 1990)

IM *An Introduction to Metaphysics*, tr. R. Mannheim (New Haven: Yale University Press, 1959)

Ister *Hölderlin's Hymn 'The Ister'*, tr. W. McNeill and J. Davis (Bloomington: Indiana University Press, 1996)

N   *Nietzsche*, 4 volumes, tr. D. F. Krell (San Francisco: Harper-
Collins, 1979–82). Roman numerals refer to volume numbers

OWL *On the Way to Language*, tr. P. D. Herz (San Francisco: Harper
and Row, 1982)

P   *Pathmarks*, ed. W. McNeill (Cambridge: Cambridge University
Press, 1998)

PLT   *Poetry, Language, Thought*, tr. A. Hofstadter (New York:
Harper and Row, 1971)

QCT *The Question Concerning Technology and Other Essays*, tr. W.
Lovitt (San Francisco: Harper and Row, 1977)

SvG *Der Satz vom Grund* (Pfullingen: Neske, 1978)

ZSD *Zur Sache des Denkens* (Tübingen: Niemeyer, 1976)

Secondary works

E   *Erinnerung an Martin Heidegger*, ed. G. Neske (Pfullingen:
Neske, 1977)

HPN *Heidegger, Philosophy, Nazism*, by Julian Young (Cambridge:
Cambridge University Press, 1997)

KuT *Kunst und Technik*, ed. W. Biemel and F.-W. von Hermann
(Frankfurt-on-Main: Klostermann, 1989)

HC   *The Heidegger Controversy: A Critical Reader*, ed. R. Wolin
(Cambridge, Mass.: MIT Press, 1993)

Introduction

1. Discussions of Heidegger's philosophy of art usually begin and end with his celebrated (or infamous) 1935–6 essay, 'The Origin of the Work of Art'. That they begin here is appropriate – 1935 indeed marks the beginning of Heidegger's serious philosophical engagement with art – but that they end at the same point is, for at least two reasons, highly unfortunate. The first is that, profound, original and seminal though the work is, it is also, as later on Heidegger clearly recognized, in important respects seriously inadequate. The second is that though indeed the beginning, the essay is *no more than* the beginning of Heidegger's 'path of thinking (*Denkweg*)' about art, a path which had, in fact, another forty years to run. The subsequent shape of that path, I shall argue, is largely determined by his dawning awareness of the inadequacy of its beginning.

Heidegger's thinking in the mid-1930s is overshadowed by Hegel's celebrated thesis of the 'death of art'. 'Great', non-trivial, art, he agrees with Hegel, has been, since Greece or, at best, the end of the Middle Ages, a thing of the past. Though, unlike Hegel, holding that great art *could*, one day, return, and holding that such a return (as constituting nothing less than the 'salvation' of the West) is devoutly to be desired, Heidegger agrees with Hegel that the present age is, in essence, 'art-less'. In chapter 1 I outline the conception of art – I call it 'the Greek paradigm' – which leads to this conclusion.

2. In the final decades of his life Heidegger came to have a great love for, in fact, a considerable number of modern artists: *inter alios*, Rilke, Stefan George, le Corbusier, Stravinsky, Georges Braque, Klee and Cézanne. And he developed a considerable personal involvement in the art world. Evidently, therefore, in order to bring his theorizing about art into line

with his love for, and knowledge of, modern art, something had to be done about the Greek paradigm. Yet even in 1935 theory and knowledge were already in tension. For already, at the time of writing 'The Origin of the Work of Art', Heidegger possessed an abiding and thoughtful love for the work of the early Romantic poet, Friedrich Hölderlin.

In chapter 2 I examine Heidegger's attempt to reconcile this tension in, as I call them, the 'early' Hölderlin discussions of 1935–6. I try to show how, unable to see beyond the Greek paradigm, and conscious of the impossibility of representing Hölderlin as a poet of the same type as Homer or Sophocles, Heidegger is driven to distort his importance into that of, not a poet, but rather a philosophical thinker – a thinker, moreover, whose thoughts look suspiciously similar to Heidegger's own.

In chapter 3 I show how, through a deeper and more open understanding of Hölderlin – through, as I put it, Heidegger's allowing himself to be 'educated' by the poet – the 'later' Hölderlin texts (1939–46) finally abandon, not the Greek paradigm as such – which is far too interesting, important, and, as Nietzsche would say, 'pregnant with future' to suffer such a fate – but rather its tyrannous role in his thought. From Hölderlin's metapoetical account of his own work, his account of 'what poets are for' in the 'needy times' of modernity (as opposed to the thriving times of Greece) Heidegger takes over a second paradigm of greatness – or at least 'validity' (*PLT* p. 96) – in art, a paradigm I refer to as 'the modern paradigm'. This new pluralism in his thinking, I suggest, allows him, finally, an undistorted understanding of Hölderlin's poetry.

In chapter 4 I show how it was the acknowledgment of the modern paradigm that enables Heidegger to overcome his blanket alienation from the art of his own age. I show how his Hölderlin-induced conviction that the essential task of art in the 'dis-enchanted' age of modernity is to 'found the holy' grounds his interest in, and shapes his reading of, in particular, Rilke, Cézanne and Klee. It grounds, too, I argue, his *rapprochement* with the East, with, in particular, the art of Zen Buddhism.

My story is, then, a history of intellectual development and personal integration; of how a great thinker, starting out from an account of art that condemned him, *qua* philosopher, to a stance of complete alienation from the art of his own times, thought his way out of a position which, as a passionate lover of, in the event, a great deal of modern art, and as himself a poet of no mean ability, he had always really known to be an error. The hero of my story – or rather the other hero – is Hölderlin. For Heidegger, I shall argue, it was Hölderlin who was, in the poet's own language, the 'saving power', not only with respect to art but also, as we will see, with respect to politics.

3. I shall, as I chart the development of Heidegger's 'path of thinking' about art, introduce a potentially bewildering number of different Heideggers. Let me say, therefore, something about how they are related. Heidegger himself identifies a 'turn' in his philosophy as having begun in 1930. Since, he also says, however, that it was not completed until the transition to '*Ereignis*-thinking' in 1936–8 (see *GA* 15, p. 344 and p. 366), he himself invites us to contemplate three (of course related) thinkers: an early (pre-1930) Heidegger, a middle or transitional thinker (1930–8), and a late Heidegger (post-1938). In chapter 4 (section 3), however, I shall argue for the recognition of yet another 'turn' as occurring in about 1946. So in addition to Heidegger's three, I shall identify a fourth, as I shall sometimes say, a 'post-war' Heidegger.

4. One further preliminary matter (for scholars: this section should be skipped by those with no previous acquaintance with Heidegger). A great deal of trouble in trying to understand the '*Sein*' in Heidegger's '*Seinsphilosophie*' (the 'Being' in his 'philosophy of Being') is caused by the fact that, usually without being very explicit or helpful about it, he in fact uses '*Sein*' in two central, but quite different, senses. In at least one place, however, in 'What are Poets for?', he clearly distinguishes these senses.[1] On the one hand, he says, there is 'being in the sense of lightening-unifying presence'. This is what he elsewhere calls 'the clearing', that which allows the beings of our world to be intelligible as the beings they are. On the other hand, he says, there is 'Being' in the sense of 'beings in the . . . plenitude (*Vollzähligkeit*) of all their facets (*Seiten*)' (*PLT* p. 124), including those that are unknown, and indeed unintelligible, to us; 'views of the appearances of what are to our representing

---

[1] Also at *DT* p. 76, P 309–10, and in *Martin Heidegger in Conversation*, ed. R. Wisser, tr. S. Murthy (New Delhi: Heinemann, 1970), pp. 44–5.

objects' which belong on the other 'side' of our 'horizon' of intelligibility (*DT* pp. 64–5).

The essence of '*Sein*' in the first sense is, as Heidegger puts it in *Being
and Time*, 'intelligibility' (*BT* 152). But in the second it is precisely the
opposite; unintelligibility, 'the mystery' (*P* pp. 136ff.), 'the ungraspable'
(*Ister* p. 136). Sometimes, but by no means consistently, Heidegger marks
this second sense by writing '*Sein*' with the 'i' replaced by the antique 'y'.
(The practice is more pronounced in earlier Heidegger but persists later
on as well; see, for example, *P* p. 144, footnote a). Mimicking this practice, I will, throughout this study, use the capitalized 'Being' to mark the
second sense, and the lower case 'being' to mark the first. Where I wish to
remain neutral between the senses, I shall retreat to the German '*Sein*'.

1   'The Origin of the Work of Art'

1. As mentioned in the introduction, Heidegger first turned to extended thinking about art in the mid-1930s.[1] In close proximity to each other he produced the lectures on Hölderlin's 'Germania' and 'The Rhine' (*GA* 39) of 1934–5, the *Introduction to Metaphysics* (*IM*) of 1935, in which art receives considerable attention, 'Hölderlin and the Essence of Poetry' (HE) of early 1936, the final (of three[2]) versions of 'The Origin of the Work of Art' (*PLT* pp. 17–87) of late 1936, and *The Will to Power as Art* (*N* I) (the first volume of the four-volume Nietzsche study) of 1936–7.

Of all these works, 'The Origin of the Work of Art' (hereafter 'The Origin') has received by far the greatest amount of attention, an attention which can only be described as obsessive. (Its reverie on Van Gogh's painting of shoes – a testament to Heidegger's early love of Van Gogh but almost completely irrelevant to, indeed, as we shall see, inconsistent with, the real thrust of the essay – has given rise to a baroque foliage of secondary literature that has had progressively less and less to do with Heidegger.) Discussions of Heidegger's philosophy of art usually confine themselves to this work, taking it to be the full and final statement of that philosophy. This, as already intimated, is for several reasons a highly unfortunate assumption. First, because the only hope of producing an intelligible reading of this tortuously enigmatic work lies in integrating it into the surrounding texts of the same period of thinking. Second, because, as mentioned, it is only the *beginning* of Heidegger's 'path of thinking' about art. And third, because it contains fundamental

---

[1] A significant exception to this is the substantial discussion of a passage from Rilke's *Notebooks of Malte Laurids Brigge* in the 1927 *The Basic Problems of Phenomenology* (*BP* pp. 171–2).

[2] See Jacques Taminiaux's 'The Origin of "The Origin of the Work of Art"' in *Reading Heidegger*, ed. J. Sallis (Bloomington: Indiana University Press, 1993), pp. 392–404.

deficiencies. As, *inter alia*, the forty-two mostly sharply self-critical foot-notes Heidegger insisted (*GA* 5, p. 379) on including in the final, *Gesamtausgabe* edition of the work (*GA* 5, pp. 1–74) make clear, later Heidegger was well aware of these deficiencies. In this chapter I shall be concerned to understand first the work itself, and then the most impor-tant of Heidegger's own criticisms of it.[3] One of these is of particular sig-nificance since the subsequent development of his 'path' is, I shall suggest, largely determined by his awareness of the difficulty raised by the criti-cism and the attempt to rectify it.

Hegel and the 'death of art'

2. In the 'Epilogue' to 'The Origin' (*PLT* pp. 79–81) (completed at an unknown time between 1936 and the 1956 'Addendum' (*PLT* pp. 82–7)), as well as in chapter 13 of *The Will to Power as Art*, Heidegger indicates the fundamental concerns of the essay by positioning it in relation to Hegel's celebrated thesis of the 'death of art'. As Heidegger presents it, Hegel's thesis can be represented in terms of the following four propo-sitions. (1) Art in its 'highest vocation' – 'great' art, Heidegger calls it (*PLT* p. 40)[4] – is art in which 'the truth of beings as a whole i.e. the unconditioned, the absolute, opens itself up' to 'man's historical exis-tence' (*N* I, p. 84); to, that is, a given, historically located, culture. (2) Great art (but not of course all art, or even all art of 'quality') is, for us, a thing of the past and has been since the time of Plato or, at the very

---

[3] A further reason the obsessive attention paid to 'The Origin' has proved, in the anglophone world, unfortunate, lies in the unreliable quality of the sole English translation – by Albert Hofstadter in *Poetry, Language, Thought* (*PLT*). The work contains many interpolations that correspond to nothing in the German, omissions, blunders of translation, infelicities, and moments of unintended humour arising from the translator's being a non-native speaker of English, which I shall mention as and when the need arises. (It also contains many carelessnesses that have been allowed to stand for thirty years. On p. 44, for example, '*Welt*' appears as 'word' rather than 'world', on p. 133 '*Predikation*' as 'prediction' instead of 'predication'.) The widespread anglophone belief that later Heidegger lapses into unin-telligible quasi-mysticism has, I suspect, received not a little help from the failings of the Hofstadter translation. (Conversely, the much better reception of early Heidegger has, I suspect, been significantly aided by the superb quality of Macquarrie and Robinson's trans-lation of *Being and Time*.)

[4] Heidegger says that 'great' art is the only kind of art 'under consideration' in the essay (*PLT* p. 40), meaning that he uses 'art', 'artwork', and so on as abbreviations of 'great art' and 'great artwork'. In this chapter I shall often follow him in this practice.

latest, the end of the Middle Ages. (3) Great art (in, at least, the West) is not only dead but *must remain so*. The inexorable, dialectical laws of history that led to the supersession of its 'truth'-disclosing function by religion, which was in turn superseded by science, are inexorable. History never repeats a more primitive stage of itself but is, rather, a record of uninterrupted progress, of the ever-increasing perfection of the world. (4) Since this is so, the death of art, like the passing of child-hood, while an occasion, perhaps, for nostalgia and expressions of grat-itude, is no cause for serious regret.

Heidegger's endorsement of Hegel

3. Heidegger's stance towards the Hegelian position is as follows. With regard to the first proposition – the Hegelian definition of (great) art – he is in full agreement. In the Nietzsche volume he says, to repeat, that 'great art' is great insofar as it 'makes manifest' the 'truth of beings as a whole i.e. the unconditioned, the absolute' (*N* I, p. 84). What is important here, is the 'i.e.': it is used to equate Hegel's characteristic term 'the absolute' with his own 'truth of beings'. In 'The Origin' itself, as we will see, Heidegger's leading idea is that the great artwork is 'the happening of truth', i.e. 'truth of beings' (*PLT* p. 39). It is clear, therefore, that, on the side of the content of the artwork, *what* it is that it 'makes manifest', Heidegger takes himself to be repeating (or maybe interpreting) Hegel. Moreover, on the side of the receivers of the artwork, those to whom the manifestation is made, he again agrees with Hegel. Where Hegel holds that great art manifests 'truth' to (in Heidegger's *précis*) 'man's historical existence' (*N* I, p. 84), Heidegger himself says that great art is the 'trans-porting of a people into its endowment (*Mitgegebene*)' (*PLT* p. 77). Given, as an educated guess would suggest, that 'endowment' is another word for 'truth', what Heidegger is doing here is agreeing with Hegel that nothing less than the reception of the artwork by a culture ('people') as a whole is sufficient to establish its 'greatness'. Art is only great if, like the Greek temple or medieval cathedral, it possesses *world-historical* signifi-cance.

Heidegger also agrees with Hegel's second proposition. In the *Lecture on Aesthetics* of 1828–9 Hegel says (and Heidegger quotes) that

Art no longer counts for us as the highest manner in which truth obtains existence for itself. One may well hope that art will continue to advance and perfect itself, but its form has ceased to be the highest need of the spirit. In all these relationships art is, and remains for us, on the side of its highest vocation, something past (*PLT* p. 80). The magnificent days of Greek art, like the golden era of the later Middle Ages, are gone. (*N* I, p. 84)

Heidegger says that, for us, this judgment is 'in force' (*PLT* p. 80). For him, as for Hegel, the totality of the art of the post-medieval, that is, modern, world is, even at its best, something less (actually a lot less) than great.

'Aesthetics' and the death of art

4. Why should this be the case? Why does none of the art of modernity qualify as 'great'? Heidegger's answer is contained in one word, 'aesthetics':

Aesthetics takes the work of art as an object, the object of *aisthesis*, of sensuous apprehension in the wide sense. Today we call this apprehension experience. The way in which man experiences art is taken to provide information as to its essence. Experience is the source that is the standard not only for art appreciation and enjoyment but also for artistic creation. Yet perhaps experience is the element in which art dies. The dying occurs so slowly that it takes a few centuries. (*PLT* p. 79)

As a synonym for 'philosophy of art', Heidegger observes in the Nietzsche volume, 'aesthetics' came into being as the result of a division of labour first explicitly carried out in the eighteenth century.[5] As 'logic' was understood as the establishment of systematic knowledge of *logos*, of judgment and thought, 'ethics' of character and behaviour, so 'aesthetics' was knowledge of *aisthetike*, of 'sensations and feelings and how these are determined' (*N* I, pp. 77–8). The point Heidegger seeks to emphasize is that the introduction of this synonymy (indeed, surveying the contemporary scene, the virtual *replacement* of 'philosophy of art' by 'aesthetics') is no mere matter of terminology but represents, rather, the triumph, in both theory and practice, of a particular conception of art over an older, as one might call it, 'ethical' conception which took for granted that the point of art was to be 'truth'-disclosing, to disclose to its

---

[5] Specifically by Alexander Baumgarten in his *Reflections of Poetry* of 1735.

audience, at least the outline, the shape of the proper way to live. That 'aesthetics' has displaced 'philosophy of art' reveals, Heidegger believes, that we have abandoned the ethical conception of art. Art, he holds, no longer provides, nor is expected to provide, guidance as to how to live. Rather, it is designed to provide 'aesthetic experiences'.

As *theory*, Heidegger says, the aesthetic conception of art began in antiquity (*PLT* p. 79), specifically with Plato (*N* I, pp. 80–3). Only with the advent of modernity, however, did the *practice* of art become aesthetic. For Heidegger, therefore, the history of Western art, which he outlines in chapter 13 of the Nietzsche volume, the 'few centuries' in which great art died, is the history of the slow overtaking of practice by (Platonic) theory.

5. What is the 'aesthetic' conception of art? The essential thing about art, on this approach, is that it is beautiful. Post-eighteenth-century German even builds this into the definition of art: 'fine art', as opposed to 'craft', is *'die schönen Künste'*; literally, 'the beautiful arts'. A successful artwork is one which is beautiful, possesses, that is, 'aesthetic appeal'. Art is expected to produce 'aesthetic experiences', which is to say that it, and nature too, is 'examined and evaluated on the basis of its capacity to produce the aesthetic state' (*N* I, p. 90).

What is the 'aesthetic state'? According to the tradition Heidegger holds to be dominant in the modern age, the hallmark of the proper reception of art is, in Kant's word, 'disinterestedness'. Here, for example, is the famous art historian, Erwin Panofsky:

It is possible to experience every object, natural or man-made, aesthetically. We do this when we just look at it (or listen to it) without relating it, intellectually or emotionally, to anything outside itself. When a man looks at a tree from the point of view of a carpenter, he will associate it with various uses to which he might put the wood; and when he looks at it from the point of view of an ornithologist, he will associate it with the birds that might nest in it. When a man at a horse race watches the animal on which he has put his money, he will associate its performance with his desire that it may win. Only he who simply abandons himself to the object of his perception will experience it aesthetically.[6]

On an aesthetic approach such as this, the essential thing about aesthetic experience is decontextualization. We attend to the object of perception

---

[6] *Meaning in the Visual Arts* (Garden City, NY: Doubleday, 1955), p. 11.

in and for itself, abstract, that is, from every relation it may have to our intellectual and practical interests.

What, one might ask, is left when we 'bracket' out all the connections which, in ordinary life, an object has? Only, one might suggest, its formal, abstract qualities. This, as Heidegger understands it, is what we are taken to respond to by the 'aesthetic state' theory: 'aestheticizing connoisseurship' of art, he says, is a matter of taking delight in 'the work's formal aspects, its qualities and charms' (*PLT* p. 68).

'Abstract' visual art did not, of course, exist in the eighteenth century. Art was always 'representational'. As art, however, representation was the occasion rather than the point of the work. Its point, according to the theory Heidegger has in mind, was to represent in a way that highlighted the formal qualities constitutive of beauty – harmony, balance, completeness, lack of superfluity, simplicity in perfect combination with complexity, and so on – to represent so as to facilitate entry into the 'aesthetic state'. (That the roots of twentieth-century abstractionism may well be seen as lying in aesthetic state theory is an important clue to understanding later Heidegger's antipathy to abstract art (see chapter 4 section 25 below).

Why is it that we find the decontextualized, 'disinterested', character of aesthetic experience pleasurable? Since objects, in such experience, are removed from all relation to our practical interests, they are removed, too, from all relation to care, to fear and hope. When the mind is wholly absorbed in aesthetic experience we become free of pain, anxiety and stress. We become, as Schopenhauer puts it, no longer the 'subject of willing' but rather the 'pure will-less subject of knowledge'. When we achieve such a state we enter

the painless state prized by Epicurus as the highest good and as the state of the gods; for that moment we are delivered from the miserable pressure of the will. We celebrate the Sabbath of the penal servitude of willing; the wheel of Ixion stands still.[7]

---

[7] *The World as Will and Representation*, 2 vols., ed. E. F. J. Payne, (New York: Dover, 1996), I, pp. 195–6. Schopenhauer actually believes that in the aesthetic state one achieves not only peace but also a kind of insight into the 'essences' of things (see chapter 7 of my *Willing and Unwilling: A Study in the Philosophy of Arthur Schopenhauer* (Dordrecht: Nijhoff, 1987)). This shows that the formalist conception of the aesthetic state is not the only possible conception. Nonetheless, Heidegger's assumption that the latter was the dominant conception throughout the eighteenth and nineteenth centuries strikes me as true.

Instead of being harried here and there by our hopes, fears and anxieties, we achieve a moment of stillness, a unique kind of peace.

6. Modern art, then – more precisely, the place of art in modernity – represents, according to Heidegger, the triumph of the aesthetic conception of art. Why, however, is aesthetic experience the 'element' in which great art 'dies'?

Heidegger asks why it is that we value aesthetic experience, and gives, essentially, Schopenhauer's answer, albeit in somewhat less elevated language. We value it because it 'reposes and relaxes' (*IM* p. 131). We enjoy the aesthetic state because it is a form of stress relief, a moment of lyric *stasis* in the midst of busyness, a holiday from the anxious world of willing and working.

But if that is all that is valuable about art then it becomes, for life, of peripheral importance. If, Heidegger says in 'Hölderlin and the Essence of Poetry', art has 'nothing about it of action', if it is 'harmless and ineffectual', then it fails to be something we need to take 'seriously' (HE pp. 294–6). In the Nietzsche volume he says that

What makes art great is not only and not in the first place the high quality of what is created. Rather, art is great because it is [answers to] an absolute need. (*N* I, p. 84)

Greek art answered such a need because, self-evidently, an understanding of how to live is something we all need. But stress relief, while pleasant, is no absolute necessity. We may choose to live without it, to be workaholics. And even if that is not our choice, it is still not the case that we stand in need of art as such. Heidegger says that, as aesthetic, art becomes the province of 'the art industry' (*PLT* p. 40), an industry aimed at providing pleasurable experiences for 'connoisseurs' (*ibid.*). As the fashion industry provides pleasurable objects to the consumers of fashion, so the 'art industry' provides pleasurable objects to the 'consumers' of art. As such, however, art becomes merely a 'sector of cultural activity' (*QCT* p. 34): merely *one* 'sector' of that which puts a little icing on the cake of life given that many other sectors are equally available; travel, recreational sex, sport, gossip, analytic philosophy, wine and food and so on. As stress relief, art takes its place as simply one option on a smorgasbord of offerings no one of which is any more or less valuable than any other. When art becomes aesthetics it becomes, says Heidegger, 'a matter for pastry cooks' (*IM* p. 131), meaning that the provision of pleasant experiences to 'connoisseurs' of art is neither more nor less important than the provision of pleasant experiences to connoisseurs of food.[8] (One is reminded here of Berlioz' remark that the Italians take their opera as they take their food.)

One reason, then, that 'aesthetic' art fails to be great art – becomes, in fact, a triviality – is that even in the lives of those who 'take it up' it represents, in a double way, an *option* rather than a 'need'. We do not have an 'absolute' need for stress relief of any sort, and even if we did we do not need art in order to satisfy it.

Another, related, reason, however, concerns precisely the idea of 'taking up' art. Heidegger complains that whereas the art of Homer and Sophocles gathered together and united an entire culture, art, in modernity, 'exists only for the enjoyment of a few sectors of the population' (*N* I, p. 85). This follows from what has been said already. If art exists only as a 'sector' on the smorgasbord of 'cultural activity' then, evidently, it exists only for those few 'sectors' of the population who choose to go in for that particular form of rest and recreation. Since the enjoyment of (at least fine) art requires leisure and education – the masses prefer real to metaphorical pastries – aesthetic art becomes the province of a subcultural social elite.

In two ways, then, aesthetics is the element in which great art 'dies', descends from greatness into triviality. It becomes marginal within the lives of those who choose to take it up. And it becomes marginal to the life of the culture as a whole, devoid of that world-historical significance which, for both Hegel and Heidegger, great art must have.

'Aesthetics' and 'enlightenment'

7. Aesthetics is the element in which art, as a non-trivial enterprise, dies. But Heidegger actually provides a deeper analysis of the death of art by

---

[8] This, of course, is a deliberate insult to eighteenth-century thinkers like Kant who sought to elevate aesthetic over, specifically, gastronomic experience on the grounds that while the latter is a matter of pure sensation, the former involves an element of judgment. Heidegger's implied comment is: different, maybe, but no less trivial.

providing an account of why, at the beginning of the modern age, the aesthetic approach came to be the dominant climate within which art was created.

In the *Ister* lectures he says that 'aesthetics is the way in which the essence of the beautiful and of art is delimited in terms of . . . metaphysics' (*Ister* p. 88). The aesthetic view of art, he claims, is 'metaphysics' applied to art, 'metaphysics', as we might put it, in action. By 'metaphysics' Heidegger here explains, he understands 'enlightenment', the view that knowledge of the truth about the world is the exclusive province of 'reason' (*Ister* pp. 111–12).[9] As an intellectual movement, claims Heidegger, the Enlightenment began with the Sophists, Socrates and Plato. Only, however, in the seventeenth and eighteenth centuries did it achieve world-historical dominance, which is why, as the label of an historical epoch, it names that period (*ibid.*).

'Enlightenment' is, in more current language, 'scientism' or 'positivism'. Why does this lead to the aestheticization of art?

In the 1920s the so-called 'logical positivists' confronted ethics as a theoretical problem. Convinced that only science could possibly provide access to truth it followed that ethical utterances could not be truth-bearing, since, evidently, 'killing is wrong' is not susceptible to empirical testing, a susceptibility which is the *sine qua non* of a statement's being accorded the title 'scientific'. Evidently, however, ethical utterances play an important role in human life, so some account is required of what that is. The answer the positivists produced was a more or less sophisticated version of 'emotivism': ethical utterances rather than reporting truths evince, like cries and groans, feelings. Having expelled ethics from the domain of truth the positivists, in other words, assigned it to the domain of feeling. They 'aestheticized' ethics.

It is in a way similar to this, I take Heidegger to say, that positivism aestheticizes art. Having expelled it from the domain of truth (it was the poets', in Plato's view, unmerited reputation as truth-disclosers that led to his expelling them from the ideal state) there remains no alternative but

---

[9] It is important to notice that this is a highly atypical use of 'metaphysics'. Generally, as we will see, Heidegger uses the term in such a way that 'the truth about reality is fully expressible on the "rigid grid" of "reason's concepts"' (*Ister* pp. 111–12) counts as merely one species of metaphysics.

to assign it to the realm of feeling. A great medieval altarpiece possessed, for its original receivers, at least two aspects: most importantly, it disclosed the 'truth' of the Christian cosmos but, in second place, it did so in a formally beautiful way. If, then, thinking about art in a climate of positivism, one cancels its truth-bearing function, all one is left with is its 'aesthetic' role.

For Heidegger, then, the ultimate ground of the triumph of the aesthetic view of art is the imperialism of reason, the triumph of the view that science (in the broad, German sense), and science alone, has access to truth. Notice that, in the end, this more or less repeats Hegel's analysis of the death of art. Great art died because for better or worse (better in Hegel's view, worse in Heidegger's) science took over the role that had made it great.

Heidegger's rejection of Hegel

8. With respect to Hegel's first two propositions, we have seen, Heidegger is in complete agreement. Hegel's third proposition, however, he rejects. Though currently 'in force', the judgment that great art is dead and gone *for ever* 'has not yet been decided' (*PLT* p. 80). That art might one day become, once more, 'an essential and necessary way in which that truth happens which is decisive for our historical existence' (*ibid.*) is a possibility that nothing precludes. The reason Heidegger disagrees with Hegel here is that he rejects the idea that history happens according to Hegel's – or anyone's – laws. There is no discoverable law to history, every attempt to 'calculate' it being an, at bottom, technological, control-oriented, illusion (*QCT* p. 48). History is, rather, 'sent' to us by a 'Being' we can neither comprehend, predict, nor control. The character and timing of world-historical change is therefore something

no one knows. Nor is it necessary that we know. A knowledge of this kind would even be most ruinous for man, because his essence is to be the one who waits, who attends upon the coming to presence of Being. (*QCT* p. 42)

Heidegger also rejects Hegel's fourth proposition. Far from being something we can happily do without, it is *only* if great art returns that there can occur a 'decisive confrontation' (*QCT* pp. 34–5) with the 'destitution' (*PLT* p. 91) of the age. The return of great art, therefore, is something we need more than anything else.

Heidegger says, on the final page of 'The Origin' that though reflection on the character of great art cannot force its 'coming-to-be' it is, nonetheless, the 'indispensable preparation for the becoming of art'. Only such reflection prepares a 'space' for art (*PLT* p. 78).

Unlike Arthur Danto, Heidegger does not believe that art always exists in a climate of a theory that moulds its character. The greatest age of Western art, eighth- to fourth-century Greece, existed 'without a corresponding cognitive-conceptual meditation on it'. Reflection on art only began, with Plato, as the greatest age of art came to an end (*N* I, p. 80).

Modern art, however, does exist in a climate of theory – bad theory, according to Heidegger. And though theory cannot make art, it can kill it. Given this, Heidegger's intention is to disrupt the prevailing theoretical climate by re-presenting an older theory of art – the theory, as he sees it, the Pre-Socratics would have given had they been disposed to theorize about art. Only with such a disruption is the return of great art even possible. 'The Origin' is Heidegger's contribution to creating the possibility of the rebirth of art.

The question: what is art?

9. The first of the many challenges of comprehension presented by 'The Origin' is the question of the question. What is it to which Heidegger seeks to provide an answer? According to the title it is, of course, the question of the 'origin' (*Ursprung*) of the artwork. That question is, however, answered in the first paragraph. In the sense in which Heidegger is interested, the origin of the artwork is, not the artist, but rather 'art' (*PLT* p. 17). In an, as he later admits, obscure discussion,[10] Heidegger says that 'the origin of something is the source of its nature' (*ibid.*). So the thought

---

[10] 'Capable of misunderstanding this talk of origin' a 1960 footnote dryly observes (*GA* 5, p. 1). (The footnotes in the *Gesamtausgabe* edition of 'The Origin' represent a selection from the marginal notes Heidegger wrote on his own copies of the 1957 and 1960 editions of *Holzwege*. When I refer, hereafter, to '1957' or '1960' marginalia I do not mean they were written in one or the other of those years, but rather in the margins of one or the other of those books. (Heidegger was an inveterate scribbler on books. The University of Freiburg library has, I am told, made a collection of their own books on which Heidegger scribbled – in pencil.))

is, presumably, that though the artist is undoubtedly the artwork's *causal* origin, he is not the origin of its status as an artwork and thus not the *logical* origin of its 'nature' as an artwork. In the sense that interests Heidegger, then, an 'origin' is a *logical or conceptual* origin, that in virtue of which an entity of a certain kind counts as being of that kind.

Since art, the property (or, as philosophers say, 'universal'), is fairly obviously that which enables a work of art to count as a work of *art*, 'the question of the origin of the work of art turns into a question about the nature (*Wesen*) of art' (*PLT* p. 18). Thus the initial question dissolves into the traditional question of the nature of (great) art. (After writing 'What is a thing?', 'What is art?' might well have been Heidegger's title had Tolstoy not got there first).

Traditionally, philosophers have answered this question by focusing either on the creator of art (Nietzsche's approach) or on the receiver (Kant and Schopenhauer's approach) and then extrapolating to the nature of the work from their chosen vantage point. Heidegger, however, says that he intends to do neither of these things but to focus instead on the work itself. (The reason for this, surely, is the likelihood that, on either the spectator or creator approach, the essence of art will turn out to be a psychological state and that one's philosophy of art will therefore degenerate into 'aesthetics'.) After a lot of mainly unnecessary footwork, therefore, the fundamental question that 'The Origin' seeks to answer is: 'What . . . is a work of art?' (*PLT* p. 18).

As its Socratic form suggests, this question is a request for a definition. Insofar as it possesses one, this request supplies the essay with its structure. It proceeds, in a manner vaguely reminiscent of a Platonic dialogue, by means of a series of attempted definitions of the artwork, the first rough and 'provisional' (*PLT* p. 51), the last, it is hoped, refined, deepened and completed. The initial definition, Heidegger's Hegelian *Grundgedanke* (founding idea), is that art is the 'happening of truth' (*PLT* p. 39, p. 57).

Expanding the concept of art

10. Halfway through the essay, however, Heidegger throws this understanding of the nature of his project into serious confusion. Art, it seems to transpire, is only *one* of the ways in which 'truth happens':

One essential way in which truth establishes itself . . . is truth setting itself into [the] work. Another way in which truth occurs is the act that founds a political state. Still another . . . is the nearness of that which is not simply a being, but the being that is most of all. Still another . . . is the essential sacrifice. (*PLT* p. 62)

One might, following, in part, Hubert Dreyfus,[11] think of these references as being to Hitler's founding of the Nazi state or Pericles' founding of Athenian democracy,[12] to God's covenant with the Jews, and to the crucifixion. Let us call events such as these, 'charismatic events'. The disconcerting suggestion, then, is that 'truth happens' in great art *and* in charismatic events.

Essentially the same point reappears at the end of the essay. As the 'projection' of 'truth', all art is, says Heidegger, 'poetry (*Dichtung*)' (*PLT* p. 72). Not, of course, linguistic poetry, 'poesy', but rather poetry in a 'broad' sense that is equivalent to the happening of truth. But, Heidegger now says, 'poetry is thought of here in so broad a sense that we must leave open whether [i.e. we must deny that] art, in all its modes from architectural to poesy exhausts the nature of poetry' (*PLT* p. 74). We have yet to see why Heidegger associates 'poetry' so closely with the projection of truth (see, further, section 18 and especially footnote 31 below). But whatever the reason, the point here, too, is that charismatic events, as much as artworks, count as poetry in the 'broad' sense, i.e. as 'happenings of truth'.

This apparent allowing of the happening of truth to occur outside artworks is disconcerting for two reasons. The first is that since definitions are supposed to provide necessary and *sufficient* conditions for identifying that which they define, one would expect, given the character of Heidegger's enterprise, that all *and only* artworks would turn out to be occasions of 'truth'. The second reason is that if truth happens outside of art it is not at all clear why we should be *bothered* by art's demise, why

---

[11] 'Heidegger on the Connection Between Nihilism, Art, Technology, and Politics' in *The Cambridge Companion to Heidegger*, ed. C. Guignon (Cambridge: Cambridge University Press, 1993), pp. 289–316, at p. 301.

[12] Already in 1935, in the *Introduction to Metaphysics*, Heidegger had abandoned many of his illusions about Nazism, criticizing its racism, militarism and totalitarianism as well as the crassness of the Nuremburg rallies. Though it is hard to doubt that a reference to Hitler is intended here, it should be thought of as to the Hitler of Heidegger's 1933 hopes and dreams rather than to the reality of Nazism as it stood before his eyes at the end of 1936. (See *HPN* pp. 45–6, 116–17.)

we should not join Hegel in, without regret, bidding farewell to art. Yet, for Heidegger, as we have seen, it is art alone that can provide the decisive antidote to the 'destitution' of our times.

In reality, however, Heidegger is not failing to provide a sufficient condition of art, but rather expanding the concept to embrace 'world-defining' events of all sorts. Anything that provides what Hubert Dreyfus calls a 'cultural paradigm'[13] counts, for Heidegger, as an 'artwork'. That he is doing this quite deliberately is made clear by the fact that at one point, the Greek temple, Greek drama *and* the Olympic Games are offered as equally valid examples of 'works' (*PLT* p. 43).

Is a concept of art according to which a Greek temple, a medieval altarpiece, a Palestrina Mass, a football match, a rock concert, and perhaps even something not too unlike a Nuremburg rally, might all count as 'artworks', an artificial cobbling together of disparate things?

Heidegger points out in the Nietzsche study (and in many other places) that the Greeks had no concept corresponding to our notion of 'fine art'. Both art and craft, along with all other modes of 'truth'-disclosure were, for them, just *techne*. If we return, then, to thinking in a Greek way, 'we [will] understand the word "art" quite generally to mean every sort of capacity to "bring forth" truth, understand it, that is, so that it corresponds to the Greek concept of *techne*' (*N* I, p. 82).

The idea of 'fine art' as a distinct species first came into being in the eighteenth century; with, that is, if Heidegger is right, the transformation of art into 'aesthetics'. It follows, then, that from Heidegger's point of view the idea that 'art' is synonymous with 'fine art' is a product of decadence. That he should seek to displace this notion is, therefore, part and parcel of his enterprise of restoring us to an older and healthier conception of the nature and significance of art.

A related point is that, as Heidegger puts it in a 1960 marginal comment, 'the distinctiveness of art' in the modern sense is 'open to question (*frage-würdig*)' (*GA* 5, p. 60). Artists, that is, are constantly challenging the accepted boundaries of art, constantly suggesting that we should accept as art works which lie outside of the domain and power of the 'art industry', outside 'the realm of tradition and conser-

13 'Nihilism, Art, Technology, and Politics', p. 298.

vation'. Those, for example, who enshroud vast public buildings and bridges may well be intending, in part, to make the Heideggerian point that art should belong, not in the museum as an object of 'aesthetic connoisseurship', but rather in the marketplace as a public 'happening of truth'. In this regard, Heidegger's revision of the notion of art looks to be quite prescient, an anticipation of aspects of the current *avant-garde*.

Art as the 'opening up of world'

11. Art, then, in the broad, Greek sense is the 'happening of truth'. The artwork is that in and through which 'truth happens'. What does this mean?

Heidegger's first step in elucidating this provisional definition is to replace 'happening of truth' with 'opening up of world'. The artwork is something which 'opens up a world' (*PLT* p. 44).

Which world is it that the artwork opens up? Heidegger says: 'the work belongs, as work, uniquely within the world opened up by itself' (*PLT* p. 41). The temple at Paestum (*PLT* p. 40) belongs to the Greek world, Bamberg Cathedral (*PLT* p. 41) to the world of medieval Christendom. In 'The Origin' itself, painting with a fairly broad brush, Heidegger distinguishes just three (Western) worlds, the Greek, the medieval and the modern (*PLT* pp. 76–7).[14] Elsewhere, however, he distinguishes the Roman from the Greek and the world of 'early' from that of 'consummate' modernism.

Worlds come and go. The Greek and medieval worlds both succumbed to a process of decline and fall, have 'decayed' and 'perished' (*PLT* p. 41). This means that 'is a great artwork' is a predicate which comes and goes too. Since their worlds have disappeared, neither the temple nor the cathedral can do its 'work' of 'opening up' anymore. They have, rather, passed over into 'the realm of tradition and conservation' (*ibid.*), have become, in a word, museum pieces.

A work, then, can lose its greatness through 'world-withdrawal'. But it

---

[14] Notice, for future reference, that not every 'world' possesses an artwork. The age of modernity represents 'a new and essential world', yet is, of course, the age in which great art is 'dead'. This means that worlds can happen without an artwork.

Plate 1   Temple of Hera II (so-called Temple of Neptune), Paestum.

can lose it, too, by, not world being withdrawn from it, but rather the reverse, its being withdrawn from world. Thus, for example, in the nineteenth century, an American Indian totem might have lost its world-disclosing power through being removed from its site and placed in a New York museum, an African fertility symbol by being relocated on the living-room sideboard. In the 1960s, Heidegger observes of Raphael's altarpiece known as the 'Sixtina' that it belongs to its church at Piacenza 'not merely in an historical-antiquarian sense, but according to its pictorial essence'. The painting 'is the appearing of . . . the place within which the sacrifice of the mass is to be celebrated' so that were it to be uprooted and relocated in a museum, and so deprived of its world, it would lose its 'authentic truth' and become instead a mere 'aesthetic object' (*D* pp. 70–1).

There are, then, two ways in which an artwork may cease to do the work it once did and so lose, as Heidegger's sees it, its greatness: either the world is withdrawn from the work or the work is withdrawn from the world.

Notice that while the proposed connection between work and world does not commit Heidegger to the view that we cannot 'appreciate' the art of alien cultures, it does commit him to the relative triviality, the 'aesthetic' character, of such appreciation. For us, unless we become something a great deal more than tourists, the Taj Mahal is merely an 'aesthetic object'. (That, in the 1950s, Heidegger became, as we will see, deeply involved with the art of Zen Buddhism is a measure of the profundity of the changes that occurred as he proceeded down his 'path of thinking' about art.)

What is a 'world'?

12. What, though, is a 'world'? Heidegger himself poses this question, and does so against the background of the famous 'temple' passage. Here is part of it:

A building, a Greek temple . . . stands there in the middle of the rock-cleft valley. The building encloses the figure of the god, and in this concealment lets it stand out into the holy precinct through the open portico. By means of the temple[15] the god is present in the temple. This presence of the god is in itself the extension and delimitation of the precinct as a holy precinct. The temple and its precinct, however, do not fade away into the indefinite. It is the temple-work that first fits together and at the same time gathers around itself the unity of those paths and relations in which birth and death, disaster and blessing, victory and disgrace, endurance and decline acquire the shape of destiny for human being. The all-governing expanse of this open relational context is the world of this historical people. Only from this expanse does a people first return to itself for the fulfillment of its vocation.

Standing there, the building rests on the rocky ground. This resting of the work draws up out of the rock the mystery of that rock's clumsy yet spontaneous support. Standing there, the building holds its ground against the storm raging above it and so first makes the storm itself manifest in its violence. The luster and gleam of the stone, though itself apparently glowing only by the grace of the sun, yet first brings to light the light of the day, the breadth of the sky, the darkness of the night. The temple's firm towering makes visible the invisible space of air. The steadfastness of the work contrasts with the raging of the surf, and its own repose brings out the surge of the sea.[16] Tree and grass, eagle and bull, snake and cricket first enter into their distinctive shapes and thus come to appear as what they are . . . The temple,

---

[15] Hofstadter's translation is true to the German, but 'figure' surely makes more sense here than 'temple'.
[16] Hofstadter transposes 'raging' and 'surge' in a way that suggests someone who has never seen the sea.

in its standing there, first gives to things their look and to men their outlook on themselves. (*PLT* pp. 41–3)

It is important to be conscious of the fact that the overall character of this beautiful passage, like that of the equally famous (but largely irrelevant) evocation of Van Gogh's painting of shoes (*PLT* pp. 33–4), is poetic rather than analytic. A great deal of misreading of 'The Origin' derives, in my view, from a literalist reading of the temple passage. In subsequent chapters we will repeatedly encounter Heidegger's preference for philosophizing by way of interpreting poetic texts, those, for example, of Sophocles Rilke, Trakl, George and, above all, Hölderlin. In 'The Origin' however, he, as it were, provides his own text (a text we will shortly see to be modelled on Rilke's evocation of the world of his childhood in the work mentioned in footnote 1). Its purpose, I suggest, is to provide an intuitive entry into the experience the Greek might have had before his temple, an intuitive understanding which the remainder of the essay will attempt to articulate philosophically.

13. According to the passage, 'world' is the 'all-governing . . . open relational context' of an 'historical' culture, a kind of space. What kind of space?

Since 'world' is the same as 'truth' – the 'truth of beings' or 'being of beings' as Heidegger also puts it (*PLT* p. 39) – the root understanding of 'world' lies in Heidegger's theory of truth, a theory which received its first statement in 1925,[17] a major restatement in section 44 of *Being and Time*,[18] a significantly developed restatement in the 1930 'Essence of Truth' (*BW* pp. 113–42) and, more briefly, in 'The Origin' itself (pp. 50–5).

The fundamental insight contained in the theory is that truth as 'correspondence' or 'adequacy' to the facts – *the* account of truth offered, since Roman times, by the philosophical tradition – actually presupposes

---

[17] In *Plato's Sophist*, tr. R. Rojcewicz and André Schuwer (Bloomington: Indiana University Press, 1997).

[18] Though stated in *Being and Time*, its implications, I would argue, are not there properly understood. The 1930 'Essence of Truth' represents a considerable advance in appropriating those implications into his philosophy as a whole – which is why Heidegger says it constitutes the beginning of 'the turn' (*BW* p. 208) – but their full appropriation required, I believe, the rest of Heidegger's philosophical career. A helpful 'take' on his 'path of thinking' is to see it as a continuous attempt to fully think through the implications of his own theory of truth.

a more 'primordial' truth which has the task of establishing what kind of 'facts' there are to which statements may, or may not, correspond. Heidegger calls this 'truth as disclosure' or '*aletheia*' (*PLT* p. 51), which he sometimes writes '*a-letheia*' to highlight the idea of the foundation of truth as consisting in a coming-out-of-oblivion.

Consider this table on which I write. Let us call it 'Smith'. Suppose I say, pointing at Smith, 'Smith is colourless.' It might seem obvious that I say something false. But suppose that (for my own arcane reasons) I am actually referring, not to the table, but rather to the collection of molecules which Smith also is. A further possibility is that what I am talking about is neither the table nor the collection of molecules, but rather the space–time region they exactly occupy. Or maybe I refer to the demigod whose residence is just that place. And so on. The point this example makes is that truth as correspondence presupposes reference, and reference presupposes – a point often overlooked – a 'horizon of disclosure' which, through disambiguation, first makes it possible. Only when we know what kinds of beings belong to a given domain of discourse do we know what kinds of facts there are to which propositions may or may not correspond.

My example, of course, highlights issues of reference of a relatively localized kind. Heidegger, however, thinks of every human being as born into a very fundamental, 'transcendental' (*DT* p. 63) horizon of disclosure – as it were, the horizon of all one's horizons – and it is this that he calls 'world'. After 1930, as we have seen, he thinks of world (or at least Western) history as divided up, *à la* Hegel, into quite sharply distinct epochs, historical 'worlds'. These historical worlds (Heidegger also speaks of 'the clearing' and 'the open') are defined and distinguished by different horizons of disclosure. They are embodied in what Heidegger calls 'language' (see further section 18 below); hence his frequently repeated remark that 'language is the house of being'. In sum, then, 'world' is the background, and usually unnoticed understanding which determines for the members of an historical culture what, for them, fundamentally, there *is*. It constitutes, as it were, the entry conditions, the ground plan, the 'being of beings', which something must satisfy in order to show up as a being in the world in question.

In the first version of 'The Origin' Heidegger calls world a 'framework for the present-at-hand',[19] echoing *Being and Time*'s description of world as an 'ontological structure' (*BT* 74–5). We could, then, think of understanding one's world as possession of a kind of metaphysical map (world, remember, is a kind of space), a map detailing both the regions of being and the kinds of beings that dwell there, a map that is internalized by all fully-fledged members of the culture. The Greek 'map' would divide the world into (at least) earth (inhabited by mortals) and sky (inhabited by gods) (later Heidegger calls this 'the fourfold'), the medieval into earth (mortals), heaven (gods) and hell (souls of the damned).

To understand one's world is, then, to understand what, fundamentally, there is. We may call this the 'ontological' aspect of world. Heidegger often appeals to this conception in describing the disclosive activity of the artwork. The work, he says, 'make[s] manifest' what 'beings as a whole [i.e. as an organized structure] are' (*N* I, p. 84). It 'opens up . . . the being of beings' (*PLT* p. 39).

In and around the temple passage, however, Heidegger's presentation of world seems to be focused not on ontology but rather on ethics; not on what *is* but rather on what *ought to be* the case. The important thing here about understanding one's world, is understanding the difference between 'victory and disgrace', 'what is brave and what cowardly, what noble (*edel*) and what fugitive (*flüchtig*[20]), what master and what slave' (*PLT* p. 44). In general, when the artwork opens up our world for us we understand 'what is holy and what unholy' (*ibid.*), 'the shape of destiny for human being' (*PLT* p. 42), the broad outline of the 'simple and essential decisions' (*PLT* p. 48) which constitute, for us, the proper way to live, our, as I shall call it, fundamental *ethos*.

This dual character of world reflects a thesis fundamental to all phases of Heidegger's thinking: the inseparability of ontology and ethics, of 'being' and 'the ought', the necessity for the grounding of the latter in the former. (See especially the *Introduction to Metaphysics*, pp. 196–9, and the '*Letter on Humanism*' (*BW* pp. 225–39).)

There are two aspects to this claim which I shall discuss in turn: the claim that ontology is necessary to the grounding of ethics, and the claim that it is sufficient.

---

[19] '*Von Ursprung des Kunstwerks: Erste Ausarbeitung*', *Heidegger Studies* 14, 1998, pp. 6–22.
[20] Hofstadter's 'flighty' reveals the dangers of translating into a language of which one is not a native speaker.

Ontology and ethics

14. Modern thinking, thinking which has its beginnings in Plato's separation between the form of the good and the other forms, is, Heidegger holds, dominated by the separation between fact and value, between in Hume's language, the 'is' and the 'ought'. Once such a dichotomy sets in, however, once it becomes no mere philosopher's theory but rather the way in which people in general experience the values of their culture, then moral nihilism sets in. The reason, in brief, is the following. The realm of being, of 'fact', constitutes, for us, what we *discover*, simply *acknowledge* to be the case. If, then, values are expelled from that domain then, inevitably, they become assigned to the realm of what we *make* to be the case, the realm of human invention or, as Heidegger puts it in t*he 'Letter on Humanism'*, 'fabrication' (*BW* p. 279). As such, however, they cannot be genuinely authoritative for us. If they are someone *else*'s fabrications then their only source of authority is the power of the other, an authority which is quite different from, in Kant's language, the 'unconditional' character of genuinely ethical authority. If, on the other hand, one's values are one's own fabrications – Heidegger is attacking, here, in particular, Sartre's notion that one must *choose* one's own fundamental values – then, if the going gets tough, one can simply unfabricate, unchoose them so that, again, they lack genuine authority. 'Values', says Heidegger, by which he means values divorced from facts, are 'impotent'; 'no one dies for mere values' (*QCT* p. 142). What follows from this, he concludes, is that only 'the grounding of man's historical existence on beings as a whole' (*N* I, p. 90) can establish an authoritative ethic.

It might be objected to this that the choice between assigning values to either the domain of beings or the domain of choice is not one we have to make. There is, so moral 'intuitionists' insist, a third domain; the domain of 'moral facts', facts which, while being fully objective, and so independent of human choice, are yet autonomous, completely separate from the domain of non-moral facts. That killing is wrong is something we 'perceive' rather than choose to be the case yet not on account of perceiving anything about the non-moral domain.

Heidegger attacks this position, popular among his German contemporaries,[21] in the *Introduction to Metaphysics* (pp. 198–9). It is, he suggests, simply an attempt, through obfuscating their origins, to lend spurious authority to what are, in reality, nothing but human fabrications. That he is right about this can, I think, be gathered by examining the response of 'intuitionists' to disagreement. Someone who does not have the same moral 'perceptions' as themselves they are compelled to abuse as morally deviant, defective in their capacity for moral perception. They are compelled, in other words, to resort to power, thereby unmasking the true and sole authority behind their fabrications.

15. A grounding in ontology is, then, necessary to a genuinely authoritative ethics. But Heidegger also claims that it is sufficient. Properly understanding one's world does not, he says, 'consist in mere information and notions about something'. Rather, 'he who truly knows what is knows what he wills to do in the midst of what is' (*PLT* p. 67). And again: he who properly understands the 'truth of beings as a whole' knows his own 'position in the midst of beings' (*N* I, p. 88). Proper knowledge of one's 'ontology' is no merely 'theoretical' accomplishment. It is, rather, also 'practical'. It bears, in a decisive way, upon will and action.

To try to understand this claim let us focus on the word 'position' as it occurs in 'position in the midst of beings'. 'Position' is, of course, a spatial concept. But it is also, as one might put it, a 'straddling' notion, linking together the idea of a physical (or metaphysical) space with that of a moral space. On the one hand to know one's position is to know one's latitude and longitude, on the other it is to know one's moral position, one's rights and duties, one's, as it were, moral 'latitude and longitude'. Position, in this sense, means the same as 'station' as it occurs in the Victorian-sounding phrase 'my station and its duties'.

Position entails *structure*, usually hierarchy, a feature of the Greek world Heidegger emphasizes through his repeated quotations of the Heraclitus fragment 53: '*polemos*' (usually translated as 'conflict', 'war' or 'strife') is, Heidegger quotes Heraclitus as saying,

---

[21] See *HPN* pp. 206–8.

for all (that is present) the creator that causes to emerge, but (also) for all the dominant preserver. For it makes some to appear as gods, others as men; it creates (shows) some as slaves, others as free men. (*IM* pp. 61–2; Heidegger's interpolations in parentheses)

This is the passage alluded to in 'The Origin' when Heidegger says that the Greek artwork makes manifest 'what is holy and what unholy, what great and what small, what noble and what fugitive, what master and what slave (cf. Heraclitus, fragment 53)' (*PLT* p. 43).

Heidegger here parses *polemos* as *Aus-einandersetzung* – in ordinary German 'encounter' or 'confrontation', but with Heidegger's hyphen, 'setting apart' or 'establishment of difference'. It is this, he says, expanding on Heraclitus, which

first caused the realm of being to separate into opposites; it first gives rise to position and order and rank . . . In th[is] *Aus-einandersetzung* world comes into being. (*IM* p. 62)

Let us suppose ourselves to be, then, 'freemen', citizens, in the Greek *polis*. ('*Polis*', says Heidegger, is inadequately translated as 'city state'. Thought of in a properly Greek way, it is, rather, the 'place and scene of history' (*IM* p. 152), in other words, the Greek 'world'.) Understanding our world we understand ourselves to be located within a structure of which some of the nodal points can be represented as follows:

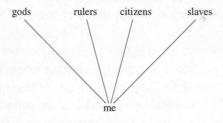

Heidegger says, to repeat, that 'he who truly knows what is, knows what he wills in the midst of what is'. In the 1942 *Ister* lectures he puts the point in a more Greek way. To truly understand the *polis* is to understand what it is that is the 'fitting', or appropriate life for oneself, since it is 'from this site and place (*Statt*) [that] there springs forth whatever is in place (*gestattet*)[22] and whatever is not, what is order and what is disorder, what is fitting and what is unfitting' (*Ister* p. 82). Thus positioned as I am, I know, for example, that I am under the following kinds of obligations:

The 'simple and essential decisions' that are the outline of my proper life are determined by my position in the structure which is my world. If I do not understand that authentic gods – and the places they visit – are to be honoured, that rulers are to be obeyed, that my fellow citizens are to be treated differently from slaves, then I do not properly understand what a god, ruler, or citizen is. (I have, in other words, an inadequate command of the 'language', am not Greek but a 'barbarian'.) Part of knowing what a god or ruler is is knowing the kind of behaviour that is appropriate to his presence.[23] Knowing, in general, the structure that is one's world is knowing, in general, the kind of life that is appropriate to one's station in it.

(Heidegger, however, says that he who properly knows 'what is', 'knows what he *wills* in the midst of what is', in other words that fully understanding one's world is not only knowing the 'fitting' life but also being *motivated* to lead such a life. Yet one could, surely, perfectly well know the kind of behaviour appropriate, in a given world, to gods, rulers, citizens

[22] In ordinary German '*gestattet*' means 'permitted'. Heidegger is trying here to point to an etymological link between place and *ethos*, to suggest that the ethical is what belongs to the place, that the right life is the 'fitting', or as we would say 'appropriate' life, the life that is 'in place' in one's place. In the 'Letter on Humanism' Heidegger claims that thought in a properly Greek way '*ethos*' simply means 'place', 'place of dwelling (*Aufenthalt des Wohnens*)' (*BW* p. 233).

[23] Of course sometimes the honour that is due to the gods and their 'laws' (HE p. 312) conflicts with the obedience owed to rulers. Sophocles' *Antigone*, at least in Heidegger's reading, is about this conflict.

and so on yet still be disinclined to act in the appropriate way. This shows that there is more to 'truly know what is' than has yet appeared. What more I shall discuss in section 24 below.)

What is 'opening up'?

16. To summarize, then, a 'world' is not to be thought of as a collection of objects. It is, rather, a structure of beings, beings of different 'rank', which endows those who properly and fully belong to that world with a moral identity, an identity which gives purpose and meaning to their lives. 'Being-in-the-world', in the language of *Being and Time*, is knowing where and so who you are, and what you have to do.

The next question is: what is it for an artwork to 'make manifest', to 'open up' a world?

There is, in the temple passage, a great deal of emphasis on the idea of 'firstness'. The temple, to repeat,

first . . . gathers around itself . . . the world of this historical people . . . *first* brings to light the light of the day . . . [allows] tree and grass, eagle and snake and cricket *first* to enter their distinctive shape . . . The temple, in standing there *first* gives to things their look and to men their outlook on themselves. (my emphases)

This repeated emphasis, together with Heidegger's talk of art as a 'beginning' (*PLT* p. 77) and an '*Ur-sprung*' (*PLT* p. 78) – 'origin' but, with Heidegger's hyphen, 'primal leap' – has led to 'The Origin''s being read as affirming the, as I shall call it, 'Promethean' view that art *creates* world. The attribution to Heidegger of such a view has important political implications: it has led to 'The Origin''s being read as a thinly disguised plea for the overcoming of European nihilism through the coming into being of a brave new world to be established by the Hitler-created artwork, by, in a word, (a refined version of) the Nuremburg rally.[24]

In what follows, I am going to argue against the Promethean reading of 'The Origin'. I must, however, concede that, though absolutely crucial to one's overall reading of the work, the matter is difficult and obscure. By emphasizing certain passages over others it is, I think, quite possible to present a Promethean reading that is both plausible and coherent.

[24] See *HPN* pp. 109–14.

Hubert Dreyfus, if I understand him, does this.[25] Heidegger himself, I think, found the matter difficult and confusing. Though, as I shall shortly show, fundamental positions worked out in *Being and Time* demand the rejection of Prometheanism, certain passages in the *Introduction to Metaphysics* as well as, as Jacques Taminiaux shows (see footnote 2 above), earlier drafts of 'The Origin', seem to affirm it. My view is that, almost certainly as a response to the spirit and rhetoric of Nazism, Heidegger flirted with Prometheanism from about 1933 to 1936, half-forgetting fundamental commitments established in *Being and Time* (1927).[26] By the time of the final draft of 'The Origin', however – here again I am in basic agreement with Taminiaux – he had, I believe, seen the error of his flirtation and returned, decisively, to the insights of *Being and Time*.

The first difficulty for the Promethean reading is that, whether or not *some* artwork might have created the Greek world, it is extremely difficult to see how it could have been *the temple*. As Heidegger, of course, well knew, behind the stone temple of the sixth century lay a long history of development: first the sacred site, then the open-air altar, later the wooden hut to enclose and protect the altar, and finally the magnificent re-presentation of the hut (and the Greek home) in the medium of stone. Theology does not always precede the sacred building. The Emperor Augustus, for example, concerned to preserve his authority and with it the integrity of the Roman Empire, declared himself a god and ordered altars to himself to be constructed throughout the empire. But in the case of the Greek temple it, of course, did. And if Greek theology – one and the same as Greek mythology, Heidegger says (*Ister* p. 111) – was in place well *before* the construction of the temples then, surely, so was the Greek 'world'. Heidegger in fact *says* this: the 'founding of Being[27] for

---

[25] In 'Nihilism, Art, Technology, and Politics'.

[26] A weakness in *HPN* is that I did not, there, acknowledge this flirtation.

[27] The infuriating things about Heidegger's frequent use of genitive phrases such as 'house of B/being', 'truth if B/being', 'openness of B/being' and, here, 'founding of B/being' is that they are almost always ambiguous between the objective and subjective genitive ('Tales of Hoffman' construed as 'Tales about Hoffman' is an objective genitive while construed as 'Tales told by Hoffman' is a subjective genitive). This ambiguity makes '*Sein*' ambiguous between 'Being', 'that which genuinely is' (*QCT* p. 44), in other words 'reality' (*QCT* p. 18), and 'being', our 'take' on reality. (Most often, I think, when he does not disambiguate by means of the '*Sein*'–'*Seyn*' convention (see Introduction section 4 above), he means both genitives and both senses of *Sein*. But the economy of expression in no way makes up for

Western[28] humanity (*Dasein*) completed itself with Homer' (*GA* 39, p. 184) – in other words, a couple of centuries before the temple was even a twinkle in an architect's eye.

If the repetition of 'first' in the temple passage is not to be read in the Promethean way how, it might be asked, is it to be read? The answer is, as I have already intimated, *poetically*. The idea of firstness is often associated with profound, art-mediated experience. Shelley, for example wrote that the essence of poetry is that it

purges from our inward sight the film of familiarity which obscures from us the wonder of our being . . . It creates anew the universe after it has been annihilated in our minds by the recurrent impressions of blunted familiarity.[29]

Again, Cézanne's paintings have been said to present us with the world 'on the day of creation'. And Alfred Brendel's performances of the Beethoven piano sonatas have been movingly and accurately described as 'admitting us into the act of creation itself'. Heidegger himself, I think, tells us that this is how firstness is to be understood. Greek tragedy, he says, 'originating in the saying (*Sagen*) of the people does not talk about (*reden über*)' 'the battle of the new gods against the old'. Rather 'it transforms the people's saying so that now every essential word fights the battle and puts up for decision what is holy and what unholy' (*PLT* p. 43). The drama, that is to say, does not refer back to some well-known event in the (mythological) past. Rather, the issue of what is holy and unholy is being *decided right now* – before our very eyes. If, for example, we become absorbed by a performance of *Henry V* then, sharing in Henry's tension on the eve of Agincourt, we do not know the outcome of the battle. Phenomenologically speaking, the struggle between Henry and the French is being decided *for the first time*, before our very eyes. Similarly the Greek. Profoundly moved by the temple, or by the worship occurring in it, the 'simple and essential' outlines of his world present themselves to

the loss of clarity.) In the present case, however, since Heidegger here uses '*Seyn*', I take the genitive to be a subjective one: since being but not Being can be 'founded', 'Being' needs to be read as the subject which (through Homer) completes the founding of – another word Heidegger uses, as we will see, is 'destining' – our world. (This is a footnote for scholars. It is not essential.)

[28] The dubiousness of the idea that not just the Greek but the *Western* (in other words, our) world was somehow *fully* in place in the eighth century BC is a matter to which I shall return.

[29] Quoted in *The Times Literary Supplement* 5016, 21 May 1999, pp. 14–15.

him, in pristine freshness, 'for the first time'. And they do this – one might think, here, of the emphasis on the importance of *regularity* of worship in Christian practice – over and over again. Throughout his life, the artistic or religious person repeatedly experiences his world 'for the first time'.

17. The second reason the Promethean reading of 'The Origin' is untenable is that, as already intimated, it is inconsistent with fundamental positions Heidegger had already worked out in *Being and Time*.

In *Being and Time*, 'world' is the same as the 'thrownness' which every human being (*Dasein*), as it grows to adulthood, finds itself 'already' in. Being human *means* 'already being-in (a world)' (*BT* 327). In the *Basic Problems of Phenomenology*, which like *Being and Time* belongs to 1927, Heidegger connects the latter work's doctrine about world explicitly to art.

It does so in a passage (*BP* pp. 171–3) which begins by repeating *Being and Time*'s thesis: 'as existent we already understand world beforehand'. Since the 'intelligibility' of shoes, for example, depends on that complexly interconnected totality of human practices which provides shoes with the function which makes them shoes, only his prior understanding of world allows the cobbler to understand what he is doing. For the cobbler, however, for 'average everydayness', world is shrouded in background 'inconspicuousness' (*BT* 70), merely implicitly, never explicitly, known. Only 'original' Dasein is able 'to *see* expressly the world that is *always already unveiled with its existence*, to verbalize it, and thereby make it expressly visible for others' (my emphasis). And then Heidegger identifies who 'original' Dasein is: 'Poetry, creative literature, is nothing but the elementary emergence into words, the becoming-uncovered, of existence as being-in-the-world.'

To illustrate the point, he quotes Rilke's evocation of the world of the urban squalor of late nineteenth-century Prague in which he was brought up. Rilke's evocation proceeds by expounding the context in which the remaining walls of a demolished house had been the walls that they were:

You could see the walls of the rooms on the different stories to which the wallpaper was still attached and here and there the place where the floor or ceiling began. Along the whole wall, next to the walls of the rooms, there still remained a dirty-white area, and the open, rust-stained furrow of the toilet pipe crept through it in unspeakably nauseating movements, soft, like those of a digesting worm. Of the paths taken by the illuminating gas, gray dust traces were left at the edges of the ceiling . . . The tenacious life of these rooms refused to let itself be trampled down . . . it was still there . . . There stood the noon days and the illnesses, the expirings and the smoke of years, . . . the fusel-oil smell of fermenting feet . . . and the sultriness from beds of pubescent boys.

Heidegger asks us to notice (his quotation of Rilke is much longer than this) 'in how elemental a way the world – being-in-the-world – Rilke calls it life – leaps towards us from the things' that the poet describes.

The point here concerns, as *Being and Time*'s discussion of 'world' puts it, 'thematizing' (*BT* 74–5). The cobbler knows world implicitly since he knows what shoes are. But he does not know that he knows. It takes the 'original' eye of the artist to 'thematize', to render 'expressly visible', that of which we are, in our 'average everydayness', unaware.

This passage is very important since it contains, so I suggest, the model for both the Van Gogh shoes and the temple passages in 'The Origin' (notice the shoe link between it and the Van Gogh). In both passages – imitating, as I suggest, Rilke – Heidegger presents the object in such a way as to thematize the world or 'environmentality' (*BT* 60) to which the shoes and the temple belong. (Notice, too, the association of 'originality', in other words, 'firstness', with art in the Rilke passage.)

What follows, then, is that – unless the Heidegger of 1936 rejected these ideas of 1927 – the role of the artwork is not to create but rather to 'make expressly visible', to 'thematize' a world *which is already in existence*.

In fact, in spite of, as indicated, an earlier period of confusion, Heidegger did not finally reject these products of his early thinking since they reappear, quite explicitly, in the final version of 'The Origin' itself. 'Genuinely poetic projection', it says, 'is the opening up of that into which human being, as historical, is already cast', namely, 'everything that already is' 'for an historical people', 'though still hidden from [unthematized by] itself' (*PLT* p. 75). The artwork's 'opening up of the open', it says, consciously reusing *Being and Time*'s technical terminology, 'makes its advent in thrownness' (*PLT* p. 71).

But that 'thrownness' is – here 'The Origin' repeats *Being and Time*'s thesis of the normal 'inconspicuousness' of world – not an 'object'. Unlike shoes, 'world is never an object that stands before us and can be seen' but is rather, 'ever non-objective' (*PLT* p. 44). Since everyday consciousness is geared to objects, this is why it requires something special, the 'originality' of the artwork, to make it 'visible'.

The artwork's 'opening up' of world is, then, not Promethean creation but rather, 'thematizing', 'making expressly visible'. This kind of language is repeated throughout the writings of late 1936. The artwork 'clears' what normally 'veils and withdraws itself' (*PLT* p. 74), it 'make[s] manifest' (*N* I, p. 84) the normally obscured, 'articulates' (*N* I, p. 88) the normally implicit.

18. If, it might be asked, the artwork does not create its world, what does? Heidegger's answer to this question is clear: not the artwork but rather 'language' creates world. The artwork makes its advent 'within the clearing of what is, which has already happened unnoticed in language' (*PLT* p. 74).

In 'Hölderlin and the Essence of Poetry', Heidegger says that the essence of language is the 'name'. Contrary to naïve assumptions, however, a name does not christen something already in existence. Rather, naming is 'the establishing of being by means of the word' (HE p. 304). This represents some version of what can be called 'linguistic Kantianism' – a fairly routine position for any post-Kantian German philosopher, which Heidegger embodies in the slogan that 'language is the house of being'.

What, however, is 'language'? Heidegger manages to confuse the situation by calling it poetry (*Dichtung*) (*PLT* p. 74). Given this identification, 'language creates world' becomes 'poetry is the inaugural naming of the gods and of the essence of things' (HE p. 306). Since 'poetry' seems to presuppose a poet, this looks to say that world is the creation of the poet and seems to take us back once more to the Promethean understanding of the work–world relationship. In the 'Germania' lectures Heidegger says that 'poetry is the primordial language (*Ursprache*) of a people' (*GA* 39, p. 64). This raises the spectre of the ur-poet, Homer perhaps, as the creator of the West.

Actually, however, all Heidegger means by 'language is poetry' is that language *posits* rather than christens beings, that it, in a use of the word introduced by Nietzsche, 'poeticizes' them.[30] 'Language is poetry' means

---

[30] Heidegger, of course, is well aware of this Nietzschean use of 'poeticize'. In the *Introduction to Metaphysics: Thought and Poetry* of 1944, he explains that Nietzsche calls man a 'poet' since – so Heidegger reads Nietzsche – the whole world is the creation of his 'will to power' (*GA* 50, pp. 109–10).

that language does not simply *acknowledge* world but rather 'projects' it – analogous to the way in which a system of map-making 'projects' its 'world'. Language is 'poetry' because, remember, poetry at this period in Heidegger's thinking, poetry in the 'broad', 'essential' sense (*PLT* p. 74), is simply *defined* as any kind of 'projective saying' (*ibid*.).[31] In brief, then, 'language is poetry' is neither more nor less than a (in the context of a discussion of art confusing) statement of linguistic Kantianism. It does not imply that 'language' is a creator-implying artwork nor, therefore, that world is the creation of any artist.

We do not need, then, to think of 'language' as the creation of some ur-poet. But if not the poet, what does bring 'language' into being? Heidegger says, in 'Hölderlin and the Essence of Poetry', that, *qua* philosophically interesting, world-creating ('constructing', in today's jargon) phenomenon, language is not to be understood as an abstract system of vocabulary and rules of syntax. Rather, it is a 'conversation (*Gespräch*)' (HE p. 301), an integration, I suggest, of words and things and actions that slowly comes together and grows into a comprehensive way of life. As such, it is not the creation of any individual or even 'committee' of individuals (compare *QCT* p. 23), but is, rather, in the title of one of Hölderlin's poems, 'The Voice of the People'. Heidegger repeats this point in 'The Origin' itself when he says that 'the linguistic work', Greek tragedy, 'originating in the saying (*Sagen*) of the people', brings that saying to vivid presence (*PLT* p. 43). The poet's task is not to create the people's voice but to 'remind' them of it when, as it is always inclined to do, it 'grows dumb and weary' (HE p. 312).

What this says about the nature of 'language' is, I believe, very much what section 34 of *Being and Time* says; that it is, in a word, social practice, a complex integration of words, things, moods, feelings, actions and commentaries on actions which constitutes, in Wittgenstein's phrase, a

---

[31] The decision to use 'poetry' in this Nietzschean way in an essay on art was a bad one for at least three reasons. First, it encourages the Promethean reading of the role of the artist. Second, it allows, for example quantum mechanics, to appear as 'poetry'. And, third, a related point, thinking that 'projective saying' captures the 'essence' of poetry prevents Heidegger from paying proper attention to the difference between poetry and prose. (Later on, as we will see, once he starts to think properly about the nature of poetic language as such, nothing is more important to him than this distinction.) It is, I suggest, with all these deficiencies in mind, that, in a marginal comment of 1960, he calls 'The Origin''s use of 'poetry' 'questionable' and 'inadequate' (*GA* 5, p. 59).

'form of life'. As such it is something we receive rather than create, something whose genesis lies in neither individual or collective human intention but in, rather, extraintentional reality. Languages constitutive of historical cultures are always, as we say, 'natural' rather than 'artificial' (or artifactual) languages. In Heidegger's way of speaking they are 'sent' or 'destined' to us by Being. There are, therefore, no Promethean artists involved in the creation of world by language. At least no *human* artists; one might, if disposed to metaphor, think of the relation of Being to world as that of artist to work – an artist whose artwork is himself.

19. Not the artwork, then, but rather 'language' creates world. The artwork's role is not to create but rather to thematize, to render explicit, to bring the 'inconspicuous' into salience. Two questions now confront us. First, *why* is it that 'world' is normally inconspicuous? Second, how does the artwork disrupt its inconspicuousness?

Heidegger says, as we have seen, that 'world' does not belong among things with which we are 'familiar' since it is 'ever non-objective', 'never an object that stands before us and can be seen' (*PLT* p. 44). What we notice in everyday life are the 'objects' of our practical concerns, never the background 'framework' (*PLT* p. 42) that allows them to be the objects that they are.

Heidegger's point, I believe, is one that was also seen, in his own way, by Nietzsche. Nietzsche writes – notice that he, too, sees that art has something to do with overcoming the everyday inconspicuousness of world – as follows:

What should win our gratitude – only artists, and especially those of the [Greek?] theatre, have given men eyes and ears to see and hear with some pleasure what each man is . . . only they have taught us to esteem the hero that is concealed in everyday characters, only they have taught us the art of viewing ourselves as heroes – from a distance and, as it were, simplified and transfigured – the art of staging and watching ourselves. Only in this way can we deal with some base details in ourselves. Without this art we would be nothing but foreground and live entirely in the spell of that perspective which makes what is closest at hand and most vulgar appear as if it were vast, and reality itself. Perhaps one should concede [grudgingly, in Nietzsche's case] a similar merit to the religion that made man see the sinfulness of every single individual through a magnifying glass, turning the sinner into a great, immortal criminal. By surrounding him with eternal perspectives, it taught man to see himself from a distance and as something past and whole.[32]

[32] *The Gay Science*, tr. W. Kaufmann (New York: Vintage Press, 1974), section 78.

In everyday life we are, as it were, so close up to our lives that we lose ourselves in a maze of everyday details, demands and decisions. In worrying about the train to catch, the assignment to finish that is already late, the morning's quarrel over the washing up and how it is to be resolved, we lose sight of the 'simple and essential decisions' (*PLT* p. 48)[33] that constitute our world, lose sight of the wood on account of the trees. Heidegger speaks of the 'clearing' as permeated by 'concealment'[34] or 'dissembling' (*PLT* p. 54). The 'essential' 'withdraws itself' into a 'veil[ed]' and 'dim confusion' (*PLT* p. 74). The best word to use here, I think, is 'camouflage'. Everyday life camouflages our foundational values in somewhat the way in which, in (to my mind relatively useless) foreign-vocabulary-learning exercises, a word is camouflaged by random letters thus:

azomanopt.

In daily life what vanishes from our existence are the 'simple and essential' meanings which establish our 'position in the midst of beings' and give, thereby, meaning and direction to our lives.

In *Being and Time* Heidegger speaks of situations in which some kind of breakdown interrupts the smooth flow of everyday existence as the point at which world stands forth out of its usual inconspicuousness (*BT* 74–5). The car, for example, fails to start. In such a situation, he suggests, one is likely to become suddenly aware of the network of life-connections that is one's world and in which the car plays a vital role.

Though 'The Origin' does not think of the artwork as any kind of breakdown, it does, in a similar way, think of world becoming conspicuous when and only when the flow of everyday existence is disrupted. When we come under the power of the work we undergo, Heidegger says, 'displacement'. The work 'transport[s] us out of the realm of the ordinary', out of *Being and Time*'s 'average everydayness', and into 'the openness of beings' of which it is the locus (*PLT* p. 66).

---

[33] It is essential to realize that the use of the word 'decision', here, lends no support whatever to the Promethean reading of 'The Origin'. What Heidegger is referring to are 'the rare and the simple decisions of history [which] arise [not from any human being but] from the way the originary essence of truth essentially unfolds' (*P* p. 146). *History*, in other words Being in its 'destining', 'decides' on our world, not us.

[34] Heidegger is very careful to distinguish two modes of concealment: concealment *by* the clearing of world – concealment of all those alternative 'horizons of disclosure' which are occluded by our current one – and concealment *within* the clearing. Only the latter is 'dissembling' (*PLT* p. 60), and only dissembling concerns us in the present context.

How does this disruption of the 'dim confusion' of everydayness in which world 'veils and withdraws itself' happen? Heidegger introduces the verb 'setting up (*aufstellen*)' as a synonym for 'opening up' on the basis of the fact that the opening up of world bears a partial analogy to the 'setting up' of something on display in an exhibition (*Ausstellung*) (*PLT* p. 43). Somewhat in the way in which a normally inconspicuous object is brought to salience by being put on exhibition, so the work can be thought of as putting its world 'on exhibition'.

To illustrate this phenomenon one might, for example, think of the role played by the church – or rather the worship that occurs in it – in Christian practice; of the way in which the clarity and simplicity of the Creed and the Mass restores the individual, dispersed, distracted, harassed and compromised by the seeming urgencies of daily existence, to the 'simple and essential decisions' of the Christian life. In spite of his hostility, this virtue, as we noted, Nietzsche grudgingly concedes to Christianity.

What is 'earth'?

20. The artwork, then, 'sets up' a world, brings it out of inconspicuousness and into salience, places it 'on display'. But it does not, says Heidegger, *just* do that. The setting up is not 'bare placing'. Rather, the work 'consecrates' its world, invests it with 'dignity and splendour', allows it to stand forth 'as holy' (*PLT* p. 44). The artwork, as one might put it, brings its world to *charismatic* salience.

It is to do justice to this aspect of the work, so I shall argue, that Heidegger introduces into the discussion an entirely new term – 'earth'. The fundamental character of 'earth' as it occurs in 'The Origin' is, I believe, that it is the principle of holiness.

Heidegger introduces earth by, halfway through the essay, revising and expanding the definition of the artwork. The work, he now says, does not merely 'set up' a world. It also 'sets forth' (*herstellen* – literally, 'places here, *towards* us') 'the earth' (*PLT* p. 46). What is the effect of this revision? What does 'earth' mean?

21. Heidegger's *Grundgedanke*, let us remember, is that the artwork is the 'happening of truth'. The heart of his conception of the work must,

therefore, lie in his account of truth. The world–earth duality, I shall argue, is introduced to correspond to a duality in that account. Let us, therefore, return briefly to that account.

Truth as correspondence, we know (from section 13 above), presupposes truth as disclosure, truth as '*aletheia*'. Such a disclosure is embodied in a 'language' and constitutes a 'world'.

As we saw in my (rather drab) 'Smith' example, one and the same, as we may call it, 'region of Being', can have a number of different disclosures. George may be disclosed as a table, a congregation of molecules, a space–time position or as the house of a god. Even if we confine ourselves just to disclosures of Smith which we contemporary human beings can make intelligible to ourselves, even if we leave aside the possibility that Martian physics might disclose him in ways utterly unintelligible to us, it is clear that there is no upper limit to the number of possible disclosures a region of Being may receive.

Only one disclosure – or as, following Nietzsche, Heidegger, on occasion, also says, 'perspective' (*P* p. 304) – may, however, be inhabited at any one time. Just as the ambiguous figure, disclosed as a duck, cannot simultaneously be disclosed as a rabbit, so Being, disclosed in the manner of atomic physics cannot be disclosed as everyday objects. Truth is thus always, as Heidegger puts it, 'concealment'. For one horizon of disclosure to be inhabited, to be, as it were, favoured, is for all others to be 'denied' or 'refused' (*PLT* pp. 55, 60), occluded.

'World' is, of course, not just any 'horizon', just any old 'perspective' on things. It is, as I put it, the horizon of all our horizons, the horizon within which all perspectives available to us are contained, the outermost limit (like Kant's 'categories') of what, to us, is intelligible.[35] Yet the axiom that truth implies concealment applies to it too. This means that, through reflection on the character of truth, we know that belonging to our 'truth', in the sense of 'world', is an indefinitely large totality of other possible 'truths', alternative horizons of disclosure, 'views' disclosing other 'sides' of our world of beings (*DT* pp. 64–5) that are equally

---

[35] This is the reason that cubism is not a counter-example to the principle that truth is always concealment. Arguably, a cubist portrait allows us to inhabit several visual perspectives at the same time. Yet representation occurs, nonetheless, within specific, post-Renaissance conventions of visual intelligibility which exclude indefinitely many alternative 'languages': the language, for example, of Maori art.

disclosive of Being (reality),[36] itself, yet blocked by our disclosure and, in fact, utterly unintelligible to us. It is this region of ineffability, the, as it were, epistemological 'depth' to Being, which Heidegger calls 'earth'. Earth, he says, is that which is 'closed . . . not [conceptually] mastered . . . concealed, [conceptually] disconcerting (*Beirrendes*)' (*PLT* p. 55).[37] Earth is the area of 'unfathomable' (*PLT* p. 128, compare p. 180) darkness which constitutes the other 'side' of the 'clearing' that is world, 'the side of . . . [Being] that is averted from us, unilluminated by us' (*PLT* p. 124). Being is thus 'world' and 'earth' taken together. In an image which later Heidegger takes over from Rilke, it resembles the moon: behind the side illuminated by and for us lies an immeasurable – 'ungraspable' (*Ister* p. 136) – area of unperceived darkness (*PLT* p. 124).

Notice that Heidegger's world–earth duality looks very like Nietzsche's duality between the 'Apollonian', the conceptually grasped and articulated, and the 'Dionysian', that which lies beyond conceptual articulation, beyond intelligibility.[38] This is no accident since at the end of the lectures on Hölderlin's 'The Rhine' (and throughout the Hölderlin lectures of the thirties and forties) Heidegger makes clear that he subscribes to this fundamental Nietzschean distinction. The only qualification to the acceptance is his insistence that the distinction was discovered earlier and the relationship between the two terms thought more profoundly, by Hölderlin. For this reason he prefers Hölderlin's terminology to Nietzsche's, prefers to express it as a distinction between 'clarity of presentation (*Klarheit der Darstellung*)', on the one hand, and 'the fire from heaven' or 'holy pathos', on the other (*GA* 39, pp. 290–4).

Heidegger's world–earth duality is, I suggest, identical with Hölderlin's 'clarity of presentation'–'fire from heaven' duality.[39] Later on, as we will see, 'earth', in the signification it has in 'The Origin', disappears from

---

[36] To repeat, 'that which genuinely is . . . is uniquely Being' (*QCT* p. 44), 'reality' (*das Wirkliche*).   [37] See footnote 34 above.

[38] See further my *Nietzsche's Philosophy of Art* (Cambridge: Cambridge University Press, 1992), chapter 2.

[39] The acute reader, noting that on the Rilke image, 'earth' turns out to be, as I put it (in the paragraph before last), 'unfathomable darkness', may wonder how it can also be 'fire from heaven'. This combination which 'for everyday thinking is . . . a crude contradiction', however, is exactly how, under Hölderlin's influence, Heidegger does come to conceive the Dionysian. To experience it is to experience the 'dark light' of ecstatic intoxication, something which (like, one might suggest, a ruby) 'comes to shine through its darkness' (*GA* 52, p. 149; cf. *GA* 4, p. 117).

Heidegger's vocabulary. But the concept it expresses does not. It becomes expressed, rather, by more directly revealing phrases such as 'the secret', 'the ungraspable', 'the Other', 'divine radiance', and, most centrally, by 'the holy'.[40]

'Earth' in the artwork

22. Since truth is always concealment, since 'untruth' (*PLT* p. 54) is always its other 'side', since world is but the illuminated 'surface' of an uncharted and unbounded region of epistemological darkness, truth is essentially a 'mystery' (*P* p. 148ff.), 'uncanny' (*PLT* p. 54). Ordinarily, however, we forget the mystery of truth. We believe we dwell in 'the immediately surrounding circle of beings', of things, that are 'familiar, reliable, ordinary' (*PLT* p. 54). (Elsewhere Heidegger calls this '*Seinsvergessenheit*' – 'forgetfulness of [the 'depth' of] Being', forgetfulness that our realm of beings is just one disclosure of a reality that contains within itself the possibility of infinitely many alternative realms of beings.) In terms of the moon image, our everyday experience resembles the child's understanding of the moon as a flat, illuminated disk. The impoverished, everyday drabness (or scientistic *hubris*) which supposes our own clearing to be everything that there is – the drabness which finds philosophical expression in the idea that all there is to truth is correspondence – forgets the concealment that belongs to unconcealment, forgets the dark side of the moon.

The artwork, on the other hand, disrupts, 'displace[s]' (*PLT* p. 66), such forgetfulness since in it, earth 'rises up through (*durchragt*)'[41] world (*PLT* p. 49), 'rises up as self-closing' (*PLT* p. 55), rises up, that is to say, *in* its incomprehensibility. Through the work, to put the point in terms of an elegant paradox from the 1942 *Ister* lectures, we 'grasp . . . the ungraspable' and ourselves 'in the face of the ungraspable' (*Ister* p. 136).

The question that confronts us, however, is: why should we believe this?

---

[40] With no doubt Hölderlin's line 'Full of merit, yet poetically man dwells upon this earth' in mind, Heidegger offers something like a definition of 'earth': it is 'the ground' 'on which man bases his dwelling' (*PLT* p. 42). 'The Origin' never explains the connection between dwelling and the idea of the numinously incomprehensible. But, as we will see in chapter 4, it becomes central to Heidegger's later thinking about dwelling.

[41] Hofstadter's 'juts through' is, I think, too localized and too violent.

Why should we believe that great art, *in particular*, initiates us into a proper understanding of truth, disrupts our normal forgetfulness of 'earth'? Why should we believe that it is part of the proper reception of great art that through it we grasp our lives as lived in the face of 'the ungraspable'?

Heidegger says, to repeat, that the great artwork does not simply bring world to salience but brings it to salience in 'dignity and splendour', 'as holy'. (Notice that Rilke's description of the wall is not, in terms of *this* condition, 'great' art. Far from coming forth in splendour, his world comes forth as seedy and disgusting. *Great* art, for Heidegger as for Nietzsche, is life-*affirming*.) Later on Heidegger makes the same point by saying that, in the work, 'truth happens' – world comes to salience – 'with extraordinary awesomeness' (*PLT* p. 68). Truth happens awesomely because world presences as holy. Awe and reverence is the receptive-active response which necessarily accompanies – is – the reception of the holy as the holy. 'Earth', so I suggest, is introduced to explain this aspect of the artwork.

23. The crucial axiom in Heidegger's thinking is, I suggest (to put it rather formally), that

x is grasped as holy, as 'awesome',[42] if and only if x is grasped in its infinite mystery, its unintelligibility.

An important sentence, repeated three times in Heidegger's 1946 essay 'The Saying of Anaximander' (*GA* 5, pp. 321–74) is : 'Being withdraws as it reveals itself in what is.' This is the idea captured in the moon simile presented in the Rilke essay of the same year. The part of the quotation which needs emphasizing in the present context is the statement that it is 'Being . . . *itself*' which is apprehended when we apprehend world. Unlike the Kantian 'appearance' or 'phenomenon', world is not something ontologically separate from Being. This is part of the appropriateness of the moon image. For what we see when we look up into the night sky is not some entity distinct from the moon, not a moon 'appearance' or 'representation' behind which the 'moon-in-itself' lurks (as the TV hardware lurks behind

---

[42] This identification of the holy and the awesome is problematic. I shall articulate and address the problem in chapter 3 (sections 20–1).

the TV image) as something completely unknown. What we see, rather, is simply *the moon* – the moon, if one wishes to speak this way, 'in itself'.

On the other hand, however, world is only one aspect, one 'facet' (*PLT* p. 124) of Being, of a reality which, since it is a 'plenitude' of such facets (*ibid.*), remains infinitely 'withdrawn', 'closed', 'concealed', unintelligible. That something possesses – possesses *itself* – such unfathomability, depth and mystery is what, according to Heidegger, renders it 'awesome', 'holy' or, as I would say, using a traditional term from the philosophy of art, 'sublime'.[43] (In eighteenth- and nineteenth-century philosophy of art the heart of the sublime is the idea of a magnitude so vast as baffles conceptual comprehension.) This, it seems to me, is a compelling analysis of the holy or sublime. The novice and the experienced mariner have the same visual experience. But whereas the former sees an ice floe – something belonging to Heidegger's realm of 'the familiar, reliable, ordinary' – the latter sees an iceberg[44] and in doing so experiences something sublime. Awesomeness lies in concealment. 'God', says Heidegger, remains something 'exalted and holy' only so long as he preserves 'the mysteriousness of his distance' (*QCT* p. 26), his beyond-the-horizon-of-our-conceptual-understanding-ness. People, too, are sublime on account of their mystery. If one feels one has plucked out the heart of another's mystery, that one has a complete conceptual mastery of what makes her 'tick' – that she has become, as Heidegger would say, completely 'calculable' – then she cannot command awe or even respect. Antigone or (in the right production) Madam Butterfly are sublime characters because they operate according to principles that are beyond the standards of everyday calculation, present themselves, in terms of such standards, as unintelligible. Similarly that other traditional image of the subime (one of great interest to Heidegger (see, for example, *GA* 9, pp. 309–10)), the warrior; one who risks and even sacrifices life for the nebulousness of 'people' or 'homeland'.

---

[43] I take 'sublime' to be a synonym for 'awesome'. Heidegger does not use the former term partly because it is subsumed under his most preferred term 'holy', but partly too, I think, on account of a reluctance to identify with anything in the Western tradition of philosophizing about art, a tradition which, remember, he officially holds to be nothing but 'aesthetics'. (This characterization, of course, conveniently ignores the traditional dichotomy between the sublime and the beautiful and the side of the tradition that is concerned with the former.)

[44] Compare Rilke's image of everyday consciousness as the 'tip of a pyramid', quoted by Heidegger at *PLT* p. 128.

Heidegger's claim that 'truth happens awesomely' in great art is corroborated by the way in which art has traditionally been received and thought about. The artwork – the temple with its statue of the god, the cathedral with its altarpiece – was the traditional focus of religious worship, the medium through which the *sacred* word was spoken. As formal religion declined, art changed its character. Yet awe before both the creator of the work and the work itself remained undiminished. The creator was someone possessed by a muse or as even, himself, (as Hölderlin describes the poet) a 'demigod'. Even the sober Kant describes the great artist as a 'genius', that is, someone for whose activity 'no definite rule can be given'.[45] And still today we speak of 'maestros' and 'divas'. In traditional philosophy of art the awesomeness of the work itself is acknowledged in the recognition of conceptual bafflement as a defining condition of great art. Kant, for example, says that great art is art which expresses a content

that induce[s] much thought, yet without the possibility of any definite thought whatever, that is *concept*, being adequate to it, and which language, consequently, can never quite get on level terms with, or render completely intelligible,[46]

and Schopenhauer says, more succinctly: 'we are entirely satisfied by the impression of a work of art only when it leaves behind something we cannot bring down to the distinctness of a concept' (*The World as Will and Representation*, II, p. 409).

Given, then, the observation that truth happens awesomely in great art, and his analysis of the awesome, Heidegger reasons, I believe, in somewhat the following manner:

(1) world or 'truth' is grasped as holy or awesome by the authentic receivers ('preservers' (*PLT* pp. 66–8)) of great art
(2) something is grasped as holy or awesome if and only if it is grasped in its infinite unintelligibility, i.e. as the 'self-disclosure' of the infinitely 'self-concealing'
so
(3) world is grasped as holy or awesome if and only if it is grasped in its infinite unintelligibility, metaphorically, that is, as the illuminated 'side' of that of which the other 'side' is 'earth'
and therefore
(4) earth presences and 'rises up through' world in the great artwork

---

[45] *The Critique of Judgment*, tr. J. C. Meredith (Oxford: Oxford University Press, 1952), pp. 168–9.   [46] *Ibid.*, p. 210.

'Rises up through' I take to be a phrase intended to capture what, for example, the hidden part of an iceberg does when the ice floe is apprehended as an iceberg. The hidden part, though not part of visual experience, is nonetheless, in a sense, seen – seen 'in the mind's eye' – to be there. Another metaphor later Heidegger sometimes uses to convey the same idea is that of 'transparency', of the clearing's 'clearing' (*QCT* p. 44). In everyday experience world is, he says (following Rilke), 'opaque' (*PLT* p. 108). As experienced in and through great art, on the other hand, it becomes translucent, transparent to 'earth'. Experienced as the self-disclosure of an unfathomable 'mystery' it acquires radiance, becomes, as one might also say, *numinous*, a 'holy' place.

24. What does the artwork's 'setting forth' of earth add to its 'setting up' of world? What does the idea of the work as the *transparent* 'happening of truth' add to its conception as the mere happening of truth? Why, that is, is it important that the work not only brings its world to salience but brings it to salience as a *holy* world, a world invested with 'dignity and splendour', (a world in which, as later Heidegger puts it, things 'thing' (*PLT* pp. 177ff.))? In a word, because 'dignity', 'splendour', charisma, is *authority*.

The artwork, we have seen, brings to 'clarity of presentation' the fundamental ethical 'laws' (HE p. 312) of its culture. But clarity alone is not enough – not enough to produce *observance* of those laws. Finding oneself in Creon's Thebes, Nazi Germany, Stalin's Russia, Milosevic's Serbia (even, perhaps, the world of Rilke's wall), one is liable to receive constant and clear reminders of the culture's fundamental values yet at the same time to find oneself deeply alienated from those values. Or one might be a visiting anthropologist, recording with detached curiosity the ethical customs of the natives yet with no commitment at all to live by those customs oneself.

What this discloses is that knowledge of and commitment to a fundamental *ethos* are two different things. In Kant's language 'respect' for the 'moral law' is different from, and additional to, knowledge of that law.

This is where 'earth' comes into the picture. Because 'world' is transparent to 'earth', because it presences as the self-disclosure of the infinitely 'awesome', it itself presences charismatically, as a 'holy' place. This endows its laws with the unconditional authority characteristic of ethical obligation. For while it makes perfect sense for Antigone to ask why and whether she should abide by the laws of Creon's state, it does not make sense to ask why one should do what is *holy*, abide by, as Heidegger calls them, 'the *divine* destinings' (*QCT* p. 34: my emphasis).[47] As 'preserved' throughout the culture, therefore, the artwork not only makes clear the 'simple and essential' outlines of what is to be done, but endows its imperatives with absolute authority. Individuals achieve 'the resoluteness intended in Being and Time' (*PLT* p. 67), become committed to 'restrain[ing] . . . all doing and prizing, knowing and looking . . . within the truth that is happening in the work' (*PLT* p. 66), and the culture, so long as the work retains its power to bring both 'world' and 'earth' to presence, endures. In *The Brothers Karamazov* Dostoyevsky's Grand Inquisitor identifies 'miracle, mystery and authority' as the 'three powers' by which the church 'holds prisoner' the consciences of its flock 'for their own good'. For Heidegger, on the other hand, there is only one 'power' (a term he indeed frequently applies to the great artwork (for example at *GA* 39, p. 214)). The mystery *is* the authority.

Difficulties in the account of 'earth' in the artwork

25. One problem connected with Heidegger's introduction of 'earth' into the analysis of the artwork concerns the question of whether, as he seems to want to hold, the art of medieval Christendom can really count as great art. The problem is created by the fact that, for medieval theology, 'world' in the sense of natural world is, as Heidegger notes (*GA* 39, p. 195; *Ister*

---

[47] Heidegger's post- (or pre-)Enlightenment understanding of the character of ultimate ethical authority as essentially charismatic is, of course, *dangerous*. (It is, however, a view shared by such benign spirits as Vaclav Havel and Iris Murdoch – Murdoch speaks, in the *Sovereignty of the Good*, of morality as resting on an 'unesoteric mysticism'.) It is what led Heidegger, for a time, to think of Hitler as a new god, a new ethical paradigm, and is why, having recovered himself, he warns against the worship of false 'idols' and manufactured gods (*PLT* p. 150), the power of Hitler's charisma being the product of his and Goebbels' pioneering understanding of the manipulative powers of the mass media. The ethical task is, then, to distinguish genuine holiness from false glamour. It would be nice if, as Kant dreamt, there were rules, algorithms, for doing this. But, such is life, there are not. As the Greeks understood and Heidegger emphasizes in the *Ister* lectures, life is essentially a *Wagnis*, a risk, in which illusion – 'dissembling' (*PLT* p. 54) – constantly threatens to displace truth.

pp. 30–1, 77–8, 103–4), not a holy place but a place, rather, of corruption and exile. The response to this difficulty has to be that the 'medieval world', the world 'opened up' by, let us say, Giotto, embraces not just nature but heaven too. Yet that 'world' in this expanded sense should appear as holy requires, on Heidegger's analysis, a ground of holiness, 'earth', which lies *outside* it. God, however, in the Lord's Prayer, for example, is said to be a being who belongs 'in heaven', *within* world, a locatedness which leads towards the heresy that there is something more awesome than God himself. To avoid such heresy God has to be located outside of 'world', has to be identical, in short, with what Heidegger calls 'earth'. The insistence on God's ineffability by the mystical strand in the Christian tradition (by, for instance, Meister Eckhart, one of Heidegger's major sources of inspiration) effectively makes such an identification. And so, too, does the fact that in many traditional representations of heaven God is conspicuous by his pictorial absence, presencing only in the golden light with which everything is surrounded. (Perhaps the distinction between God the 'father' and God the 'holy ghost' has something to do with this problem.)

26. A more serious problem connected with the presence of 'earth' in the analysis of the artwork concerns the fact that Heidegger does not merely claim that earth presences in the work along with world but seeks, additionally, to explain *how* it does so.

In equipment, hammers and the like, materials, says Heidegger, 'disappear into usefulness'. This is a repetition of *Being and Time*'s point that, in normal use, items of equipment present themselves functionally (as 'ready-to-hand') rather than materially (as 'present-to-hand'). It is *abnormal* for us to be aware of the grain of the hammer's shaft, the shine of its head, the faint yet pungent smell of the steel in that head. When we respond to the artwork as an artwork, however, materials become salient, 'shine forth'. We notice the sensuous qualities, the 'lustre and gleam' (*PLT* p. 42), of the stone in the temple, the colours of a Van Gogh, the sound of the words in a Hölderlin poem. Yet the materials of the artwork are 'self-secluding'. Colours or sounds may be represented in terms of measurable wavelengths, the stone's weight in terms of numbers, yet we know that the colour, sound or weight itself is by no means fully captured in such representations.

Hence in apprehending the artwork we become aware of the inadequacy of all our 'projections' fully to capture the nature of the material, aware that there is infinitely more to nature, to beings, than we can ever make intelligible to ourselves. In the material, that is, 'earthy' element of the artwork 'earth' stands forth in its 'self-secludingness' (*PLT* pp. 46–7).[48]

In the light of his theory of truth, Heidegger is absolutely right to maintain that every material thing possesses an unlimited 'plenitude' of aspects which lie beyond the realm of what is intelligible to us. The moon simile, that is, applies not only to a world as a whole but also to the individual beings it contains. It is also true that a meditation on the materiality of humble things may lead us to experience them in their astonishing mystery. A meditation on the 'earthy' may lead us to an experience of, in Heidegger's sense, 'earth'. Nonetheless, the assumption that such a meditation *necessarily* belongs to the reception of great art contains, I think, at least two serious mistakes.

The first is the assumption that in the proper reception of art we *always* become attentive to the materials in the work, to its 'tactile' or, more generally, 'formal values'. Sometimes, often even, such attention is indeed of central importance. Heidegger's friend Braque mixed sand and other forms of 'earth' into his pigment so as to, as it were, demand a response to the earthiness of our existence. And a response to the stone in the temple is, as Heidegger points out, hard to avoid. The effect of eternal solidity could not be achieved in, for example, wood. Yet the high Gothic cathedral, on the other hand, in its gravity-defying, heavenward ascent, asks us precisely to *ignore* the stony weight of its stone, to pretend that, like the soul, it is made out of some immaterial, ethereal stuff. (Hence the ambition to construct a cathedral entirely out of glass in Peter Carey's *Oscar and Lucinda*.) And with regard to films, for instance, attention to the elegance of the spatial organization of the frames is usually a sign that the drama has failed to capture our attention – that the film has failed as an artwork – and that one is seeking diversion in order to evade boredom. Art can sometimes be in *this* respect similar to 'equipment'. It can conceal its materials or pretend that they are other than they are. And to insist that if it does it cannot count as *great* art is entirely arbitrary.

[48] The foregoing is a slightly tidied up version of, I think, a somewhat confused passage of thinking.

Setting aside this objection, there remains the problem that Heidegger's line of reasoning looks to be, in the jargon of analytic philosophy of language, an 'intensional fallacy'. He seems to claim, that is, that: (a) in responding properly to an artwork we are aware of its (e.g.) colour; that (b) colour is essentially 'self-secluding'; and to conclude that, therefore, (c), in responding properly to an artwork we apprehend the self-secludingness of its materials. But this is as fallacious as arguing that in knowing Ortcutt to be in the park one knows a spy to be in park given, merely, that it is true that Ortcutt is, in fact, a spy. (One is, of course, likely to be unaware of this fact.) And it is actually most implausible to suppose that on those occasions when one does respond to the materials in a work one has running through one's mind the thought: 'What wonderful colour and, gosh, how mysterious that such wonder can't be fully captured by science.'

The reason for this is that when we do respond to the material values of an artwork what is likely to grab us is nothing to do with conceptual inscrutability but rather sensuous beauty. The beautiful is, after all, what, according to 'aesthetics', we respond to when we abstract from the instrumental categories of normal experience. And the paradoxical fact of the matter is that Heidegger, in this passage of thinking, has effectively lapsed into 'aesthetics', into insisting that the proper response to art requires the adoption of the 'disinterested', 'aesthetic attitude'. This fact alone should be sufficient to reveal the forgettable character of the entire passage.

27. If attention to materials is not the explanation of the presence of the 'ungraspable' in the artwork, if the salience of 'earth' (the unintelligible) has no intrinsic connection to the salience of 'earth' (the material), what is the explanation of such a presence? This question, however, contains a false presupposition. For there is, I believe, no such thing as a general theory as to why art facilitates our grasping our lives as lived 'in the face of the ungraspable'.

In his discussions of Klee, Cézanne and Japanese Nô plays, as we will see in chapter 4, Heidegger is intensely interested in the way in which truth happens in these artworks, as I put it, 'transparently'; in the way in which they allow what 'The Origin' calls 'earth' to shine through world and render it numinous. In these discussions, too, he is interested in elucidating the way in which this happens. With regard to Klee, he thinks that his sparse, glass engraver's drawing is important; with regard to Cézanne, his partial deconstruction of objects; with regard to Nô plays, the fact that landscape is conjured to presence by nothing but mime performed on an empty stage. The thing to notice about these observations is, first, that there is no mention at all of attention to materials, and, second, that the formal feature identified is in each case *different*. This seems to me to reflect the truth of the matter. 'Truth', in many artworks, happens 'awesomely'. But with respect to *how* it so happens each work must be treated on its own merits. There are a thousand and one ways in which, for the right audience, 'earth rises up through world'. In the medieval cathedral stained-glass windows are a powerful metaphor for the transparency of world, in the altarpiece it is the gold which allows the numinous to shine 'through' world.

And we should not be surprised if, sometimes, we have no idea as to how the effect is achieved, and should never suppose that hints and elucidations, such as Heidegger provides with regard to Klee, Cézanne and Nô plays, represent a *theory* of the numinous, the identification of a comprehensive *technique* for bringing earth to presence. Art criticism of a technical character, so long as it remains tentative and *ex post facto*, is, of course, possible. But art theorizing – in the sense of plucking out the heart of its mystery – is not. Great art not only brings 'the mystery' to presence but is itself essentially mysterious. The great work of art, to repeat Kant's definition, is something for which 'no rule can be given' (see p. 44 above). The task, as Heidegger wisely says in the epilogue to 'The Origin' – but forgets in the passage under discussion – is to see the 'enigma (*Rätsel*)' of art, not to solve it (*PLT* p. 79).

Great art is communal

28. Great art is, then, the transparent happening of truth, the co-presence of 'world' and 'earth' in the work in such a way that the latter 'rises up through', becomes visible through, the former. This, however, is not yet the completed definition of the artwork. One further condition remains to be added.

To be a 'great' artwork the work must, says Heidegger, be received; in his own language, 'preserved'. There must be those who come under its 'power' (*GA* 39, p. 214), those who 'stand within the openness of beings that happens in the work' (*PLT* p. 67), and have their lives, 'all [their] usual doing and prizing' (*PLT* p. 66), decisively affected as a result.

This is a somewhat startling condition since it leaves no room for the idea of great but unappreciated artworks. (In popular mythology, of course, it is almost a defining condition of great works that they are unappreciated in their time: Beethoven's late quartets were considered unplayable by his contemporaries, Van Gogh sold only one painting during his lifetime, authentic poets starve in garrets, and so on.) Yet Heidegger, quite explicitly, rejects such a possibility:

Just as a work cannot be without being created so what is created cannot come into being without those who preserve it. However, if a work does not find preservers, does not at once find them such as respond to the truth happening in the work, this does not at all mean that the work may be a work without preservers. Being a [great] work . . . always remains tied to preservers. (*PLT* pp. 66–7)

Heidegger reasons as follows. To be, in the full sense, an art*work*, the work must 'work', that is, be effective. (The '*werk*' in '*Kunstwerk*' is etymologically connected to '*wirken*', to 'work' or 'have an effect'.) If it is not yet received then it does not yet 'work' – it lacks a 'work-being' (*PLT* p. 39) and is at best a *potential* artwork. (If it *no longer* 'works', if it has 'passed over into the realm of tradition and conservation', then it is, presumably, like John Cleese's ex-parrot, an *ex*-artwork.)

Who are the 'preservers'? Not isolated individuals but rather an entire culture. 'Whenever [great] art happens', says Heidegger – repeating his Hegelian starting-point that great art is the disclosure of truth to 'man's historical existence' – 'history either begins or starts over again.' Since 'history is the transporting of a people into its appointed task as entrance into that people's endowment' (*PLT* p. 77), only when it makes sense to speak of the work being received by an entire culture, a 'people',[49] does it count, for Heidegger as being 'preserved'. The paradigmatic role played by temple and cathedral is, here, very evident.

[49] In the 'Germania' lectures Heidegger bitterly attacks the racial and biological conceptions of 'people (*Volk*)' of racist thinkers such as Rosenberg and Kolbenheyer (*GA* 39, pp. 26–7). It is clear, therefore, that 'people' is, for him, not a racial, but rather a cultural – above all, linguistic – concept. Heidegger would have had no difficulty in accepting Turks born and educated in Germany as 'Germans'.

This requirement, the requirement, as I shall put it, that the artwork be 'communally' received, reveals a great deal about Heidegger's conception of 'greatness'. Greatness, as he points out (*N* I, p. 84) is a matter of 'magnitude'. But the magnitude he has in mind in connection with art is world-historical significance. The great work is great in the way in which 'great men' of history are great. Like them, it bestrides its epoch as a colossus.

29. How, it might be asked, can a *single* artwork bestride an entire epoch? What it is important to notice, here, is that when Heidegger speaks of 'the temple' he is not speaking, at least, not only speaking, about the temple at Paestum. Neither are his thoughts about 'the cathedral' confined to thoughts about Bamberg Cathedral. 'The temple' and 'the cathedral' are not, that is, particular buildings but are, rather, building *types* repeatedly instantiated throughout their cultures by particular buildings. These particular buildings and the forms of worship that take place in them are never, of course, exactly the same. As authentically Greek *techne*, 'bringing forth', they respond to local landscape, local materials and local cultural differences. The god or saint venerated as the guardian of one city is different from the god or saint venerated in another. Yet in Greece or Christendom there is enough similarity between the buildings and forms of worship to justify speaking of a single artwork (type) as being repeated throughout, and so binding together, the entire culture.

The artwork creates a people

30. Before us, now, lies the completed definition of the artwork. The great work, to recapitulate, is something which, first, brings 'world' out of background inconspicuousness and into the clarity of foreground salience, second, allows it to be transparent to 'earth' so as to appear as 'holy' (and hence commanding), and third, gathers together an entire culture to bear witness to the numinous salience of world which happens in the work. The next question that needs an answer is: why, exactly, is the work, thus understood, important? Why is it something for which we have, in the words of the Nietzsche volume, an 'absolute need' (*N* I, p. 84)?

Heidegger's answer (as opposed to the meaning of that answer) is relatively clear:

Whenever art happens – that is, whenever there is a beginning – a thrust enters history, history either begins or starts over again. History means here not a sequence of events of whatever sort, however important. History is the transporting of a people into its appointed task (*Aufgegebene*) as entrance into that people's endowment (*Mitgegebene*). (*PLT* p. 77)

And again:

Poetry [i.e. art] founds the ground of the possibility that man . . . can become historical, in other words can become a people. (*GA* 39, p. 216)

Formally speaking, these answers are inconsistent since while the second speaks of art as creating a 'people' the first speaks of art as doing something to an already-existent people. Fairly clearly, however, the inconsistency is a superficial one, to be resolved by understanding 'people' in the first quotation as 'potential people' and in the second as 'actual' or 'fully-realized' people. The artwork's 'transporting a [potential] people into . . . its endowment' will thus be the occasion of its becoming an actual people, a – to change the terminology – potential community's[50] becoming a *living* community.

Thus, though I have rejected Prometheanism with respect to world, there is, after all, a kind of Prometheanism in 'The Origin': the artwork creates (realizes) a 'people', a living community. Why should this be the case?

A people's 'endowment' is, reasonably clearly, what section 74 of *Being and Time* calls its 'heritage' (the words are virtual synonyms), what 'The Origin' calls its 'simple and essential decisions', and what I have called its 'fundamental *ethos*'. In *Being and Time* 'inauthentic Dasein' is one who, in his life, 'forgets' the fundamental values of both his culture and (since he is, at bottom, a 'construct' of that culture) himself, allows himself to become a function of the fluctuating fashions of current public opinion ('the One'). Authentic Dasein, by contrast, actively 'remembers' heritage. In doing so she achieves two things. First, critical distance from current public opinion – she achieves self-determination – and second, a projection of herself, of her 'task', into the future, a projection determined by the conjunction of heritage with her own concrete situation – her talents, limitations, historical context and so on. These two features together (in

---

[50] At *BT* 384 Heidegger identifies 'people' and 'community'.

chapter 2 of *HPN* I call them 'autonomy' and 'focus') constitute what *Being and Time* calls 'becoming resolute', becoming, that is, '(authentically) historical'. What liberates one to heritage and from the 'dictatorship of the One' is authentic 'being-towards death', facing rather than evading the fact that one dies alone and soon and possibly at any moment.[51]

By the time of 'The Origin' two changes have occurred in Heidegger's thinking. First, his focus has shifted from the authenticity of individual to that of collective Dasein. Second, the agent of this is no longer 'being towards death' but rather the artwork. In spite of these changes, however, the account of Dasein's becoming authentic – becoming the 'people' that it potentially is – is, in the collective case, structurally identical to that given in the individual case. Thus collective Dasein's authenticity is a matter of, first of all, its actively remembering, appropriating, its heritage – 'entering into its endowment'.

In *Being and Time* every society, even an inauthentic one, in a sense, remembers its heritage. Its foundational values are preserved in its literature, its folklore, its myths and its cultural mood. Particularly important will be its account – typically largely or wholly mythical – of its own origin. If it pictures itself as having 'fallen' from a golden age in the past then it is, and knows itself to be, deeply inauthentic; not itself, not living out its own proper life. Later Heidegger pictures Western modernity as deeply inauthentic. Though its heritage, 'the divine in the world of the Greeks, in prophetic Judaism, in the preaching of Jesus', exists and is known, it is no longer 'appropriated' (*PLT* p. 184), does not 'any longer gather men and things unto [itself] . . . visibly and unequivocally and by such gathering dispose the world's history and man's sojourn in it' (*PLT* p. 91). To become authentic, to become once more a living community, we must re-enter our 'endowment'. We must overcome the disguised, 'dissembled' version of heritage that governs our current life (later Heidegger, as we will see, identifies the agent of modernity's 'dissembling' as 'enframing', the reduction of everything to 'resource'), heritage must be once more seen and appropriated.

When, through the artwork, heritage is appropriated it determines for

---

[51] This, of course, is a very crude and incomplete summary of division II of *Being and Time*. For a fuller treatment see *HPN* chapter 2.

the culture, in conjunction with the current situation (its own political and social condition, the world-historical situation, and so on), the outline 'shape' of its proper future, its 'destiny'. That culture's 'entrance into its endowment' is also its being 'transported' into its 'appointed task', its 'becoming historical'. Through their appropriation of heritage, the members of a culture become united by commitment to a common project. Through such commitment a society becomes a living 'people'.[52]

This is a conclusion already previewed in the discussion of authentic community, 'authentic being-with-one-another', in section 26 of *Being and Time*. There Heidegger contrasts the 'being-with-one-another of those who are hired for the same affair' which 'often thrives on mistrust' (clearly an account of, in the language of German social theory, *Gesellschaft*, society) with the being together of those who 'devote themselves to the same affair in common, their doing so [being] . . . determined by the manner in which their Dasein, each in its own way, has been taken hold of'. In the latter case (clearly *Gemeinschaft*, community), individuals become 'authentically bound together' (*BT* 122). The realization of genuine community, of, that is, a 'people' (*BT* 384), is, then, a matter of shared *commitment*, a common project. *Being and Time* itself has no account of how this shared commitment comes about. But 'The Origin' fills this gap by telling us that it is the artwork which makes shared commitment possible. It is the artwork, therefore, which makes authentic community, makes a 'people' possible.

The artwork, then, realizes a people, brings forth authentic community. But why, to return to the question of the importance of the artwork with which I began this section, should *this* be important? Why should a society's becoming a 'people' be an 'absolute need'?

As we saw, 'One essential way in which truth establishes itself in the beings it has opened up . . . is the act that founds a political state' (*PLT* p. 62). As noted, the salient reference here is to Hitler – not the actual Hitler of 1936 but the, as it transpired, fictional Hitler of Heidegger's 1933 dreams (see footnote 12 above). As scholars such as Philippe

---

[52] Hegel maintained that a people only begins to 'make history' when it organizes itself into a political state. Heidegger makes the same claim save for attributing the key role to the artwork rather than the state. This difference reveals the fundamental ground for Heidegger's rejection of Hegel's thesis that the death of art is no cause for regret.

Lacoue-Labarthe have rightly emphasized, Heidegger's 1933 dream was of a National Socialist state which, as a great 'artwork', would restore a fallen Germany to authentic community, would bring about its realization through, in Heidegger's own words, 'an inner self-collection of the people' (quoted in *HPN* p. 17). (Only through the temple, Heidegger says in the temple passage, 'does the people first return to itself for the fulfillment of its vocation' (*PLT* p. 42).) If, then, we can discover why that is important, we will have discovered why the artwork is important.

In the 'Rectoral Address' and other political speeches of 1933–4, it is authentic 'science', specifically the university reformed so as to become 'the will to science as the historical-spiritual mission of the German people' (*HC* p. 30), which is to bring about the German people's self-realization. By 'The Origin' Heidegger has abandoned his faith in science – 'science is not an original happening of truth' (*PLT* p. 62) – and turned instead to art. This, however, is all that changes. Everything he had demanded in 1933 of science, in 1936 he demands of art.

What he demands, as he demanded of the reformed university, is that there should come into being a 'concentrated centre' that is a 'site of spiritual legislation' (*HC* pp. 37–8). In other words, that there should be a being which establishes, for the Germans as a whole, a clear and compelling knowledge of the 'German essence' (heritage) and hence of its 'historical destiny' (*HC* p. 36). In other words, the centre of legislation is to be the site of a 'spiritual leadership' that will lead the Germans – and through their becoming a 'centre' out of which unfold 'new spiritual energies', the entire West (*IM* p. 39) – out of the night of nihilism and back into its 'historical-spiritual mission'.

Why is *that* important? Because, first of all

True comradeship only arises under the pressure of a great common danger or from the ever-growing commitment to a clearly perceived common task; it has nothing to do with the effusive abandonment of psychological (*seelische*) inhibitions by individuals who have agreed to sleep, eat, and sing under one roof. (*HC* p. 26)

Only, in short, in the context of a people which has fully realized itself in shared commitment to a clearly articulated 'task' through the appropriation of heritage, is true community with others possible. Not in the face-to-face encounter of soul with soul but only in the side-by-side commitment to a shared project is authentic 'being-with-one-another' possible.

The realization of a people is important, therefore, because it is the precondition of the obtaining of genuine 'I–thou' relationships. Equally, however, it is important as the precondition of meaning. Meaningful work, says Heidegger, is simply 'the title of every well-ordered action that is of service to the people' (*HC* p. 59). Individual life acquired meaning by and only by the individual's contributing, 'each in its own way' (*BT* 122), to the 'historically' determined mission of the people. Only this can rescue us from the night of contemporary 'meaninglessness' (*GA* 39, p. 135).

Thus the artwork's realization of a people is important because through it and it alone is either integration or meaning possible. In the 1940s Heidegger's paradigm of a society marked by both alienation and meaninglessness is America: he calls it 'ahistorical' (*Ister* p. 55). Interestingly, the American writer Norman Mailer suggests his country's lack of a living heritage to be connected with the lack of a great artwork. Reviewing Tom Wolfe's *A Man in Full* as, in the end, a blockbuster rather than 'the great American novel' it aspires to be, Mailer laments the American condition as due to the fact that 'no American writer [has] succeeded . . . in doing the single great work that would clarify the nation's vision of itself as Tolstoy has done perhaps with *War and Peace*, or with *Anna Karenina* and Stendhal with *The Red and the Black*'.[53]

The artwork preserves a people

31. The artwork, then, by bringing forth its world to clear and commanding salience allows an inauthentic society, one that is either not yet or no longer a people, to become, or become once more (history's 'starting over again' (*PLT* p. 77)) a people. Its importance does not, however, lie merely in the creation or recreation of a people. It is important, too, because it *preserves* what it has created.

The word Heidegger uses more than any other to describe the relation between world and work is 'found (*stiften*)'. The work 'founds' its world (*PLT* p. 75; *GA* 39 et *passim*), a world which, to repeat, 'has already happened unnoticed in language' (*PLT* p. 74).

[53] *New York Review of Books* 45/20, December 1998, p. 18.

This looks like a contradiction. Since 'founding' looks to be a thoroughly Promethean notion, it is hard to see how that which has 'already happened' can possibly be founded. Heidegger's repeated use of 'found' in connection with the work's work has, I think, made a major contribution to the Promethean reading of 'The Origin'. In fact, however, when one looks at the context from which 'found' is taken and which establishes the meaning it has for Heidegger, it becomes clear that its central meaning is not 'create' but rather 'preserve'. This context is the last line of Hölderlin's 'Remembrance':

> But what endures, the poets found
> (*Was bleibet aber, stiften die Dichter*)

Commenting on this line in 'Hölderlin and the Essence of Poetry' Heidegger says:

This line sheds light on our question as to the essence of poetry [i.e. art]. Poetry is the act of founding the world . . . What is founded? The permanent (*das Bleibende*). But can the permanent then be founded? Is it not that which has always been present? No. Even the permanent must be brought to stand (*zum stehen gebracht*) against the forces that would tear it away (*gegen den Fortriss*), the simple must be wrested from confusion, measure must be set before that which lacks measure. That which supports and governs beings as a whole must become manifest . . . But even this permanent is fugitive. [Hölderlin says] 'Thus swiftly passes everything heavenly . . .'. But that this remains is 'entrusted to the poet as care and service'. (HE p. 304 and *GA* 4, p. 41; Cf. *GA* 39, pp. 215–16)

This passage makes clear that the artwork does not merely 'open up' a world. It also preserves its living existence and with it the 'people' it has brought into being. This same doubleness of function is made explicit in 'The Origin' itself. The work, it says, 'opens up a world and keeps it abidingly in force (*in waltenden Verblieb*) (*PLT* p. 44). The artwork, it says, is of vital importance because a world 'establishes' itself only if there is 'some being in the open . . . in which openness [world] takes its stand (*Stand*) [against 'the forces that would tear it away'] and achieves constancy [*Ständigkeit*] (*PLT* p. 61).

Let me note, here, *en passant*, how profoundly different the Heidegger–Hölderlin spirit is from that of, for example, certain, as we might call them, anarcho-existentialists.[54] For them, *every* reality

---

54 I mean, here, some of my students.

interpretation is an oppressive power-structure, the task being to sweep it away so as to be free to 'create oneself'. For Heidegger, on the other hand, the on-going and commanding salience of 'world' is precisely what is required for integration and meaning. When world 'veils and withdraws itself' (*PLT* p. 74), when our apprehension of it falls into decay and confusion, then alienation and nihilism sets in. The task, then – precisely the opposite of the anarcho-existentialist conception – is to *preserve* world, to bring it 'to stand' against the Heraclitean flux. The Heideggerian spirit is, in the best sense of the word, a profoundly conservative one.

What is the connection between the artwork and the endurance of its world and people? In *Being and Time* authenticity is never a once-and-for-all achievement. 'Falling' remains a constant threat. Similarly with respect to collective Dasein, the 'world withdrawal and world decay' which, in the end, overtook the worlds of both the temple at Paestum and of Bamberg Cathedral (*PLT* pp. 40–1) remains always a threat. The reason is fundamentally the same as the reason individual Dasein is under constant threat of 'falling'. Because we are, perforce, everyday creatures, world, heritage, constantly threatens to disappear into the multitude of confusing and camouflaging details which are 'average everydayness'.

What must the artwork be like not only to wrest us out of 'the realm of the ordinary' but also to keep us there? Heidegger writes that an authentic culture 'can never directly preserve its full momentum'. The only possible way 'to preserve [that] . . . full momentum is to repeat, to draw once again (*wieder-holen*) more deeply than ever from the source' (*IM* p. 191), in other words from heritage. Such a drawing – *Being and Time*'s 'repetition' of heritage – must not, however, amount to slavish copying. We must 'take a creative view of tradition' (*IM* p. 38) rather than adopting the ossified conservatism which demands that 'the formerly actual may recur' (*BT* 386) just as it was. To remain relevant and compelling in the current context the artwork must constantly reinvent itself – the worlds of the temple and cathedral disappeared, presumably, when their artworks cease to be able to do this. It is in line with this demand that Heidegger says that the poet must not only 'remind' the people of their voice, when it grows 'tired and weary', but sometimes, too, 'interpret' it (HE p. 312). And also that though Greek tragedy 'originate[s] in the saying of the people' it also 'transforms the people's saying so that now every essential word fights the battle and puts up for decision [i.e. allows us to see – see p. 31 above] what is holy and what unholy, what great and what small.' (*PLT* p. 43). For fourth-century Greece, the great tragedies did not 'refer to' a battle of gods in some archaic past. Rather, the work shows what the battle between Olympian (civilized) and Titanic (barbaric) values[55] comes to in the current context.[56] (One might also think here, perhaps, of the evangelical movement, of the vernacular mass and of 'modern dress' productions of Shakespeare and Wagner – of *Richard III* as the fall of fascism, or of the Ring cycle as the triumph of socialism over capitalism.)

Clarity and the priority of poetry

32. A final expository remark concerning 'The Origin'. In the Nietzsche volume Heidegger is sharply critical of the music dramas of Richard Wagner. Not that he criticizes Wagner's *goal*. The idea behind the '*Gesamtkunstwerk*', collective artwork, was not merely to collect together all the particular arts but also, Heidegger observes, to become '*the* religion' of the people, a religion that would be a 'celebration of the national community' (*N* I, pp. 85–6). With this goal (since it is, after all, his own) Heidegger has no quarrel at all. What he criticizes, rather, is Wagner's subordination of words to music, 'the domination of art as music, and thereby the domination of the pure state of feeling – the tumult and delirium of the senses' (*ibid.*). Given this presentation of 'the absolute' as 'sheer indeterminacy, total dissolution into sheer feeling', 'Wagner's attempt had to fail' (*N* I, p. 87). For what he missed is the fact that a 'solidly grounded and articulated position in the midst of beings' is 'the

---

[55] Values, to repeat, rooted in and inseparable from the fundamental structure of 'world', which man does not 'fabricate' but finds himself 'already' in. Heidegger himself abjures the word 'value', but only on account of its divorce, in contemporary thinking, from facts, not because he thinks there are no values: 'to think against "values" is not to maintain that everything interpreted as "a value" . . . is valueless' (*BW* p. 228).

[56] Some readers, influenced by Hegel's reading of Greek tragedy, take Heidegger to suggest that it presents a dialectic between new and old values rather than any definite solution to the dilemma. But this is a mistake. For Heidegger, Greek tragedy 'brought the dialogue of *divine* and human destinings to radiance' (*QCT* p. 34; my emphasis). Between such unequal contestants there can be no equality. As conceived in 'The Origin', art is no more satisfied to merely 'raise the level of debate' than is the Catholic Mass. Its point, rather, is decisively to *direct*, to provide us with 'a solidly grounded and articulated position in the midst of beings' (*N* I, p. 88).

kind of thing that only great poetry and thought can create' (*N* I, p. 88).[57]
Words, 'poetry' in the 'narrow' sense must, in short, always be supreme
in, the organizing principle of, the artwork. For only as the clear articulation of 'truth', of 'world', can the artwork 'gather men and things unto
[itself] . . . and by such gathering dispose of the world's history and man's
sojourn in it' (*PLT* p. 91), create, in other words, a 'people'.[58]

Given these remarks, we would make the same mistake as Wagner were
we to fail to subordinate the temple and cathedral to the 'linguistic
work[s]' (*PLT* p. 43) which it is their primary function to house and which
give them their meaning. That the temple is meaningful depends on a
prior understanding of Greek theology (mythology, that is), that the
cathedral's cruciform shape is meaningful depends on a prior linguistic
grasp of the meaning of the cross. Heidegger asserts this priority of the
linguistic by describing 'poesy – or poetry in the narrow sense' as 'the
most primordial (*ursprünglichste*) form of poetry in the essential sense'
(*PLT* p. 74). What this means is that for all the salience of the temple,
Heidegger's most fundamental paradigm of great art is, as with Hegel,
Hölderlin and Nietzsche, Greek tragedy (see further, chapter 3 sections
2–5).

Heidegger's self-criticisms

33. So far, my appproach to 'The Origin' has largely been an expository
one. Now, however, I want to turn to criticism of a fundamental kind,
more specifically, to what later Heidegger himself identifies as seriously
wrong-headed in the essay, to his self-criticisms. Among these, two stand
out as of particular importance: the charge, first, that the essay distorts
its theory of truth by adding to it, more or less gratuitously, what it calls
'the primal conflict', and, second, that its understanding of what constitutes a work of art is radically incomplete. The first criticism holds, then,
that the essay contains too much, the second that it contains too little. I
shall discuss these criticisms in the order presented.

---

[57] Great poetry *which is also* great thought, I would suggest.
[58] Heidegger's thinking is too underdeveloped to provide any answer on the subject of why
music should be important *at all* to the artwork. On the inadequacy of Heidegger's thinking about music, see chapter 4 section 26.

34. In expounding its conception in 'The Origin', art, I said, is the co-presence of 'world' and 'earth', the shining of the latter through the former. In presenting it in this way, however, I deliberately suppressed something to which the essay devotes a great deal of attention: the 'primal conflict (*Urstreit*)'. According to what Heidegger actually says, the artwork does not simply bring world and earth to presence. It brings them to presence *in their 'primal battle' with each other*. Hence the character of the work is essentially one of 'agitation' (*PLT* p. 48).

It is, I think, possible to see immediately that something has gone wrong. Some works of art, certainly, are agitated. Bearing in mind that, as Vincent Scully[59] has emphasized, the Greek temple and the, typically rugged, landscape of the site were considered as a single, artistic whole, it is true that the temple embodies a dynamic tension between the serenely geometric, strongly horizontal, 'rational' lines of the building itself and the jagged, 'irrational', predominantly vertical lines of the site. Heidegger records this kind of contrast in the temple passage:

standing there, the building holds its ground against the storm raging above it and so first makes the storm manifest in its violence. The steadfastness of the work contrasts with the raging of the surf and its own repose brings out the surge of the sea. (*PLT* p. 42)

But to suppose that *every* great artwork is agitated, to suppose, for example, this to be true of Raphael's '*Sixtina*' (discussed, as we saw (p. 20 above), by Heidegger in the 1950s), is to deny the difference, for example, between the high Renaissance and the mannerist or baroque. In great works of the Renaissance it is true, in Heidegger's language, that 'earth' as well as 'world' comes to presence – that they inspire awe – but, by and large, the two come to presence, not in conflict, but in a serene *harmony* with each other.

The fundamental reason, however, that 'The Origin' is committed to the essential 'agitation' of the artwork lies not in a blinkered aesthetic sensibility but in the way it treats its theory of truth.

The *duality* of world and earth derives, as we have seen, from Heidegger's account of truth as disclosure. Like, however, the Rectoral

---

[59] *The Earth, the Temple, and the Gods* (New Haven: Yale University Press, 1962), p. 2.

Address of 1933 and the *Introduction to Metaphysics* of 1935, 'The Origin' puts a particular spin on this duality. Truth, at the end of the story, does not just 'happen'. It is, rather, 'won' as the outcome of the primal conflict between the competing imperialisms of two primeval 'strivings', 'impulses' (*PLT* p. 63), 'wills' (*PLT* p. 62) or 'powers' (*IM* pp. 149–50). The one, the 'world' impulse, cannot 'tolerate (*dulden*) anything closed'. The other, the self-secluding 'earth' impulse, strives always to keep everything closed, 'to draw the world back into itself and keep it there' (*PLT* p. 49). Since it is 'Being [which] lets the openness happen' (*PLT* p. 61), both impulses, the impulse to 'darkness' and the impulse to 'light', are internal to Being which is *itself*, therefore, an 'agitated', self-conflicted entity.

So far as there is any *argument* for putting this particular spin on the world–earth duality, it is a fallacious one. Heidegger observes that, given the understanding of truth as *aletheia*, there exists a 'curious opposition (*Gegnerschaft*)' (*PLT* p. 53) between world and earth. 'Opposition' in the sense of contrast, difference, *Aus-einandersetzung* as Heidegger often puts it, there obviously is. But, of course, the move from opposition in this sense to opposition in the sense of strife – a move Heidegger seems to make – is a mere pun. Difference does not imply disagreement or enmity.[60]

The main source, however, of the notion of the primal conflict lies not in logical error but in, rather, a kind of late-Romantic Heracliteanism for which the punning on 'opposition' is merely a kind of logical fig-leaf. In the *Introduction to Metaphysics*, Heidegger makes his Heraclitean source explicit, by saying that 'the primal conflict' and Heraclitus' *'polemos* (strife)' are one and the same thing (*IM* p. 62).

Polemos, says Heidegger, quoting the Heraclitus fragment 53, is 'for all (that is present) the creator that causes to emerge, but (also) for all

---

[60] By the *Wege zur Aussprache* (*GA* 13, pp. 15–21) of 1937 Heidegger has clearly seen this. There, too, in the context of a discussion of German–French relations, he speaks of the need for an *Auseinandersetzung* for each culture to come fully into its 'own' (*das Eigene*), to be fully and self-consciously itself. But, here, *Auseinandersetzung* is clearly 'encounter' rather than 'dispute' or 'strife', since he speaks of 'mutual understanding' and 'the courage for the recognition (*Anerkennung* – i.e., respect) of the own of the other' as the essential condition for this creative, mutually enriching interaction between 'neighbours'. In the *Ister* lectures of 1942 he sums up the character of this mutually respectful encounter as a 'conjoining in distinction' (*Ister* p. 54), something quite different from 'The Origin's battle of the hostile forces.

the dominant preserver' (*IM* pp. 61–2). In section 15, above, we concentrated on *polemos*, considered as *Aus-einandersetzung*, difference, in its role as world *preserver*. World exists and survives only so long as 'difference' is preserved. So far as the primal conflict is conceived, however, Heidegger considers *polemos* as *Aus-einandersetzung*, warfare. Being, the 1936 Heidegger thinks, is essentially warfare between the forces of disclosure and those of concealment internal to a self-conflicted Being.

It is not hard to see, I think, that the motif of the primal conflict is really both extraneous to, and a disfigurement of, the important things 'The Origin' has to say about truth and art. It has no intrinsic connection to the theory of truth, its source being found not there but, one suspects, in the militaristic *Sturm und Drang* rhetoric popular during the Nazi era. (If the illumination of 'world' has to 'battle' its way into existence, then one can easily be asked to take up arms on behalf of the 'light' and against the forces of 'darkness'.) To see this is to see that the essay stands in need of radical surgery; the excision of the *Urstreit*. And this is precisely what Heidegger performs in a marginal note of 1960: the idea of the 1936 text that 'the essence of truth is in itself the primal conflict' is to be replaced by the idea that it is the '*Ereignis*' (*GA* 5, p. 42; see, too, p. 1 footnote a and p. 25 footnote a). As we will see, there is a great deal more to Heidegger's notion of *Ereignis* than its everyday meaning of 'happening'. Yet that meaning is an important *part* of the Heideggerian meaning. 'Truth', as later Heidegger sees, does not 'battle' its way into existence. It simply – even serenely – 'happens'. Having seen this, Heidegger dismisses the *Urstreit* from his thinking. After the transition to '*Ereignis*-thinking' in 1936–8 (see Introduction section 3 above) it makes no further appearance either in connection with art or with anything else.

35. So much for the first of Heidegger's self-criticisms. The second, and for the purposes of this study, more important, is of a quite different character.

During the 1950s, Heidegger discovered the works of Paul Klee, a discovery that will be discussed in detail in chapter 4. The impact of the discovery was so great that he told Otto Pöggeler that it had brought him to see the need to write a 'pendant' to 'The Origin'.[61] The same point is recorded by Heinrich Petzet: the enormous significance of Klee's art, coupled with the fact of the partial, but only partial, success of the artist's attempt to grasp that significance in his own theoretical writings, led Heidegger to the idea of writing a 'second part' to 'The Origin'.[62] (Of course, no second part was ever completed; for, I am about to suggest, the same reason that the projected second part of *Being and Time* was never written – it would have been centrally and crucially inconsistent with the 'first part'.)

Why should Heidegger's realization that Klee (as well as, as we will see, Cézanne, Rilke, Braque, and, in fact, a great number of modern artists) is an artist of great importance, even, in some sense of the term, a 'great' artist, have led Heidegger to the conclusion that 'The Origin' is essentially incomplete?

Let us, once more, recapitulate. Great art, we have seen, is art which, first, brings world out of background inconspicuousness and into the explicitness of foreground clarity (call this the 'truth' condition); second, endows it with an aura of 'holiness' (the 'earth' condition); and, third, gathers together an entire culture to witness this charismatic presencing of world (the 'communal' condition). In view of the focal significance of Greek tragedy and the Greek temple in its construction, I shall call this conception of art 'the Greek paradigm'.

It is immediately obvious that neither Klee nor Cézanne can count, in terms of the Greek paradigm, as great art, since neither satisfy the 'communal' condition. Though painting as such is not excluded from performing a community-gathering role – the medieval altarpiece had that function – it is obvious that neither Klee nor Cézanne does so. Generally small in Cézanne's case, and almost always tiny in Klee's, their paintings were destined for museums and private homes and seem, therefore, to be paradigms of private rather than public, individual rather than communal, art. (This, of course, is also true of Van Gogh's shoes, which is why its citing in 'The Origin' as an apparent paradigm of great art is such an anomaly.)

---

[61] '*Neue Wege mit Heidegger*' in *Philosophische Rundschau* 29, pp. 39–71; p. 47.
[62] *Encounters and Dialogues with Martin Heidegger* (Chicago: University of Chicago Press, 1993), p. 149.

Of itself, this failure to match up to the Greek paradigm does not absolutely necessitate any radical rethinking of the 1936 position, since
Heidegger could simply say – as we are about to see him saying of
Hölderlin – that Klee and Cézanne's paintings are *potentially* great artworks (and their creators, as creative of such works, *actually* great artists),
artworks which are 'waiting for preservers' (*PLT* p. 67) to realize their
potential. The advent of mechanical reproduction that much exercised
Heidegger's contemporary, Walter Benjamin, makes the smallness of the
works of Cézanne and Klee no absolute objection to the thought of their
being raised to the status of communal art. In fact, however, Heidegger
cannot say this since while (in, as we will see in chapter 4, both
Heidegger's and my own view) they both satisfy the 'earth' condition,
neither satisfies the 'truth' condition.

In the case of Klee, there is a degree of difficulty in arguing this point
due to the relative obscurity of his *œuvre*. (This is, of itself, a reason to
doubt that his art ever *could* become communal art given that community-gathering art must be accessible, in some sense of the term, 'popular'
art.) Yet it is, I think, intuitively obvious that 'founding the historical existence of a people towards beings as a whole' (*GA* 39, p. 59) is much too
grandiose a language in which to talk about Klee.

One reason for this is, I think, the following. Greek-paradigm art, we
have seen, does not just disclose beings: it discloses them always, in relation to *us*, from, that is, the perspective of *our* 'absolute need' to know
how to live. The art of the Greek paradigm articulates *our* 'position in the
midst of beings', places *us* in the centre of the picture. More precisely, as
conceived in the period of 'The Origin', great art is always 'about the relationship between gods and men' (*GA* 52, p. 72), about, that is, our relationship to fundamental *ethos*, to the 'laws of the signs of the gods' (HE
p. 312), the 'divine destinings' which are our world.

Yet in terms of topic, Klee's art does not seem to be particularly – certainly not obsessively – concerned with us at all. Though it is true that
human-like figures quite frequently appear, they appear only *inter alia*,
alongside fish, seaweed, children, underwater gardens, moons and twit-
tering machines. Moreover, even when beings vaguely like us do appear,
they have a removed, dreamlike quality about them; seem more like den-
izens of the unconscious realm of the night than of the daytime world of

action. The thought of looking to Klee, as one might look to the mass, to discover the 'simple and essential decisions' one is to live by has a vaguely comical air to it.

Concerning Cézanne's failure to satisfy the 'truth'-disclosing condition, the situation is even clearer. Cézanne's art is not about us, not about our, in the language of *Being and Time*, 'being-in-the-world' because his works, with few exceptions, are essentially 'people-less'. With respect to the works that, as we will see, most impressed Heidegger, the late studies of Mont St Victoire, this is quite literally the case. On some occasions, of course, people do appear. But when they do they usually appear, not as social beings, but rather (as Cézanne told Mme Cézanne she should sit) like apples, natural objects among other natural objects. His monumental bathers, for example, are often virtually indistinguishable from avenues of trees. Far from being concerned with the 'dialogue of divine and human destinings', Cézanne, generally, is sublimely indifferent to human existence, scarcely noticing its presence.[63]

Neither Cézanne nor Klee, then, can have their significance explained in terms of the Greek paradigm. Recall now, from Heidegger's discussion of 'aesthetics' (sections 4–6 above), that there are, in Heidegger's thinking of the mid-thirties, just two categories available in terms of which art can be discussed: on the one hand there is the art of the Greek paradigm, on the other the decadent triviality of 'aesthetics'. Recall, that is, that in the Nietzsche volume's history of Western art there are just two players: on the one hand, 'art', on the other, that which is aimed at generating titillating 'experience', a kind of experience which is 'the element in which art dies' (*PLT* p. 79). Recognizing that nothing in the realm of modern art either satisfies or could satisfy the Greek paradigm – there is, in a word, no temple or cathedral of modernity – Heidegger is thus forced to the conclusion that the entirety of modern art is decadent triviality, that

---

[63] I do not wish to claim that the works of Klee and Cézanne are by any means devoid of ethical *effect*. Cézanne, in particular, was much exercised by the destruction of natural beauty by the onset of industrialization and may well communicate something of that concern to us. But for a work to have an ethical effect is by no means the same as having a world-*ethos* as its content. It seems to me plain that while a Homer or Sophocles may be said to open up for his preservers 'the unity of those paths and relations in which birth and death, disaster and blessing, victory and disgrace, endurance and decline acquire the shape of destiny for human being' (*PLT* p. 42), nothing resembling such a synoptic vision is to be found in either Klee or Cézanne.

'for us moderns' art is merely 'what reposes and relaxes . . . a matter for pastry cooks' (*IM* p. 131). Had, then, he remained stuck in the rigidities of the mid-thirties, he would have been forced to condemn Klee, in particular, and modern art, in general, as decadent junk.

The discovery, therefore, that not all modern art is of this character, the discovery that (as Heidegger might now put it) Andrew Lloyd Webber, Sarah Brightman and Andrea Bocelli are not *completely* representative of the art of modernity, necessitated a radical rethinking of 'The Origin'. Not a *rejection* of its thinking – its articulation of the nature and significance of one, very important, type of art is clearly too accurate, important and, as I put it, 'pregnant with future' for that – but, rather, a *pluralization* of its position: the development of at least one paradigm of great, or at least 'valid' (*PLT* p. 96), art according to which the works which satisfy it are required, neither actually nor potentially, to 'open up a world' to a community as a whole. What Heidegger needs is a paradigm which legitimizes, at the very least, the art of Klee and Cézanne. What is needed, in short, is a rejection of the *tyranny* of the Greek paradigm, the tyrannical dichotomy between Greece on the one hand and 'pastry cooks' on the other. Hence the need for a 'second part' to 'The Origin', for further steps along Heidegger's 'path of thinking' about art, steps towards the discovery of a middle way between the Scylla of the Greek paradigm, on the one side, and the Charybdis of 'aesthetics' on the other.

2 Hölderlin: the early texts

1. Art which is to be taken seriously, 'great' art, we saw in the last chapter, is art which satisfies the Greek paradigm. But no artwork of our historical epoch does this. There is neither a Homer nor a cathedral of modernity. So all modern art is trivial. More specifically, it is 'aesthetics', the product of 'pastry cooks'.

Thus, in the mid 1930s, Heidegger's official position. Concurrent with it, however, he was possessed by a profound admiration for the early Romantic German poet, Friedrich Hölderlin, an admiration that had begun during his student days and remained with him until his death. He records its beginning in the 1957–8 essay, 'The Nature of Language':

> In 1910 Norbert von Hellingrath, who was killed in action before Verdun in 1916, first published Hölderlin's Pindar translations from the manuscripts. In 1914 there followed the first publication of Hölderlin's late hymns. These two books hit us students like an earthquake. Stefan George, who had first directed Hellingrath's attention to Hölderlin, now received decisive inspiration from those first editions, as did Rilke. (*OWL* p. 78)

And, of course, as we will see in this and the following chapter, Heidegger himself. In the 1966 *Spiegel* interview, in his usual way, precisely and without gush, he acknowledges Hölderlin as the single most important influence on his thinking: 'My thinking', he says, 'stands in a definitive relation to the poetry of Hölderlin' (*HC* p. 112).

Like every modern poet, Hölderlin fails to satisfy the Greek paradigm. There are no communal readings of Hölderlin. And neither could he ever come to satisfy the paradigm. The idea that this byword for hermetic obscurity could ever become the Homer of modernity is an absurd one. Hölderlin, that is to say, is the paradigm of a poet who writes, not for the community at large, but for a small group of initiates – a point of some importance to which I shall return.

To Heidegger, however, Hölderlin is a poet of the utmost significance, in his own way at least, 'great'. So Heidegger's position in the mid-1930s is self-contradictory, self-contradictory in a way that somewhat resembles that of the xenophobe who hates foreigners but has foreign friends. When he thinks about modern art in broadly brushed generalizations, he dismisses it out of hand and without exception. But in at least one instance, when he turns his attention to a concrete and particular case, modern art commands his deepest respect. (And actually in more than one instance, since he had long been an admirer of Van Gogh. As we observed, the presence of this admiration in 'The Origin' brings the contradiction in Heidegger's thinking to the surface. On the one hand the essay demands communal and scorns private art, on the other it offers Van Gogh as a paradigm of greatness.)

As we are about to see in this and the following chapter, Heidegger was intensely preoccupied with Hölderlin from the mid-1930s to the mid-1940s. No fewer than four volumes in the *Gesamtausgabe* are devoted to him. The question before us is: why in these discussions did he not *see* the contradiction in his thinking? Why, given the intensity of his admiration for Hölderlin together with the unmistakable fact of the poet's failure to match up to the demands of the Greek paradigm, did Heidegger not see, already in the 1930s, the need to break out of the tyranny of the paradigm, to develop a second paradigm that could be satisfied by, at the very least, Hölderlin? Why, in other words, did he have to wait until the encounter with Klee in the 1950s for the thought of the need for a 'second part' to 'The Origin' to strike him?

The answer to this question comes, I shall argue, in two parts. The first concerns what I shall term the 'early Hölderlin texts', those written during the same period of thought as 'The Origin' (actually slightly earlier than its final version.) The second concerns, as I shall call them, the 'later Hölderlin texts', those written between 1939 and 1946.[1]

---

[1] Heidegger continued to think and write about Hölderlin until the end of his life. But 1934–46 marks, I believe, the period of his *intense* engagement, the period of his struggle to comprehend just what it was that the poet meant to him. By 1946, by 'What are Poets for?', he had, it seems to me, completed his appropriation of Hölderlin. Thereafter the relationship has metamorphosized into a kind of serene identity. The sense of struggle, of comprehension being in the process of being forged and reforged, tangible in the earlier texts, is absent from the later.

The early texts are those to which considerable reference has already been made: the 1934–5 lectures on 'Germania' and 'The Rhine' (*GA* 39) and the 1936 'Hölderlin and the Essence of Poetry' (HE). To a certain extent the *Introduction to Metaphysics* (*IM*) of 1935 may be included among these texts since, though it contains no extended discussion of Hölderlin himself, it does contain a long examination of Sophocles' *Antigone*, a work to which, Heidegger believes, Hölderlin stands in an essential relationship (see *Ister* sections 9 and 10).

With respect to these texts, so, in this chapter, I shall argue, Heidegger's admiration for Hölderlin does not initiate an escape from the tyranny of the Greek paradigm because, though he treats Hölderlin as a poet who is of the utmost importance, he does not treat him as being important *as a poet*. Without being properly alive to the fact that this is what he is doing, he treats the work of the 'thinking poet' (*GA* 52, p. 197) as the work of a thinker who happens to express his thoughts in verse but might just as well have done so in prose.

The later texts, however, understand the inadequacy of this treatment of Hölderlin's work. They recognize that his importance is *essentially* that of a poet. Understanding, too, that that importance can never be captured by the Greek paradigm, they therefore develop a second paradigm of great, or at least 'valid' (*PLT* p. 96), art, a paradigm that allows Heidegger's theorizing to accommodate what, *qua* poet and receiver of poetry he had always known; that Hölderlin is a great *poet*. What I shall suggest, then, is that, in effect, Heidegger actually *did* write the 'second part' to 'The Origin' already in 1942–3 as a result of the deepening of his encounter with Hölderlin. (The thought of a 'second part' generated by the encounter with Klee was, I think, the thought of a second part concerned specifically with the *visual* arts.)

Heidegger's breaking out of the tyranny of the Greek paradigm did not occur simply as the result of *thinking about* Hölderlin. It occurred rather, I shall suggest, as the result of his deepened grasp of Hölderlin's own poetry and poetic metapoetry – the thinking about the nature and task, or rather task*s*, of poetry that permeates a great deal of Hölderlin's work. In a deep sense, I will argue (a sense which has nothing to do with plagiarism), Heidegger's breaking through to the idea of a second poetic 'essence' was unoriginal, the result of a further and more accurate reading of Hölderlin. Hölderlin, I want to argue, *educated* Heidegger, educated him about the nature of poetry and about, as we shall see in the next chapter, other things too. Heidegger's deepening understanding of the poet led him out of several disastrous intellectual – and political – positions of the mid-1930s and into the serenity (the *'Gelassenheit'*) of his later thought. One mark of this tremendous debt to Hölderlin is the fact that the distinctive, and highly poetic, language in which that later thought is couched, the language of the 'fourfold', of 'earth' (in a different meaning from that which it had in 'The Origin'), 'sky', 'gods' and 'mortals' is, as Heidegger acknowledges (*GA* 4, p. 170), taken directly from Hölderlin. It is in acknowledgment of this spiritual education, on account of the, at the deepest level, unoriginality of his later thinking that, in the *Spiegel* interview, Heidegger identifies his relationship to Hölderlin as the 'decisive' one.

'The Essence of Poetry'

2. My claim, then, is that the early Hölderlin texts treat Hölderlin as a thinker *rather than* a poet – as someone whose work, though *formally* speaking that of a poet, is, when it comes to *content*, indistinguishable from that of the (philosophical) thinker. What, then, in Heidegger's representation, does Hölderlin think?

As the title 'Hölderlin and the Essence of Poetry' indicates, he thinks, first of all, 'the essence' of poetry. Uniquely among poets, Hölderlin is the poet to be consulted about what makes authentic poetry poetry since

Hölderlin's poetry was borne on by the poetic vocation to write expressly of the essence of poetry. For us Hölderlin is, in a pre-eminent sense, *the poet of the poet*. (HE pp. 294–5; see, too, *GA* 39, pp. 214, 220)

Hölderlin's answer to the question of essence, as Heidegger reads him, is given in a line we have already encountered (chapter 1 section 31), the last line of 'Remembrance': 'What endures . . . the poets found.' 'Poetry', as Heidegger rephrases it, 'is the act of founding by word . . . that which endures' (HE p. 304); in other words a 'world'. What Hölderlin thinks, therefore, is, in a word, the Greek paradigm. It is this which constitutes 'the essence' of poetry.

Notice the definite article here – the assumption that there is one and only one measure of authenticity in poetry. Heidegger says that the question of essence is crucial since it determines whether or not we are to take poetry 'seriously'. Should it turn out, for example, that poetry is merely a kind of escapist 'dream' or 'play', that it is 'ineffectual', avoids 'seriousness' through having 'nothing about it of action' (HE pp. 294–6), then it would *not* be something to be taken seriously. *Either*, therefore, poetry is life-directing ('ethical') after the manner established by the Greek paradigm *or* it is the stuff of pastry cooks. Unsurprisingly, therefore, given its proximity to 'The Origin', 'Hölderlin and the Essence of Poetry' is completely taken over by the tyranny of the Greek paradigm.

'The absence and arrival of the gods'

3. The second thing Hölderlin thinks, according to Heidegger, is contemporary man's spiritual 'distress', his 'destitution' (*PLT* p. 91) or 'need'. The poet, he says, 'founds the need (*Not*)' (*GA* 39, *passim*).

Modernity, Heidegger quotes Hölderlin as saying, is the age of the 'flight of the gods', a time of 'spiritual decline' (*IM* p. 38). 'The gods', Heidegger–Hölderlin[2] holds, are the indispensable foundation of authentic community. Only by dwelling 'in the sight of the gods' – in the visible and charismatic presence of the 'divine destinings', that is[3] – can 'man . . .

---

[2] At no point in any of Heidegger's Hölderlin discussions does he set any critical distance whatever between himself and the poet (something true of his relationship with no other thinker save, perhaps, Sophocles.) Though the later discussions provide a different account of the character of Hölderlin's thinking to that provided in the earlier, in every discussion, the rubric 'Hölderlin thinks/says/means' always implies 'I, Heidegger, think'. Hölderlin is, for Heidegger, an almost divinely guaranteed goldmine of unalloyed truth. The task is always to discover the gold, never to question its authenticity.

[3] Greek tragedy, says Heidegger, 'brought the presence of the gods, [i.e.] brought the dialogue of divine and human destinings to radiance' (*QCT* p. 34). 'The gods' and the fundamental *ethos* of a community Heidegger always thinks of as equivalent. He is not, however, always consistent as to why they are equivalent. Sometimes he seems to think of the figures of the gods as the way in which a community embodies its sense of the *authority* of the laws. In this conception the gods are primarily the *sanctioners* of the laws. Mostly, however – this is certainly his best and his final view – he thinks of them as *exemplars* of the laws, 'messengers' (*PLT* p. 150) who give 'voice' (*GA* 4, p. 169) to their 'unwritten' (*Ister* p. 116) content by being the beings they are. (In this respect, later Heidegger's 'divinities' are a reappearance of the *ethos* ('heritage')-embodying 'heroes' (very roughly, role models) of *Being and Time* (*BT* 385).) For a fuller discussion of Heidegger's gods, see my 'What is Dwelling? The Homelessness of Modernity and the Worlding of World' in *Heidegger, Authenticity, and Modernity: Essays in Honor of Hubert L. Dreyfus* (Cambridge, Mass.: MIT Press, 2000), pp. 187–203.

become historical, become, that is to say, a people' (*GA* 39, p. 216). Since individuals only find integration in community and meaning in commitment to communal 'destiny', modernity, as we have already seen, is the age of alienation and 'meaninglessness', of, in Nietzsche's language, 'nihilism' (*IM* p. 203).

Most people, however, like the 'last man' in Nietzsche's *Zarathustra*, are oblivious to the conditions of their times. Insensible to the decayed condition of the present, they sleep the sleep of the complaisant, sleep soundly through godless night.[4] This is because – at this point (*GA* 39, p. 109) Heidegger explicitly invokes *Being and Time*'s account of 'temporality'[5] – they inhabit 'inauthentic temporality'. 'Forgetting' the past and so unable to 'project' into the future, the horizon of their life options is confined to the (specious) present. Poets, however, belong among those few remaining 'authentic creators' who climb out of the valley of inauthenticity to stand 'on the mountain peaks of time', stand in the rarefied but clear air of 'authentic temporality' (*ibid.*). From this elevated vantage point they are able to survey not only the present but also the past. Authentic poets are, as it were, the insomniacs of modernity, the authentic few who, remembering the past, are truly alive to the desolation of the present. What makes Hölderlin alive to the spiritual poverty of the present age is '*Andenken*' (remembrance), the title of one of his major poems but also the heart of all his poetry. It is the memory of the Greek 'festival', the celebration of the 'betrothal' of men to gods, the memory of the 'richness' (*PLT* p. 184) of our Greek origin, which establishes the poverty of the present age.

Because of this aliveness to the contrast between past and present, Hölderlin's poetry is permeated by a deep sadness, a profound sense of loss or absence. The '*Grundstimmung*', the 'fundamental mood' of all of his mature poetry, is 'holy mourning (*heilige Trauer*)', a mourning of the departure of the gods (*GA* 39, p. 146). Like all moods, Heidegger emphasizes, this mood is not to be understood as a '*seelische*' (psychological) but rather as a '*geistige*' (spiritual–intellectual) phenomenon (*GA* 39, pp. 82,

---

[4] 'Blessed are those who sleep well, for they shall drop off', writes Nietzsche in *Zarathustra*'s burlesque on the Sermon on the Mount. As will be discussed, Heidegger's early readings of Hölderlin are deeply influenced by his reading of Nietzsche, on whom he was working simultaneously.   [5] See *HPN* chapter 2, sections 7–19.

89). It is not an 'inner' state but rather the way the world as a whole is disclosed. In Hölderlin, our world is disclosed, above all, as a world permeated by *absence*.

Holy mourning, says Heidegger, should by no means be confused with idle nostalgia. It is, rather, precisely the opposite: not 'ineffectual melancholy' (*GA* 39, p. 170) but something, rather, essentially 'creative and productive (*schöpferisch-erzeugend*)' (*GA* 39, p. 94). It is creative because, in that it is a 'remembering', or better 'commemorative thinking',[6] of the gods that have been, it is also a projective founding of 'the future historical being of the Germans' (*GA* 39, p. 146). In the language of 'The Origin', by recovering for us our 'endowment', Hölderlin shows us our 'task'.

4. According to Heidegger, then, Hölderlin thinks two important thoughts. The first, the focus of 'Hölderlin and the Essence of Poetry', is about poetry; about what it is that renders poetry important, worthy of 'serious' attention. The second, the focus of the 'Germania' and 'Rhine' lectures, is about society; about the desolate way we are now and what we are to do about it. How, we need now to ask, are these two thoughts related?

The place, we know, where the gods come to presence, that which 'brings the dialogue of the divine and human destinings to radiance' (*QCT* p. 34) is the Greek-paradigm artwork. What Hölderlin discloses, therefore, discloses as 'our' task, is the restoration of such a work, the creation of a new artwork which satisfies the Greek paradigm. This is why Hölderlin is important. No merely academic analysis of Greek poetry, no mere nostalgia for a lost paradise, his work has about it the 'seriousness' of action. It provides both a diagnosis of the sickness of our age and a prescription of how we are to go about remedying it, a clear and unmistakable account of our 'task'. Hölderlin is, says Heidegger,

not yet the power in the history of our people. Because he is not yet that he must become it. (*GA* 39, p. 214)

Our business is to bring Hölderlin to 'power'.

---

[6] This is McNeill and Davis' illuminating translation of *Andenken* (which Heidegger often hyphenates as *An-denken*, literally, 'thinking-on') in their *Ister* translation. It makes clear Heidegger's debt – evident in section 74 of *Being and Time* – to the idea of history as 'memorializing' aspects of the past in the creation of (roughly) 'role models' for the future, which is outlined by Nietzsche in his *On the Uses and Abuses of History*.

Poetry, thought and politics

5. But who are the 'we' in question? And just what does 'bringing Hölderlin to power' mean? How, in concrete terms, are we to create the new Greek-paradigm artwork? Here Heidegger steps out of his role as Hölderlin interpreter and speaks entirely in his own voice: Hölderlin's

fundamental mood, and that [as world-disclosure rather than inner feeling] means the truth of the existence (*Dasein*) of a people, is originally (*ursprünglich*) founded by the poet. The thus disclosed being of beings is, however, grasped and ordered as being, and so first opened up, by the thinker. The thus-grasped being is [then] given the last and first seriousness of beings, which means to be formed into a definite (*be-stimmt*) historical truth so that the people is brought to itself as a people. This happens through the creation of the state – which in its essence has already been determined (*seinemWesen zu-bestimmten Staat*) – by the state-creator (*Staatsschöpfer*). (*GA* 39, p. 144)

It is impossible not to connect these remarks with Heidegger's involvement with Nazism and with Hitler. What he is outlining is a plan of action, a programme for the rebirth of a properly spiritual Germany, for a 'self-collection' of the German *Volk*. Through that, as we have seen, his aim was nothing less than a rebirth of the West as a whole. As 'the most metaphysical of nations' it is, he says, the particular task of the Germans to restore 'the history of the West . . . to the primordial realm of the powers of Being' by means of 'new spiritual energies unfolding historically from out of the [German] centre' (*IM* pp. 38–9). The beginning of this process, the self-collection of the Germans, is to happen through the poet, Hölderlin, the 'founder' of our 'truth of beings', the thinker, Heidegger, who articulates – in, presumably, more literal and therefore more accessible language – the poet's truth, and finally the state-founder, Hitler, who determines the final details and puts into practical effect poetically disclosed truth. It is because of this thinker-mediated link between poetry and politics – and because of the posited supremacy of the poet (a 'poet king' in place of Plato's 'philosopher king') – that Heidegger says that poetry is 'politics in the highest and most authentic sense' (*GA* 39, p. 214).

But what, in concrete terms, *is* this 'highest politics'? What *is* the Hölderlinian programme which, aided by the thinker, the practical politician is to put into effect?

The poet's 'founding' is what we have just rehearsed: his 'projective', forward-looking 'remembering' of 'our' Grecian origin. But Hölderlin is a writer of extraordinary obscurity. The thinker's work is necessary to make him accessible to more than a tiny coterie of literary scholars. The paradigmatic examples of this work of clarification are, of course, Heidegger's own 'Elucidations of Hölderlin's Poetry' (the title of *GA* 4).

But what is the statesman to do with these elucidations? His task, clearly, is to create a new community-'collecting', Greek-paradigm artwork. But how and of what kind? Is it, for example, intended that *Hölderlin himself* should become the 'poet of the Germans' (*GA* 39, p. 214) in precisely the same sense as that in which Homer or Sophocles was the 'poet of the Greeks'? Are we to envisage the rebirth of the nation through, for example, nightly broadcasts of readings of Hölderlin's 'hymns' in the newly discovered mass medium of radio? The idea is absurd for, as already observed, Hölderlin is the paradigm of a poet who can be accessible only to a select, highly educated, few. As Heidegger explicitly recognizes in 1946, it would be entirely

mistaken to believe that Hölderlin's time will come only on that day when 'every-man' will understand his poetry. It will never arrive in such a misshapen way. (*PLT* p. 142)

The point underlying these remarks is that the art of the Greek paradigm is, however sublime, also, as we have observed, essentially *popular* art.[7] A work can never gather the community as a whole unless it is *accessible* to the community as a whole. But Hölderlin can never become, in this sense, popular. His art is not, therefore, and never could be, the art of the Greek paradigm.

So what *is* the statesman to do? As is his Olympian wont, Heidegger never descends to details. Yet the outlines of what he wants are clear. If Hölderlin's 'remembering' of Greece is a projection of 'our' future then what, for Heidegger, as for so many thinkers and artists associated with Nazism, we need is, in a word, a 'Greek renaissance' (see section 8 below). So the task of the statesman is to sponsor artworks couched in a popular

[7] Gertrud Fussenegger (*Die Flucht ins Pianino* (Graz: Styria, 1995), pp. 138–9) on the Catholic mass: 'It is a building which accords with a sublime yet at the same time highly popular aesthetic; any child can sense what it announces yet inquisitive curiosity can never fathom what it enacts.'

idiom, artworks which will gather together the whole community in a reaffirmation of classical values. The films of Leni Riefenstal – *Triumph of the Will* and *Olympiad*, in particular – something like the architectural programme of Albert Speer, a revised version of the Wagner–Nietzsche conception of Bayreuth, and something perhaps not completely unlike a Nuremberg rally seem to be examples of the kind of thing Heidegger had in mind. Let me once again stress, however, that whoever these 'poets of the Germans' are, Hölderlin himself cannot belong among their number.

Not poet but thinker

6. In spite of the many fine insights contained in the early Hölderlin texts, insights which are carried over into Heidegger's later thinking, the early texts, taken as a whole, are seriously deficient in a number of more and less obvious ways. Some of these deficiencies are best left for discussion in connection with the later Hölderlin texts in which they emerge in the course of implicit self-criticism. Here I want to mention just two.

7. The main criticism is the point intimated at the beginning of this chapter, that though ostensibly aimed at conveying the tremendous importance of Hölderlin's poetry, what actually happens in the early texts is the disappearance from them of Hölderlin *the poet* and his replacement by Hölderlin *the thinker*, a thinker whose thoughts, moreover, turn out to be indistinguishable from those of Heidegger himself. Heidegger's programme for the renewal of the German people, we have seen, is supposed to be led by a triumvirate, an (un)holy alliance of 'H's, the alliance between Hölderlin, Hitler and himself. But the threefoldness of this structure is actually a fake threefoldness since there is no real distinction between poet and thinker. The so-called 'poet' is nothing other than a social thinker who happens to write (somewhat tiresomely, one might think) in elusive and picturesque verse but might just as well, or better, have written in prose. The thinker liberates the poet's meaning into (relatively!) clear and literal prose. All we really have, therefore, are two thinkers, one metaphorical and obscure, the other literal and supposedly clear.

In the 1942 *Ister* lectures Heidegger satirizes the 'Enlightenment' (positivistic) view of the relationship between 'poeticizing' and thinking as the view that considers philosophical thinking as liberating the mythological poem from the mythical and as recasting its remaining content into the rigid grid and debris of empty concepts. According to this view, thinking in general is nothing other than the 'demythologizing' of the myth. One represents this process as though it were the draining of a marshland, a process that, when complete, leaves 'dry' ground remaining. As though thinking already lay waiting within poeticizing and needed only to be liberated from the 'poetic'. (*Ister* pp. 111–12)

The Heidegger of 1942 rejects this kernel-and-husk view of poetry absolutely: it 'neither knows what poeticizing is nor does it understand the essence of thinking' (*ibid.*). What he fails to report, however – fails, perhaps, even to notice – is that it is precisely the view he himself fell into in his own treatment of Hölderlin seven years earlier.

In the 'Germania' lectures, Heidegger claims to distinguish two aspects to the poet's work. Hölderlin is, he says, not only 'the poet of the poet' but also 'the poet of the Germans' *GA* 39, p. 214). But the distinction is actually a fake one. As Heidegger ends up representing him, Hölderlin's sole importance is that of the metapoet – someone who outlines the poet's task in the present age, a task which, however, can be accomplished only by *other* poets, poets of an essentially different kind to himself. The only content Heidegger provides for 'poet of the Germans' is the idea that the programme of cultural regeneration he claims to discover in Hölderlin is one 'we' Germans can and should put into effect now.

The ultimately underlying cause of this elimination of the poet, this reduction of Hölderlin to himself, is the tyranny of the Greek paradigm. Since, quite patently, Hölderlin can never be represented as satisfying what is taken to be the one and only paradigm of significance in *art*, within the theoretical framework Heidegger imposes on himself, Hölderlin's importance can never be represented as that of an *artist*. All that is left, therefore, is to represent him as a great *thinker*, as someone who, standing on the 'mountain peaks of time', understands our past and is hence able to 'project' our future and our task.

Notice that there is nothing especially *poetic* about standing on those peaks. To do so is simply to be 'authentic' in the sense established in *Being and Time*, and there is, of course, no necessity that the authentic person be a poet. As with 'The Origin''s definition of poetry as *any* kind of 'projective saying' (*PLT* p. 74), the elimination of Hölderlin the poet is a necessary result of the attempt to comprehend his significance in terms of the inadequate structures of *Being and Time*.

Graecocentricism

8. The second criticism of the early texts I wish to make concerns the Greeks. Hölderlin's 'remembering' of the Greeks' festive celebration of their 'betrothal' to the gods is, Heidegger maintains, a projection of 'our' future, a projection of the future it is our task to bring into being. Why, however, should we believe this? Why should we believe that Hölderlin's 'commemorative thinking' of the Greek 'gods' is at the same time a disclosure to us of *our* 'gods'? Why should we believe that 'the absence [of the Greek] *and the arrival of [our]* . . . gods discloses itself in [Hölderlin's] . . . fundamental mood' (*GA* 39, p. 146; my emphasis)?

A clue is provided by the fact that, nearly always, Heidegger refers not, *à la* Nietzsche, to the 'death' of gods, but rather to 'the flight and arrival of *the gods* of a people' (*ibid*.; my emphasis) – as if the departed gods of the Greeks were the *very same ones* as our own true gods, the ones that will arrive given the proper implementation of the 'Hölderlinian' programme of cultural regeneration. And this, in fact, is how Heidegger thinks. The Olympians, properly understood, are not, he says, '*vergangene*' (past) beings, concrete singularities locked into a vanished past, but rather '*gewesene*' (having-been) beings (*GA* 39, pp. 108–9), eternal archetypes which, as such, are capable of 'return', of reappropriation. Of course, any such a return must be in modern dress. We must, as we have already seen, 'take a creative view of tradition' (*IM* p. 38): the authentic 'repetition' (*Wiederholung*) of the past is not the attempt to clone the past in the present, to bring it about that 'something which was formerly actual may recur' (*BT* 386–7). In 'Germania', the poet resolves no longer to call out to 'pictures of the gods of the ancient land' (*GA* 39, p. 10), the point being, as Heidegger understands it, that the old gods must be pictured, the divine archetypes instantiated, in new ways that make sense in the contemporary context (see further, chapter 1 section 31 above).

Heidegger's 1934–5 answer to the question as to why Hölderlin's 'remembering' of the Greek gods is also a projection of 'our' task is thus, in a word, that the Greek 'world' or 'heritage' and our own proper (yet forgotten, repressed) heritage are *one and the same*. Hölderlin's 'remembering' of Greece is, in the language of 'Hölderlin and the Essence of Poetry', a 'reminding' us of *our own* authentic 'voice', a voice which, in the modern epoch, has 'grown dumb and weary' (HE p. 311). The Greek gods and our own true gods, the 'simple and essential decisions' of Greek *ethos* and the simple and essential decisions that establish our own, are one and the same. In 1934–5, then, what Heidegger wanted was, to repeat, a 'Greek renaissance'. Not, of course, the superficial and vulgar literalism of most of Nazi classicism, but a renaissance, rather, that captures the inwardness, the 'inner truth and greatness' (*IM* p. 199), that was – and is – Greece. (It follows, therefore, that Heidegger's emphatic rejection of any kind of a 'Greek renaissance' in the later Hölderlin texts, his repeated insistence on the 'foreignness', the complete 'otherness' of the Greeks (see, for example, *Ister* pp. 80–1, 124, 136), is, *inter alia*, an implicit *self-criticism*).

9. The exaggerated Graecophilia of the early texts, the view that our true ethical commitments are the very same as they were in Greece – that anything not implicit in Greek *ethos* is, somehow, a falling away from the 'greatness' of our 'beginning' (*IM* p. 191) – is really quite extraordinary. Yet Heidegger, as we have seen, enunciates it quite explicitly:

The poet founds Being. For Western existence this founding of Being was *completed* by Homer, whom Hölderlin [therefore] calls 'the poet of poets'. (*GA* 39, p. 184; my emphasis)

Homer was the first to 'found' the Western world. All that remained for subsequent poets to do – Sophocles no less than Hölderlin – was to refound it, to represent, in ways that make living and relevant sense to their own generation, the unchanging essence of the West. Authentic poetry, one might say, is a series of footnotes to – re-presentation of – Homer.

It is clear that, already in the final version of 'The Origin', Heidegger had rejected this extraordinarily static view of Western ethics. For he recognizes there that, with the rise of Christianity, the Greek world did not simply go into decline but rather 'perished' in a way that 'can never be undone' (*PLT* p. 41). It disappeared once and for all as it was replaced by the 'new and essential world' of medieval Christendom (*PLT* p. 77).

The ethical heritage of the West is, of course, deeply indebted to Greece. Yet this heritage was profoundly modified by its confluence with

Judaeo-Christian practice and thought, a confluence that eventually found its charismatic articulation in the medieval cathedral. Painting the confluence with a broad brush, what occurred, one might suggest, was that the 'gentle' virtues of Christianity came to take their place alongside the 'hard' (as Nietzsche calls them, 'master') virtues of the ancient world and by so doing profoundly altered the scope and nature of the latter.

Because *our* ethical tradition is the thus-modified one, Heidegger's Graecocentrism is not only arbitrary but also oppressive. The reason Riefenstal's films, for all their cinematic genius, have an oppressive feel to them is that they are, in fact, a state-funded exercise in 'political correctness' – an attempt by a power-elite to enforce upon society at large a set of highest values that are different from – and alien to – its own. That Heidegger, in proposing the unholy alliance of Graecocentric 'poet, thinker and state-founder', envisaged a kind of state-imposed – or at least state-sponsored – Greek renaissance, reveals that his thinking did, for a brief period, fall into a perilous proximity to fascist totalitarianism.[8]

10. Not only is Heidegger's Graecocentrism (in the form it takes in the early texts) oppressive, it also leads to a bad misreading of Hölderlin. Given that the founding of the West was 'completed' by Homer, Heidegger has to explain away the fact that, by identifying the 'united three' whose departure signalled the onset of the world's 'night' as 'Herakles, Dionysus, and Christ' (*PLT* p. 91), Hölderlin attributed to Christ a status at least equal to that of the Greek gods. Hölderlin's so-called 'Western turning (*Wendung*)', his supposed turning away from the 'Easternness' of Greece was, Heidegger claims, no 'flight to Christianity', since 'insofar' as he mentions Christ at all he simply treats him as one of the Greek gods (*GA* 39, p. 220; *GA* 52, pp. 140–1).

---

[8] Proximity, it needs to be emphasized, is not identity, political correctness is not, of necessity, totalitarianism. As already remarked, like Wagner, Heidegger looked for the creation, through the rebirth of the art of the Greek paradigm, of a new 'national religion' (*N* I, p. 86). But just as there was nothing *fascist* about Ludwig of Bavaria's involvement in the Bayreuth project, so there is nothing *necessarily* fascist about Heidegger's programme of cultural regeneration. The crucial question is whether Heidegger looked for the new national religion to be state-*sponsored* or state-*imposed,* but the texts are far too abstract to convict him of favouring the latter over the former. Nonetheless it is a weakness in *HPN* that, in it, I did not sufficiently acknowledge the proximity to fascism of the mid-1930s – albeit, as we will see in the next chapter, one from which Heidegger quickly liberated himself.

This, presupposing as it does Hölderlin's blindness to the profound difference between Greek and Christian ethics, is extremely unconvincing. Hölderlin included Christ in his 'united three' because, surely, he understood the radical modification that Greek ethics underwent through its encounter with the gentler virtues of Christianity. Hölderlin's own gods, the kinds of gods he imagines being celebrated by us in our future 'festival', are far removed from the powerful, often violent, lustful, greedy and capricious gods of Greek mythology. They are, rather, powerless 'angels', 'messengers' or embodiments of, above all, the virtues of *caritas* (*GA* 4, p. 20). Hölderlin, in a word, *Christianized* the Greek gods, synthesized the Greek and the Christian in such a way that within the 'united three' it is Christ who finally takes precedence.

Traces of Heidegger's discounting of Christianity persist into the 1940s. In the 1950s, however, he finally recovers from oppressive Graecocentrism and acknowledges the essential place of Christianity within the Western tradition, speaking of that tradition as 'the hidden fullness and wealth of what has been . . . of the divine in the world of the Greeks', but also in 'prophetic Judaism [and] in the preaching of Jesus' (*PLT* p. 184). At the same time, Hölderlin's Christianized gods are appropriated as his own, become the 'message'-bringing divinities of 'the fourfold' (*PLT* p. 150).

What these reflections show is that the attempt to portray Hölderlin's 'remembrance' of Greece as a reminding us of *our* true gods is a bad mistake. Whatever its point may be, it is not to demand that we institute a 'Greek renaissance'. What Heidegger needs, therefore, is to think in a deeper and more sophisticated way about the character and purpose of Hölderlin's *Andenken*. In the next chapter we will see how, in the later Hölderlin texts, such a deeper thinking is carried out.

3   Hölderlin: the later texts

1. Under 'later texts' I include, in chronological order: the lecture 'As when on holiday . . .', first delivered in 1939 (*GA* 4, pp. 43–78); *Hölderlin's Hymn 'Remembrance'*, a Freiburg lecture series delivered in the winter semester of 1941–2 (*GA* 52); *Hölderlin's Hymn 'The Ister'*, delivered in the summer semester of 1942 (*GA* 53 and *Ister*); 'Remembrance', a second discussion of that poem in the form of an essay written in 1943 to commemorate the 100th anniversary of Hölderlin's death (*GA* 4, pp. 79–151); and 'Homecoming', a lecture delivered in 1943 also to commemorate the anniversary of Hölderlin's death (*GA* 4, pp. 9–32). Finally, I include the first five and a half pages of the 1946 lecture 'What are Poets for?' (*PLT* pp. 89–142). Though the lecture is mainly concerned with Rilke rather than Hölderlin, its introductory pages provide an important summary of the final results of a decade of intense Hölderlin research.

As I mentioned at the beginning of the previous chapter (footnote 1), Heidegger continued to think and write about Hölderlin until the end of his life. Particularly significant contributions are the 1954 '. . . Poetically Man Dwells . . .' (*PLT* pp. 211–29) and the 1959 'Hölderlin's Earth and Sky' (*GA* 4, pp. 152–81). However, 1934–5 to 1946 remains, I believe, *the* period of Heidegger's engagement with Hölderlin, the period during which, as I put it, Heidegger's *education* by Hölderlin was undertaken and completed.

The festival

2. Though their surface is variegated and complex, the underlying structure of the later Hölderlin discussions – as, for that matter, of the earlier – is relatively simple: the statement of a problem followed by the provision of a solution – or of, at least, a partial solution.

The problem, as before, consists in our 'destitution' (*PLT* p. 91), the fact that our age is a time of 'night' (*GA* 52, p. 92), or, to change the metaphor, 'winter' (*GA* 4, p. 54). As before, the reason for this is, in Hölderlin's phrase, the 'default of God', the fact that, in Heidegger's elaboration, 'no god any longer gathers men and things unto himself, visibly and unequivocally, and by such gathering disposes the world's history and man's sojourn in it' (*PLT* p. 91). As before, the fact that Hölderlin's 'united three' – Herakles, Dionysus and Christ – have left the world, the fact that 'the gods and the god' have fled (*PLT* pp. 91–2), entails the absence of a 'history'-determining *ethos* and hence, it seems, the absence of both community and meaning from our lives.

What, however, is different in the later texts is a new, and richer, way of describing the spiritual poverty of our age, a description couched in terms of our lack of what Hölderlin calls 'the festival'. This is worth exploring since it enhances our understanding of the Greek paradigm and of, therefore, Heidegger's conception of our ultimate 'salvation' contained in the suggestive but vague assertion that 'only a god can save us' (*HC* p. 91).

3. In 'Remembrance' the poet experiences a 'golden dream' (*GA* 4, pp. 112–13; *GA* 52, pp. 20, 117–19), a dream of 'the festival': in the first instance of the festiveness of Southern French 'holidays', days on which 'the brown women' of the Dordogne walk out on to 'silken ground' (the festive place), but, mediated by this, of, too, the festivals of that other 'Southern' place, ancient Greece. The ultimate object of Hölderlin's 'remembrance' is, claims Heidegger, the 'meeting of gods and men' that occurred in the Greek festival.[1]

What are 'festivals' or 'holidays'? In the first instance, says Heidegger, to 'celebrate the holiday (*feiern*)' means 'setting oneself outside everyday (*alltäglich*) activity, the cessation of work' (*GA* 52, p. 64). In the modern

---

[1] Heidegger has been frequently criticized for imposing his own Graecocentric concerns on a poem which, read with impartial eyes, is quite obviously about France and France alone. Heidegger's evidence, however, that his reading is true to the poet's intention – a letter from Hölderlin to his friend Böhlendorf written shortly after the poet's return from France – seems compelling. Hölderlin writes: 'The athleticism of the Southern [French] people, in the [in fact, Roman] ruins of the antique spirit, made me more familiar with the authentic essence of the Greeks. I came to know their nature and their wisdom, their bodies, the way in which they grew in their climate, and the way in which they protected the high-spirited [Dionysian?] genius from the power of the [Apollonian?] element' (*GA* 52, pp. 80–1).

age this is *all* there is to the holiday. It has become a mere 'break from work (*Arbeitspause*)' (*GA* 4, p. 102), (mere, as we say, 'R and R', stress relief[2]). This, however, completely fails to capture the proper and original essence of the holiday, an essence that is still preserved in the etymological components of the term '*Feier-tag*', day of celebration, holiday, or better, 'holy-day'.

On the authentic holiday, says Heidegger, we 'step into the . . . intimation of the wonder (*Wunder*) that around us a world worlds at all, that there is something rather than nothing, that there are things and we ourselves are in their midst, that we ourselves are' (*GA* 52, p. 64). We celebrate world, life, existence as such. To step into this festive mood (or mode, mode of disclosure – see pp. 74–5 above) is, *a fortiori*, to step out of the 'everyday' since, by definition, the everyday is a matter of drab and 'wearisome' care (*GA* 52, p. 65).

That is one aspect of the authentic holiday. The second is that from within the festive mode things and people are apprehended, not as they are, in everydayness, 'in the perspective of . . . usefulness', but rather as they are in themselves, according to their 'essences'. The '*Eigentlichkeit*', the 'ownness' of things becomes for the first time accessible to us so that 'care' ceases to be mere technological manipulation and becomes, instead, a *caring for*, 'obedience to a protecting' derived from 'a belonging to the essential in all beings' *(ibid.)*. This, says Heidegger, is the original and proper meaning of the term (*Sorge*). In the festive mode, we may say, using the language of *Being and Time*, care becomes for the first time authentic care.[3]

The linking of 'everydayness', here, to 'the perspective of usefulness' is, surely, a preview of Heidegger's later characterization of modernity as the age of '*Gestell*': the world-'enframing' epoch defined by the fact that, for most people, most of the time, the beings – including human

---

[2] Notice that this is just what the charge that modern art is 'aesthetics' amounts to. Heidegger's critique of modern art could also be expressed as the charge that it has become nothing more than an *Arbeitspause*, a holiday from work.

[3] Notice that although the authentic holiday is opposed to 'everydayness', unlike the modern holiday, it is not opposed to work, not, *of necessity*, an *Arbeitspause*. Although (to put the point in the manner of *Being and Time*) the *ontic* festival is a cessation of work, the *ontological* festival, the festive mood and mode of world-disclosure, can continue into work which becomes *authentic* work precisely because it is 'festive'. Heidegger makes this point at *GA* 52, p. 65.

beings – in whose midst we find ourselves, show up as, and only as, 'resource'. As resource, though things may be conserved in the sense of being stored up for future use, they are never conserved in the sense of being cared for. As resource, things are simply used and – usually the same thing – abused. In everydayness, one experiences the other not, as he is, a man with a character, temperament, feelings, aspiration and life situation that is uniquely his own but as, simply, 'consumer', 'customer' or 'worker', as 'human resource' (*QCT* p. 18). Or else one experiences him as a *negative* resource – as something that impedes the efficient organization of things – as 'Jew',[4] 'geriatric' or 'foetus'. And the same with non-human nature. Animals show up merely as food or as pests, trees as either timber or as obstructions to real-estate development. Things and humans are denied the space in which to exist and flourish according to their own natures for the simple reason that those natures are never allowed to appear.

Heidegger's anticipation of *Gestell* in the discussions of 'Remembrance' is important because it reveals it to be simply 'everydayness' raised to epoch-defining status, everydayness *unmitigated* by 'the festival'. *Gestell*, this discussion makes clear, is *always* an incipient threat – even in Greece. The Greeks, however, because they possessed the festival, were protected from its world-historical take-over.

4. How so? How do we recover understanding of the 'essence' of things in the festival? The authentic festival is, says Heidegger, a day for 'coming to ourselves' (*GA* 4, p. 102); not in the sense of becoming self-obsessed or self-indulgent, but in the sense of a, as we say, 'coming to one's senses' or 'putting things into [their proper] perspective'.[5] The authentic holiday is redemptive, as we say, 'time out', a stepping out of all usualness into the 'unusual' or better (to adopt McNeill and Davis' illuminating translation of *ungewöhnlich* (*Ister* p. 184)), the 'inhabitual'. It is not, however, a stepping into the exotic or 'sensational'. Rather, 'the opposite':

---

[4] This is Heidegger's analysis of the industrialized genocide that was the Holocaust (see *HPN* pp. 181–8).

[5] In an illuminating television interview given in the late 1980s, the then CEO of Club Med explained that the founding concept of the enterprise was the idea that what people need from holidays is not stress relief but, rather, self-collection. Hence, I take it, the deliberate inaccessibility of newspapers and television.

The inhabitual is the permanently essential, simple and ownness (*Eigene*) of beings in virtue of which they stand within the measure (*Mass*) of their essence and so demand of men that they observe this measure (*das Masshalten*). (*GA* 52, p. 66)

Of course, the fact that individuals show up as the beings they are rather than as mere resource does not, by itself, have any bearing on action, on how we behave towards them. What has to be remembered, however, is that in the festive mode (mood) we stand not just in the 'essence' of things but also in the 'wonder' of the world's worlding (see p. 86 above). We step into wonder and adoration of the things that there are, into gratitude for the fact that they are and that we are among them. Heidegger returns to this point in the passage under discussion. In the festive mood, he says, things possess a special 'gleam (*Glanz*)', a gleam which comes from 'the lighting and shining of the essential' (*GA* 52, p. 66).[6] In the festive mode, that is, things show up as belonging to a *sacred* order and since they themselves share in this sacredness, command of us love and respect.

The festival, says Heidegger, is 'the bridal feast between men and gods' and, as such, '*the Ereignis*' (Heidegger's emphasis),[7] the occasion on which 'gods and men' are 'greeted' by 'the holy' and, as so greeted, 'able once again to greet each other and in such greeting, able to hold onto each other' (*GA* 52, p. 70). And he also says (with Nietzsche) that Greek tragedy was not 'theatre' in the modern sense, but precisely such a festive betrothal (*GA* 52, p. 72).

This makes it clear that 'the festival' is nothing other than a more developed description of what 'The Origin' calls 'the artwork'. For that which constitutes the festival is: first, the coming into salience of 'world', its coming out of obscurity, out of the 'dissembling' (*PLT* p. 54) that belongs

---

⁶ Heidegger emphasizes the point that the festive light shines *through* 'the essential'. ('World', as I have put it, becomes transparent to 'earth'.) The consequence, he says, is that though dance and play are an essential part of the festival, they are to be understood not as 'boundless tumult' but as, rather, 'being bound into the hidden obedience and rule of beings' (*GA* pp. 66–7). Not, then disco dancing but, rather, Flamenco or Latin-American; celebratory narratives of the world to which the dancers belong. Reflecting on the Greek festival, Heidegger thus in effect emphasizes (Nietzsche's point, but thought through more deeply) that the authentic festival is not the chaos of pure Dionysianism but rather the Dionysian mediated by, and in essential unity with, the Apollonian.

⁷ In ordinary German '*Ereignis*' means 'event' or 'happening'. As we will see in section 19 below, however, Heidegger wishes us to connect with it the idea of 'appropriation (*aneignen*)', which renders the term untranslatable by any short phrase. (For the kind of unintelligibility that arises from attempting to translate it, see *PLT* p. 179). This is the reason I leave the term untranslated throughout this study.

to everydayness[8] and into its true 'essence' and 'measure' (the 'world' condition of the Greek paradigm); second, that world's standing forth as a *holy* and hence authoritative order of things – its fundamental ethical structure, our 'gods' or 'divine destinings', is 'greeted' by the holy (the 'earth' condition); and third – the essential character of any festival – the gathering together of community within that 'wonder' that happens in the work (the 'communal' condition).

Thus the description of our age as the age that has forgotten the festival – the age that retains only its 'withered' (compare *PLT* p. 173) husk, the 'break from work' – is a richer description of one and the same 'lack' or 'destitution' that 'The Origin' describes by presenting modernity as the age without an 'artwork'.

5. Given this analysis the solution seems, as it did in the earlier Hölderlin texts, obvious: to found a new festival, a new artwork. And Heidegger indeed says, in the later no less than the earlier texts, that the poet's goal is the arrival of the 'coming' festival (*GA* 4, pp. 87, 148),[9] the founding of the future 'settlement (*Ausgleich*) between men and gods' (*GA* 4, p. 105). As in the earlier texts, the poet's task seems to be to build 'the house into which the gods are to come as guests' (*GA* 4, p. 148), to build, with a little help from his friends, the thinker and state founder, a new Greek-paradigm artwork.

The modern poet's exclusion from 'the highest essence of art'

6. The question arises, however as to whether modern poets, in general, and Hölderlin in particular, are capable of achieving such a goal, of fulfilling this 'highest . . . essence' (*QCT* p. 35) of art. Unlike the earlier texts

---

[8] Notice that Heidegger's 1941–2 discussion seems to offer a new account of the way in which everydayness 'dissembles'. In 'The Origin', it seemed (chapter 1 section 19), dissembling is a matter of 'the simple and essential' disappearing in the *detail* of everyday life. But by the 'Remembrance' discussion it has become the *enframed* character of the everyday that is important. I think these accounts should be seen as complementary rather than conflicting: supposing one to have escaped the reduction of beings to resource, the living of a clear and coherent life will still require the capacity to abstract from detail to the 'simple and essential'.

[9] The question of how the poet knows the festival to be 'coming', why it is a 'coming' rather than 'hoped for' festival, will be addressed in section 24 below.

– where this question is never properly articulated – the later texts explicitly confront it and provide an unambiguously negative answer. The 'default (*Fehl*)' of gods means, as Hölderlin puts it, that 'holy names are in default' (*GA* 4, pp. 27–8). The poet of modernity, finding himself thus 'wordless', can only 'sing' (*ibid.*). He cannot 'found the festival' because there exists no appropriate *language* in which to do so.

A clue to the meaning of this is provided by an explanatory remark made in 1950, part of which has already been quoted:

> The default of God and the divinities is absence. But absence is not nothing; it is rather precisely the presence, which must first be appropriated, of the hidden fullness and wealth of what has been and what, thus gathered, is presencing of the divine in the world of the Greeks, in prophetic Judaism, in the preaching of Jesus. (*PLT* p. 184)

The absence of the gods is, then, 'presence', yet a presence that is 'unappropriated'. Translated into talk of 'names' what this means is that though there are plenty of names of gods available to the poet none of them are, any longer, *holy* names. None of them, that is, is any longer 'awesome', charismatic, or, therefore, authoritative. In an age, one might observe, in which the only culture-wide use of 'Christ' is as an expletive, the poet, evidently, cannot conjure the sacredness of the sacred by appealing to 'the Christian'.

What this reveals is a profound shift between the earlier and later diagnosis of the destitution of modernity. In the earlier texts the problem, it will be remembered (from chapter 2 section 3), was that we have become 'inauthentic', forgotten our 'heritage', our authentic gods, the gods of Greece. All we need, therefore, is the poet's 'reminding' us of our Greek heritage – followed by the propagation of his 'remembrance' throughout the culture by the machinery of the state. The problem, in a word, concerned the 'world' condition of the Greek paradigm, the fact that our authentic world has sunk into obscurity.

In the later texts, however, the ground of the 'default of God' is something 'even grimmer' – the fact that, in our culture, the 'divine radiance', that 'aether . . . in which alone gods are gods', has become 'extinguished' (*PLT* pp. 91–2). In the dis-enchanted world of *Gestell*, the age in which, as resource, everything 'obtrude[s] and accumulates in a dry, monotonous and therefore oppressive [claustrophobic] way' (*QCT* p. 17), nothing at all stands forth, for modern man, as holy and so, in particular, the names of the gods fail to do so. From the later perspective, therefore, the problem concerns not the 'world' but rather the 'earth' condition of the Greek paradigm.

It follows from this that in the age of modernity it is impossible to create a Greek-paradigm artwork since it can never be the case that it finds 'preservers', satisfies the 'communal' condition. Modernity makes, as late Heidegger repeatedly says, no 'space' (*KuT* p. xiii) for art, no space of the right kind, on account of the fact that we have become insensible to 'earth', to 'the holy'.

Nothing, of course, prevents us building a large, Greek-looking amphitheatre or temple. If, however – as envisaged in the early texts – one does so in the absence of the 'divine radiance', then all one ends up with is a building which is either empty, or else full of people herded there by storm-troopers but who, once inside, simply (like Niezsche's 'last man') blink before the statue of the god, or else full of tourists who admire the statue 'aesthetically'.[10] In the age of the 'de-divinization' (*Entgötterung*) (*QCT* p. 116) of the world there is no more point in building a temple to the gods than there is, in the Amazon rainforest, to building an opera house.

7. As I have said, the later texts, while outlining the return of the Greek paradigm as Hölderlin's final goal, are quite explicit that this 'highest essence' of poetry is something he himself cannot achieve. As an articulation of the Greek paradigm, therefore, Hölderlin's metapoetry is to be read as being non-self-referential. Rather than describing himself, or any poet of the present, Hölderlin's concern is to outline the task of *future* poets. Hölderlin, Heidegger says repeatedly, 'founds the essence of the *coming* German poets' (*GA* 4, p. 115; my emphasis):

Hölderlin has poeticized the essence of the coming poet and encapsulated everything in the single word: 'But what endures, the poets found.' (*GA* 52, p. 193)

---

[10] A further possibility is that within the temple a genuine escape from the everyday occurs, an escape into a *Rausch* (ecstasy, intoxication) generated by alcohol, the media, or some other kind of drug. This describes what happened in Nazi Germany. Notice, however, that far from being an authentic illumination of 'the essential' in the Western tradition, this way is an instance of the 'boundless tumult' mentioned in footnote 6 above.

8. But what, then, is the point of Hölderlin's 'dream' of a future festival founded by a future poetry, given the impossibility of either of them coming to pass in the present, world-historical epoch? If the 'dream' is not a 'politics in the highest and most authentic sense' for the present, not blueprint for action, must not Heidegger reaffirm 'Hölderlin and the Essence of Poetry''s assertion that if poetry is 'like a dream' then it is ineffectual, lacking the 'seriousness of action' and so, nothing we need to 'take . . . seriously' (HE pp. 294–6)?

The first point to make is that, as in the earlier texts, Hölderlin's 'remembrance' of Greece is 'multidirectional' (*Ister* p. 151), a 'thinking back' which, as 'commemorative' or 'memorializing', is also a 'thinking forward' (*GA* 52, p. 194), a 'projecting' into the future of the '*gewesene*' (but not '*vergangene*' – see chapter 2 section 8) festival. There is, however, a difference between the earlier and later interpretations of the *content* of Hölderlin's 'remembering'. In the earlier texts the poet is taken to remember specific 'gods' – albeit gods who require reinterpretation to make sense in a contemporary context. This was the reason Hölderlin's thought was seen as a 'politics', as possessing the specificity necessary to a plan of action, a plan for the creation of a 'Greek renaissance'. In the later texts, however, Heidegger focuses on the poet's statement that though he is 'prophetic' he is no 'seer', that 'though his dream is divine he dreams no god' (*GA* 4, p. 114). Though the poet 'thinks forward' to 'what belongs to the building of the house' 'to which the gods are to come as guests', he is not to be confused with the 'carpenters' who will build it and celebrate 'the festival of dedication (*Richtfest*)' when it is completed. Neither is the poet to be confused with the architect who will design the building. Rather, his task is the preliminary one of 'stak[ing] out the site' on which it will, one day, be built (*GA* 4, pp. 148–9).

What this later reading of 'Remembrance' boils down to, it seems to me, is the view that the poet anticipates, nothing to do with the *content* of the future festival, but only rather, its *structure*. Whatever its content, whatever may actually appear as sacred, whatever divinities are actually worshipped, Hölderlin is read as saying, our 'saving power' (*QCT* p. 33) will be a gathering of community in ecstatic affirmation of its own sacred foundations, the coming into being of a new Greek-paradigm artwork.

Notice that this shift in interpretation is a profound one. If Hölderlin refuses to anticipate the *content* of the future festival then, even were the 'thinker' and 'state-founder' to wish to discover in him a plan for the cultural regeneration of the West, his thought would be too abstract to provide them with the necessary purchase. The later texts thus mark a retreat from the link between art and politics, from the political activism of the early texts, a point to which I shall return.

9. Still, what, to repeat, is the point of Hölderlin's 'projection' of the future festival, the projection, as we now understand, of its *structure* alone? What use is this to *us*? Is it not, as Heidegger himself poses the suspicion, mere 'froth (*Schaum*)' (*GA* 4, p. 112)?

The point, Heidegger answers, is to provide 'a measure of actuality (*das Wirkliche*)' (*ibid.*). Thinking, that is to say, about what we have been, and may again become, provides a measure against which we can remain alive to the 'destitution' of the present, prevents us falling into the complacent sleep of Nietzsche's last man. *Andenken* preserves insomnia. And that, obviously, is important because being alive to our destitution is a precondition of any kind of action directed towards its alleviation. (If one has no inkling of the glory of the musical life then one cannot experience its absence from the lives of one's children as a *lack* and hence cannot be motivated to seek to remedy it.)

There is, however, another way in which Heidegger takes Hölderlin's 'dream' to be important. In the 1951 'Building Dwelling Thinking' he says that though we cannot *make* the gods return, we can care-for (*schonen*) the coming gods by 'waiting for intimations of their coming' (*PLT* p. 150); by, that is, waiting *on*, cultivating, such intimations. As he explains in 'The Question Concerning Technology' of 1955, though it is beyond our unaided power to create our own salvation, we nonetheless can, 'here and now and in little things . . . foster the growth of the saving power in its increase' (*QCT* p. 33). We have, then, the capacity to promote the 'return of the gods' by, on a small and localized scale ('in little things'), cultivating the 'intimations' of such a return.

In what might such a cultivation consist? In the acknowledgment and securing of localized appearances of the sacred, 'untimely' exceptions to the predominantly secular character of the present age. The high number

of beatifications and canonizations carried out by Pope John Paul II
(whose thinking has, I think, many Heideggerian affinities) might be
offered as the kind of thing Heidegger has in mind: an acknowledgment
of local cults of benign character, and a willingness to celebrate and
secure them in institutional and artistic forms.

The point, however, is that one can neither 'wait' nor 'care' for the
return of the gods unless one has some idea of what one is waiting for,
trying to 'foster'. As *Being and Time* points out, no intentional activity
can be carried out without the possession, in advance, of some rough
'fore-conception' (*Vorgriff*) of the intended outcome (*BT* 150ff.).
Heidegger's point, then, is really the same as that made at the end of 'The
Origin' where he says that, though we cannot 'force' great art to happen,
meditation on its character of the sort carried out in the essay is the 'indispensable preparation' for its return (*PLT* p. 78). Unless we have some
notion of what would count as such a return, we cannot undertake any
kind of action aimed at promoting it.

What are poets for in needy times? The modern paradigm

10. Hölderlin is, then, important. He is important as an authentic thinker,
as someone alive to the 'destitution' of the present and as someone who,
by thinking the Greek paradigm, gives us (in Nietzschean language) a
'signpost' to the proper future of both art and society.

But surely Hölderlin cannot be presented as *just* a thinker, as just a philosopher of life and art who happens to possess an unusually pleasing
turn of phrase? If we do this then we fall back into the failure of the early
texts to accommodate the fact that what is above all important about
Hölderlin is that he is, first and foremost, a *poet*. Surely Hölderlin cannot
be read as outlining a unique 'essence' of poetry, a set of conditions under
which alone it is to be taken 'seriously', according to which he himself is
disqualified from counting as a serious poet?

To avoid this – and here, it seems to me, we arrive at the most crucial
of all turning points in Heidegger's path of thinking about art – what is
required is the development of a *second* paradigm of great, or at least
'valid' art, a paradigm which will allow the possibility of a modern writer
counting as a genuine poet. As 'poet of poets', as metapoet, we have seen,

Hölderlin outlines the nature and the task of the poets of the future. What we need now, however, is an account of the nature and task of the poets *of the present*. Though the art of the Greek paradigm may be 'dead' in modernity, there has to be a way of allowing that art of another – 'valid' – kind is alive.

The age from which 'the gods' are absent, and in which, consequently, the Greek-paradigm artwork is impossible, is, we have seen, an age of 'destitution' and 'need'. What we need, therefore, is to be able to answer the metapoetic question Hölderlin himself poses in 'Bread and Wine': 'What are poets for in *needy* times' (*PLT* p. 91; my emphasis), as opposed to the, as we might call them, 'thriving' times of, for example, Greece?

11. At the beginning of 'What Are Poets For?', writing in 1946, amidst the rubble of the Second World War and beneath the already advancing shadows of the Cold War and the hydrogen bomb, Heidegger sums up his thinking concerning the 'destitution' of modernity. We live, he says, in a time of 'nameless sorrow', 'peacelessness' and 'mounting confusion' (*PLT* p. 93). Since God is in 'default', since there is no shared commitment to a 'clear and unequivocal' Western *ethos*, no 'eccentric' centre of action (*Ister* p. 28), the West has fragmented into the world of the 'will to power' – the naked or disguised conflict of rival power constellations, the conflict of individuals and nations each pursuing their own, self-aggrandizing, and therefore conflicting, ends.

There is, however, as already noted, something 'even grimmer' than the absence of a 'history'-disposing (*PLT* p. 91) deity: the 'extinction' of the 'divine radiance' (*ibid.*), of, in other words, 'the holy' (*PLT* p. 94).

The holy, Heidegger emphasizes throughout the later texts, is neither identical with, nor dependent on, the gods. They, rather, are dependent on it: 'The holy is not holy because it is divine (*göttlich*), but, rather, the divinities are divine because they are, in their own way, holy' (*GA* 4, p. 59). The holy is prior to the gods in that it is, in Hölderlin's word, the 'aether' in which alone gods can find an 'abode' (*PLT* p. 92), the element 'in which alone the gods are gods' (*PLT* p. 94). Thus the 'grimmest' fact about modernity is not the flight of the gods but rather the ground of both that flight and – grimmest fact of all – the impossibility of their returning during the present age: in Max Weber's word, 'disenchantment', dis-enchantment.

As a culture, nothing is any longer sacred to us, we have lost our sense of the holy, and for *this* reason – since gods are, by definition, holy – we have no living gods.

The Apollonian and the Dionysian

12. This diagnosis is the summation of an extended meditation on Nietzsche's Apollonian–Dionysian distinction which, as mentioned in chapter 1, runs through all the Hölderlin texts, both early[11] and late. For reasons already mentioned, however (chapter 1 section 21), Heidegger prefers to mark the distinction in Hölderlin's rather than Nietzsche's language, presenting it as the distinction between 'clarity of presentation', on the one hand, and 'the fire from heaven', or 'holy pathos', on the other.

The archaic Greeks, says Heidegger, lacked, in a certain way, balance. Though endowed with a powerful openness to the 'fire', they were weak in their capacity for 'clarity of presentation'. The result was that though their 'fitting destiny' was indeed already 'assigned to them', it appeared to them only in a 'veiled and equivocal manner' (*Ister* p. 130). In the language of 'The Origin', what the archaic Greeks could not do was 'open up' their world, bring its 'simple and essential' features out of background inconspicuousness and into foreground salience. 'In a certain manner', therefore, they were 'excluded from the origin of [their] . . . own essence', 'closed off from that which was fittingly destined to them' (*ibid.*). The result was that they lacked control over their own lives, suffered from an 'excess of fate' (*Ister* p. 135). With individuals driven here and there by the impulse of the moment (like, one might add, children or the Irish of the ancient stereotype), their communal life lacked the disciplined and integrated wholeness necessary to constitute them an 'historical people' (*Ister* pp. 135–6). Unable to turn what was 'natural' to them into a 'nature' (*ibid.*) – unable to 'appropriate', in the language of 'The Origin', their 'endowment' (*PLT* p. 77) – they were not yet (in Hegelian language) an 'historical humankind' (*Ister* p. 130).

---

[11] Though an important discussion of the Apollonian–Dionysian distinction appears in the 'Germania'–'Rhine' lectures (*GA* 39), it does so only in the concluding five pages, tagged on as a kind of afterthought and not at all integrated into the body of the text. If it had been, as will appear, the work would have been of a very different character, specifically, would not have been committed, as it is, to the Greek paradigm as providing an account of *the* essence of art.

Their task, therefore, was to learn from their neighbours 'clarity of pre-sentation', the ability to 'articulate' their own 'position in the midst of beings as a whole' (*N* I, p. 88). Their greatness was that they not only did so but eventually surpassed their teachers in the capacity for articulation. (Heidegger's surprisingly contemporary 'out-of-Africa' thesis, here, I take it, is that the Greeks learnt their art and literature from their neighbours, from, in particular, Egypt.) By doing so they were able (through the artwork) to bring their world to 'the still radiance of pure lucidity' and so, for the first time, to 'appropriate' (*aneignen*) their 'own' (*Eigene*), to become properly at home in their '*Heimat*', that is, their world (*Ister* p. 125).

We,[12] however, are out of balance in precisely the opposite way to the archaic Greeks and so our 'task' is exactly the reverse of theirs (*Ister* p. 136). It is 'to fight the battle of the Greeks but on the opposite front' (*GA* 39, p. 293). We find ourselves pre-eminently endowed with 'the ability to grasp and delimit' (*Ister* p. 136), to bring the veiled and con-fusing to the clarity of conceptual articulation. We have, however, become 'consumed' by our power, caught up in a frenzy of forming 'pro-jects, enclosures, frameworks, divisions and structuring' (*ibid.*), a frenzy in which we have destroyed our environment and enslaved ourselves (turned everything, including ourselves, into 'resource'). So alienated from the holy 'fire' have we become that we possess no measure of, or limit upon, what to do with our power. Since nothing appears to us as sacred, nothing halts the omnivorous progress of *Gestell*, the transfor-mation of everything into resource, of the world into a 'gigantic petrol station' (*DT* p. 50).

Our task, then, the opposite of the Greeks', is to recover the 'fire'. Rather than be consumed by the seeming importance of providing ever finer grained, ever more powerful, articulations so as to gain ever greater control over the world (entry into 'the knowledge economy' as the pre-condition of ever-ascending 'economic growth', the unquestioned *summum bonum* of contemporary politics), our primary task is to allow the articulatedness of world to become transparent to – in the language

---

[12] Following Hölderlin, Heidegger says 'we Germans'. But he means, too, 'we of the West'. Writing in the 1930s and 1940s it surely made sense to think of the Germans as the most extreme manifestation of the ills of Western modernity.

of 'The Origin' – 'earth', to, as Heidegger now puts it, 'grasp the ungraspable and . . . [our]selves in the face of the ungraspable' (*Ister* p. 136).

This task provides the narrative theme of most of Hölderlin's major poems. In both 'Remembrance' and 'The Ister', for example, the poets are compelled to travel South, to 'the source', to recover the fire so that, one day, their successors will be able to refound the *Heimat*. 'Remembrance' begins:

> The Northeast blows
> The dearest of the winds
> To me, for a fiery spirit
> And a good journey it promises the sailors. (*GA* 52, p. 19; *GA* 4, p. 80)[13]

And Heidegger comments that in order to appropriate their 'own'

The Germans must be struck by the fire from the heavens. This is why the North-East is the auguring of their poetic destiny. This is why the North-East is greeted. (*Ister* p. 136)

13. In 'What Are Poets For?' Heidegger makes clear the relevance of recovering the fire to overcoming the 'destitution' of our age. The 'turning of the age', the transition to a postmodern epoch 'does not', he says, 'take place by some new god, or old one renewed, bursting into the world from out of ambush at some time or other'. Where, he asks, would such a god

turn on his return if man had not first prepared an abode for him? How could there ever be for a god an abode fit for a god, if a divine radiance did not first begin to shine in everything that is? The gods who 'were once there', return only at the 'right time', that is, when there has been a turn among men in the right place, in the right way. (*PLT* p. 92)

The task, then, for the poet of 'needy' times is clear. Though the Greek paradigm remains the 'highest . . . essence' (*QCT* p. 35) of art, the production of such works is, in the modern age, impossible. Rather than this, a more preliminary task must be undertaken: the preparation of the *possibility* of such a return by recovering, retaining, and through the word, infecting others with the sensibility to experience those, in Hölderlin's ter-

---

13 Although I have consulted existing translations, all the translations of Hölderlin's verse in this study are my own. Though I have made no attempt to capture metre or rhyme, I have matched my punctuation and line division to Hölderlin's.

minology, 'traces (*Spuren*)' of the holy that still remain with us, left over from the age of the presence of the gods (*PLT* p. 94). The poets of modernity are not, to repeat, the 'carpenters' who build, and live to see the completion of, 'the house into which the gods are to come as guests'. Their task, rather, is to 'consecrate the ground' (*GA* 4, p. 148) on which alone such a house can be built. It is to scent out that 'aether' in which alone gods can breathe and to communicate it to others by 'founding', allowing it to come to presence, in their poetry.

The task of the poet in modernity is, then, in a word, to 'found the holy' (*GA* 52, p. 193; *Ister* p. 138; *GA* 4, p. 148); the holy not in the restricted sense of 'the holy in society' – the sacred foundations of community, the divine destinings, that is, 'the gods' – but in, rather, the wider sense of *holiness*. The poet's task is to bring to presence that 'aether', aura, that 'holy sway' (*PLT* p. 150) which, as a matter of definition, of course surrounds gods but which, as we will shortly see, can be a 'wonderfully all-present' 'encirclement' (*GA* 4, p. 49) of other beings, too, even in the age of the absence of the gods. In other language, poetry which 'founds the holy', which validates itself in terms not of the 'Greek' but rather, as I shall call it, the 'modern paradigm', is poetry which preserves and communicates 'the Dionysian'. As Heidegger notes, Hölderlin himself gives this answer to his own metapoetic question:

'and what are poets for in needy times?' Hölderlin shyly puts the answer into the mouth of his poet friend Heinse, whom he addresses in the elegy ['Bread and Wine']. 'But they are, you say, like the wine-god's holy priests, / Who fared from land to land in holy night'.

'In Hölderlin's experience', Heidegger continues, 'Dionysus the wine god' brings 'traces' of holiness 'down to the godless amidst the darkness of the world's night':

for in the vine and its fruit the god of wine grounds the being towards one another of earth and sky as the site [the 'consecrated ground' (*GA* 4, p. 148)] of the wedding feast of men and gods. Only within this site, if anywhere, can traces of the fugitive gods remain for godless man. (*PLT* pp. 93–4; cf. *GA* 52, p. 143)

I shall comment on the introduction, here, of 'earth' and 'sky' in the next section.

The epic and the lyric

14. In 'Homecoming', as noted earlier (section 6 above), Hölderlin says that his own poetry cannot found a world because of the 'default of holy names'. Hölderlin's poetry is, therefore, in a certain sense 'wordless', something, as he puts it, 'sung' rather than said, sung on, or to the accompaniment of, a 'string instrument'. (It is a *'Saitenspiel'* (*GA* 4, p. 11)). Actually, comments Heidegger, though he lacks 'holy names' the poet cannot be *completely* 'wordless' since otherwise he could not have succeeded, as he does, in 'saying the holy' (*GA* 4, p. 27). In spite, therefore, of the absence of 'holy names' Hölderlin possesses, nonetheless, certain 'holy words' (*ibid.*). The words Heidegger has in mind, I believe, are, above all, *nature* words, the words which, in the quotation at the end of the previous section, allow the 'god of wine' to appear in 'earth' and 'sky' and so to 'consecrate' the 'site' on which the wedding feast of gods and men will one day again take place. And the 'string instrument' to which these words are sung is, I suggest, the lyre.[14] In other language, then, the poet who 'founds the holy' is the *lyric* poet, the poet who is concerned not with 'history' but typically, rather, with nature.

This gives us a new way of describing the difference between the Greek and modern paradigms: the poetry of the former is *epic* poetry, of the latter, *lyric*.[15] Put in these terms, we may say that while the epic is, for Heidegger, the art of yesterday and tomorrow, the lyric is the art of today.

---

[14] Michael Hamburger, acknowledged as the finest translator of Hölderlin into English, actually *translates* Hölderlin's *'Saitenspiel'* – 'play of a string instrument' – as play of a 'lyre', a translation for which, strictly, there is no justification. I can only think that Hamburger is moved by precisely the kinds of considerations outlined in this section (see *Hölderlin*, edited and with plain prose translations by Michael Hamburger (Harmondsworth: Penguin, 1961), p. 134).

[15] 'Lyric' and 'epic' can, or course, be defined in different ways. 'Epic', for example, might be understood to mean simply 'large-scale'. I, however, following Nietzsche, use 'epic' to mean something like 'tale of a culture's gods and heroes possessing redemptive communal import' and – again following section 5 of *The Birth of Tragedy* – 'lyric' to mean, roughly, 'work the primary content of which consists in the expression of profound feeling or emotion': feeling or emotion, that is, which, as profound, is not an 'inner', psychological state but rather a mood or mode of disclosure, as Hölderlin calls it, a *Grundstimmung*.

Is Hölderlin a poet for 'needy times'?

15. What we have seen so far is that Heidegger, by attending to Hölderlin's distinction between the present, on the one hand, and the past and future on the other – his distinctions between 'needy' and thriving times and the difference in the poetic task appropriate to each – breaks free of the tyranny of the Greek paradigm, discovers a new paradigm which gives him a theoretical position that allows him to do something other than pretend that the whole of modern art is the lightly entertaining product of 'pastry cooks'.

But does Hölderlin merely articulate the modern paradigm or does he also satisfy it? Is Hölderlin *himself* a 'poet for needy times'? And if he is, does Heidegger see this, does he, in the later texts, read him as satisfying, as well as announcing, the modern paradigm, and so, finally, acknowledge him as a writer as well as philosopher of poetry? Only the briefest attention to Heidegger's reading of the poems which he chooses to make the focus of his later attention is needed to establish that the answer to both these questions is an affirmative one, attention, in particular, to his readings of 'As when on holiday' and 'Homecoming/to the Relatives'.

'Holiday' (as I shall abbreviate its title) begins as follows:

> As when on holiday, to view the fields
> Forth goes a farmer, at break of day,
> When all through the sultry night cooling flashes
> Have fallen and the thunder still rumbles afar
> And back into its channel the stream retreats
> And newly grows the grass,
> And heaven's gladdening showers
> Drip from the vine, and gleaming
> In peaceful sunlight stands the grove of trees
>
> So they [the poets of modernity] stand under propitious weather
> They whom no master alone, whom the wonderfully
> All-present, educates (*erzieht*) in a light encirclement
> The mighty one, divinely beautiful nature. (*GA* 4, p. 49)

And 'Homecoming' begins:

> In there, in the Alps, it is still bright night, and the cloud,
> Poeticizing joyfully, covers the yawning valley within.
> Hither, yonder the skittish mountain-wind roars and tumbles

Sheer through the firs a shaft of light gleams and is lost.
Slowly it hurries and wars, this joy-trembling chaos,
Young in appearance, yet strong, it celebrates loving conflict
Amidst the rocks, seethes and reels in its eternal bounds,
For more bacchantically rises the morning within. (*GA* 4, p. 9)

Though metapoetic concerns are manifest, particularly in the passage from 'Holiday', these, evidently, are poems of intense lyricism, poems in which 'the wonderfully all-present', joy-filled 'chaos', 'holy chaos' (*GA* 4, p. 49)[16] come to presence. So they are, of course, poems which, in Heidegger's language, 'found the holy', poems which satisfy the modern paradigm. And Heidegger is fully alive to this. Commenting on the fact that Hölderlin called his late poems 'hymns', he says that they are not to be understood as hymns in the usual sense of being written to or *about* the holy. They are, rather, 'hymns of the holy' where this is to be understood as a subjective rather than objective genitive.[17] The speaker in the poems, that is, is to be understood not as the particular human being, Hölderlin, but as, rather, the holy itself. In Hölderlin's hymns, says Heidegger,

The holy gifts (*verschenkt*) the word and comes itself into the word. The word is the *Ereignis* of the holy. (*GA* 4, pp. 76–7)

Poetry and prose

16. One question concerning the modern paradigm remains outstanding: why is it *the poet* who is 'the wine god's holy priest', charged with the mission of refounding the holy, of re-enchanting the dis-enchanted age?

---

[16] Hölderlin writes in 'Holiday' that visible nature, which operates 'according to fixed laws', was 'once created out of holy chaos' (*GA* 4, p. 49). Elaborating on this paradoxical conjunction, Heidegger points out that Hölderlin's 'all-creating' holiness cannot be 'chaos' in the sense of 'wildness and confusion' since that could 'provide no footing for [the] distinctions' actually present in the visible world. The truth, rather, is that the holy must contain 'all fullness and every structure in itself' (*GA* 4, p. 63), being *itself* 'the firm law in which all beings and relations are arranged' (*GA* 4, p. 73). It follows, Heidegger in effect points out, that 'chaos' must be read epistemologically rather than ontologically: the holy cannot be intrinsically chaotic. It is merely *by our lights* 'chaotic', ungraspable in terms of our standards of intelligibility.

[17] 'Hymns of the holy', in other words, resembles 'tales of Mary' parsed as 'tales told by Mary' rather than as 'tales about Mary'. I owe this way of putting Heidegger's point to André Schuwer's sensitive 'Nature and the Holy: On Heidegger's Interpretation of Hölderlin's Hymn "*Wie wenn am Feiertage*"', *Research in Phenomenology* 7, 1977, pp. 225–37.

Why is it uniquely he who possesses 'holy words' (see section 14 above)? Why not the 'thinker' or even 'state-founder'?

The answer to this question must have to do with *language* – with the difference between poetry, on the one hand, and prose on the other. A major failing of both the early Hölderlin texts and 'The Origin' is that the question of the nature of this difference is never explicitly confronted. Poetry is injudiciously defined as just any kind of 'projective saying' (*PLT* p. 74), which makes any future-prescribing thinker as much of a poet as Hölderlin. The later Hölderlin texts, and in particular the 1941 discussion of 'Remembrance' (*GA* 52), remedy this deficiency by explicitly confronting the question of the special relationship between the holy and the *poetic* word.

17.   Ordinary language, language used as a tool for information exchange (*GA* 52, p. 15), is, says Heidegger, '*eindeutig*'. The ordinary 'name' is, or at least aspires to be, 'unambiguous', an ideal which is increasingly being realized in practice and which reaches its culmination in the one-to-one correspondence between words and concepts that occurs in the artificial language of 'cybernetic representation' (*D* p. 142), 'computer information language' (*D* p. 159). The poetic 'name', on the other hand, is '*vieldeutig*'. If we were interested only in information transference we might understand this expression in terms of its everyday, pejorative meaning: 'ambiguous'. Evidently, however, information-transference is not the point of poetry (which is not the same as saying that poetry lacks 'cognitive import'). If we are to use '*vieldeutig*' to understand the essence of poetry we must, says Heidegger, decompose the term into its literal meaning: 'of many meanings', possessed of a 'multiplicity' or 'richness of meaning'. For to every 'genuinely' poetic word belongs an 'inexhaustible' range of 'complex spaces of [semantic] vibration (*vielfältige Schwingungsräume*)', from which it follows that, unlike the word of (at least ideal) information exchange, the poetic word has no 'definition' (*GA* 52, p. 15; see, too, *OWL* pp. 64, 192). It communicates, means, more than can ever be captured in words, is, to use a familiar word from the philosophy of art, unparaphrasable.[18]

---

[18] Though the word is familiar the connection between poetry and the holy is less so, suggesting that Heidegger's understanding of the phenomenon is different from, say, Kant's. The

Eindeutig language is the language of drab everydayness. In *eindeutig* world experience the richness of many-faceted (*PLT* p. 124) Being is shut out by the cage of language, by the one-dimensionality of a horizon of disclosure that is taken to be the only horizon there is, the only *possible* horizon. (As we will see in the next chapter, Heidegger calls this drabness 'metaphysics'.) Poetic language, by contrast, opens up. When poetry 'works', when, for example, under the power of Hölderlin's 'Remembrance' or of Trakl's 'A Winter Evening'

> Window with falling snow is arrayed
> Long tolls the vesper bell,
> The house is provided well
> The table is for many laid . . . (*PLT* p. 194)

we are brought to experience the world poetically, then beings start, as later Heidegger puts it, to 'thing' (*PLT* pp. 199–200); to sing the song of Being, to ring with its 'inexhaustible' and 'unfathomable' (*PLT* p. 180) 'richness'. Beings which, in the *eindeutig* representations of everydayness are 'opaque' (*PLT* p. 108), become, in poetry, transparent to Being, to, that is, the holy. Though, like all good poetry, Trakl's poem is an absolute 'clarity of presentation' (see section 12 above) – there is no ambiguity about 'bell', 'house' or 'table' – its 'names' nonetheless 'vibrate' with the richness of meaning that is their inexhaustible range of poetic spaces, are vibrant with the holy itself. In poetic naming, therefore, we experience the 'self-secluding' in things, the infinitude, the unfathomability, the 'secret' life that belongs to every being. The being, as it were, through the transparency of its presence, allows us to sense the infinitude of its depth. It acquires an aura, ceases to be a mere being, but becomes, rather, numinous. In its naming the holy shows itself. This is the reason why poets, and

---

footnote 18 (*cont.*)

difference is, I suggest, the following. Kant, while thinking of the poetic word (or 'aesthetic idea', as he calls it) as resonating indefinitely, thinks of all those resonances as occurring within an ultimate ('transcendental') horizon of intelligibility, the 'horizon of all our horizons', as I put it. They are all 'worldly' resonances, one might say. Heidegger, on the other hand, thinks of the poetic word as, in addition to resonating in the way Kant recognizes, bringing additionally to presence the sense of its designata as possessing indefinitely many 'facets', belonging to indefinitely many 'spaces', that *transcend* our ultimate horizon of intelligibility. To name one's true love poetically, for example, is to name a face, a character, a deportment, a rose, a summer's day, a blessing a. . . . What is important here are the '. . .'s. Read in Heidegger's way, they indicate not only that her 'worldly' qualities are uncountable, but also that the range of those qualities extends beyond what either we or the poet can grasp.

poets alone, possess 'holy words'. Only the possessors of poetic language can name the unnamable, 'bring the enigma as enigma close . . . to us' (*Ister* p. 35), allow us to 'grasp the ungraspable' and ourselves 'in the face of the ungraspable' (*Ister* p. 136).

The *Ereignis*

18. So far, we have found two connected contrasts between the early and later Hölderlin texts, two transitions in Heidegger's thinking, two aspects to his Hölderlinian 'education'. First, through the later texts' expanded and deepened reading of the poet, he discovers the modern paradigm and through it escapes from the tyranny of the Greek. And, second, simultaneously and inseparably connected with this, he ceases to treat Hölderlin's significance as indistinguishable from that of the authentic, philosophical thinker and properly recognizes, for the first time, his greatness as, above all, the greatness of a *poet*.

A third contrast consists in a striking transformation in Heidegger's understanding of the fundamental character of Hölderlin's poetry itself. According to the early texts, it will be remembered, the 'fundamental mood' of *all* of Hölderlin's mature verse is 'holy mourning' (chapter 2 section 3). According to the later texts, however, it is 'gratitude' or 'thankfulness' (*das Danken*) (*GA* 52, p. 197). This is a clear and immediate consequence of Heidegger's coming to read Hölderlin in terms of the modern paradigm. If Hölderlin discloses the world as a holy place, then it follows that, even in the face of the absence of the gods, the *Grundstimmung* of the poetry and of its proper reception is, of necessity, one of 'thankfulness'. To experience one's world as a holy place is, as a matter of conceptual necessity, to inhabit the mood of cosmic gratitude, to 'give thanks' for the 'gift' of such a world and for one's own existence in it.

Moods, as we have seen Heidegger emphasizing from his earliest discussions of the *Grundstimmung* (*GA* 39, pp. 82–3; see chapter 2 section 3) are not 'inner feelings' tacked on to cognitive experience as causal by-products. They are, rather, the way 'beings as a whole' are disclosed. From this it follows that to be in the *Grundstimmung* of cosmic gratitude is to experience the world as a whole as full of the presence of, in Hölderlin's words, the 'wonderfully all-present' (see p. 101 above and *GA* 4, p. 52), as sparkling with the 'divine radiance' (*PLT* p. 91), as, in the language of 'The Origin', transparent to 'earth'. It is, in other words, to experience the world as a holy place. In short, therefore, experiencing the holiness of world and cosmic gratitude are not merely connected. They are one and the same phenomenon.

19. As mentioned in section 3 of the introduction, Heidegger identifies a second 'turn' in his thinking as occurring in the *Contributions to Philosophy* of 1936–8, a turn to '*Ereignis*-thinking'. '*Ereignis*' is, there-fore, the central concept in his post-1938 thinking. What, however, does this mysterious word mean?

It means, first of all, what it means in ordinary German; 'event' or 'hap-pening'. *Ereignis* is, for Heidegger, the happening of, as he variously calls it 'truth', 'the clearing', 'being', 'the being of beings', 'presence' or 'pres-encing' (*P* p. 302). It is, in other words, the happening of that ultimate horizon of disclosure which defines the 'world' of an historical culture. In calling being or world a 'happening' Heidegger makes the point that intel-ligibility, the fundamental structure in terms of which beings show up as the beings they are, is not something independent of human beings. It is, rather, something that 'happens' in 'language', in, that is, human practices or 'forms of life' (see chapter 1 section 18) and is, therefore, dependent on human beings (*P* p. 310).[19] Because it is thus dependent, being 'happens', and happens again and again as human practices undergo historical change – as, for example, the ancient world is replaced by the 'new and essential' world of medieval Christianity.

Ereignis is, then, the happening of world. But this is only part, the less essential part, of the concept. Heidegger indicates this by saying that, for him, *Ereignis* means 'event of appropriation' (*BT* p. 19). The 'Event' appropriates us. When we are aware of this appropriation we have an *Ereignis* 'experience' (*GA* 65, p. 70). What is 'appropriation' and what is it to experience it?

In the *Contributions to Philosophy*, in a section entitled 'Das Ereignis', Heidegger says that when the 'lighting-concealing' that is truth is 'experi-ence[d] as *Ereignis* (appropriation)' it happens as 'transport and enchant-

---

[19] Of course *B*eing (reality) – see section 4 of the introduction – cannot be thus dependent, otherwise one ends up with an *absurd* kind of idealism.

ment (*Entrückung und Berückung*)' (*GA* 65, p. 70). In 'Holiday' he uses exactly the same words, '*Berückung und Entrückung*', to describe the poet's experience of the presence of the 'wonderfully all-present' (*GA* 4, p. 54). What follows, I suggest, is that to share in the poet's 'epiphany' (*ibid.*), his ecstatic experience of the holiness of the world (in other words the festive mood that celebrates 'the wonder that around us a world worlds, that there is something rather than nothing, that there are things and we ourselves are in their midst' (see p. 86 above)) *is* the *Ereignis* experience. Properly experienced, the *Ereignis is*, as Heidegger puts it, 'the *Ereignis* of the holy' (*GA* 4, pp. 76–7).

Since the experiencing of the holiness of world – its radiant 'world-ing', as later Heidegger most often puts it (for example at *PLT* p. 179) – and the *Grundstimmung* of cosmic 'gratitude' are the same, it follows that the *Ereignis*-experience and the world-disclosing mood of cosmic gratitude are one and the same. Heidegger says, to repeat, that his second 'turn' is a turn to '*Ereignis*-thinking': the kind of thinking appropriate to and informed by, *appropriated* by, the experience of the world as the *Ereignis* of the holy. The time of this turn, 1936–8, it is important to note, precisely marks the division between the earlier and later Hölderlin texts, between the apprehension of the Hölderlinian *Grundstimmung* as 'holy mourning' and its apprehension as cosmic gratitude. What I suggest, therefore, is that the turn of 1936–8 and the transformation in Heidegger's understanding of Hölderlin are one and the same process.[20]

The transformation, that is, is no mere transformation in Heidegger's *interpretation* of Hölderlin. Given the identity of voices throughout the Hölderlin discussions, it is a transformation in Heidegger himself. The description, then, that embraces all the aspects of Hölderlin's education of Heidegger is to say that it is in and through Hölderlin's self-reflective lyricism that Heidegger discovers both the concept and the experience of 'the *Ereignis*'. He discovers it because, to repeat, '[Hölderlin's] word *is* the *Ereignis* of the holy' (*GA* 4, pp. 76–7; my emphasis).

---

[20] If this is right then it follows that the '*Contributions to Philosophy*' – often described, for unclear reasons, as 'Heidegger's second-greatest work' – is actually less fundamental than the later Hölderlin texts. Though it precedes them in the order of writing, their content, I suggest, precedes it in the order of thinking.

From the sublime to the holy

20. At this point, however, a question (one which has actually been with us since the discussion of 'The Origin''s conception of 'earth' in chapter 1) presents itself as urgently in need of an answer; the question of why we should in fact *believe* the claim that the world is a holy place. Granted that reflection on the fact that truth is disclosure and disclosure always concealment – or a prereflective grasp of the content of such reflection – reveals the world to be a sublime, 'awesome', 'earth'-ridden place, still the sublime, one would think, is not the same as the holy. For while the holy – as at least *we* understand the term – is, as a matter of conceptual necessarily, benevolent, in some sense morally perfect, the sublime can be morally ambivalent, perhaps even demonic. With Hölderlin, Heidegger repeatedly insists on the 'gracious', 'gift-giving' character of the holy (*GA* 4, p. 55; *GA* 9, pp. 309–10) as he has to if it is to be truly the holy. But why should we actually believe that the world, life, existence as we know it, is a gift rather than, as, for example, Schopenhauer famously maintained, a curse? Why, then, should we believe that the sublime is also the holy? Why should we prefer Heidegger to Schopenhauer?

Hölderlin, of course, presents the sublime as supremely gracious. In 'Holiday', the poet, in festive mood and so standing outside the drabness of 'everydayness', ascends to what Heidegger sometimes calls 'the other side' (*GA* 52, p. 178), ascends, that is, 'from out of the space (*All*) of beings to Being' (*ibid.*). He experiences Being as, in his own words, 'all-creating' (self-disclosing) and therefore 'mighty'. As a consequence, says Heidegger, he is acquainted with the 'terror' (*GA* 4, p. 63) of the holy. Yet because the terror is, as the poet puts it, 'hidden under the mildness of the light encirclement' (*ibid.*) of everything by the 'wonderfully all-present', the holy is experienced as not only supremely powerful but also supremely 'gracious' (*GA* 4, p. 55). And in 'Homecoming', as Heidegger points out, 'the highest' is described variously as 'the serenely cheerful' (*das Heitere*), 'the joyful' (*das Freudige*), as one which 'greets' the poet with tidings of 'joy'. Heidegger's later Hölderlin readings are absolutely right: there is no doubt at all that Hölderlin's fundamental mood is one of cosmic, and ecstatic, 'thankfulness'. The question remains, however, as to why should we take Hölderlin's mood to be anything more than – Hölderlin's mood?

Why should we accept it as anything more than one man's *Gestalt* on 'beings as a whole' possessing no less, but also no more, claim to verisimilitude than, say, Schopenhauer's fundamental mood of cosmic despair? Are we not entering the well-trampled domain of the unanswerable question as to whether the beer glass is half full or half empty? Yet if Hölderlin's (and Heidegger's) mood is to be of any *philosophical* interest it must be possible to say that, in some sense or other, it is the *right* mood to inhabit.

21. Paul de Man suggests that Hölderlin's role for Heidegger is that of a 'witness'.[21] Being is holy because Hölderlin is a man of semi-divine powers of insight (inhabits the *Nähe*, is 'near' to Being) and allows the content of his insight to come to presence in his poetry. But that, of course – this is de Man's point – advances the argument not at all. A Schopenhauerian could equally well set up Thomas Hardy as a poet of semi-divine insight and conclude that Being is demonic.

When it comes to providing a thoughtful validation of the Hölderlinian vision Heidegger is somewhat indistinct on the question of whether it is the *that* or the *how* of the world that is of focal importance. Sometimes it seems to be only the former. Recall once again, for example, the remark that, on the festive occasion, we step into 'the wonder (*Wunder*) that around us a world worlds at all, that there is something rather than nothing, that there are things and we ourselves are in their midst, that we ourselves are' (see p. 86 above). This reflects a theme which goes back to the 1929 lecture 'What is Metaphysics?'; the claim that the truly philosophical mood is 'wonder' that there is something rather than nothing, a claim that links Heidegger to Aristotle, who said that philosophy begins with 'astonishment' at the ordinary (though according to Heidegger, Aristotle himself did not properly understand the character of that astonishment), and to Wittgenstein, who wrote that

How things are in the world is a matter of complete indifference for what is higher. God does not reveal himself in the world . . . it is not *how* things are in the world that is mystical but *that* it exists. (*Tractatus Logico-Philosophicus* 6.432–6.44)

[21] 'Heidegger's Exegesis of Hölderlin' in *Blindness and Insight* (Minneapolis: University of Minnesota Press, 1983), pp. 246–66.

The trouble with this line of thinking, however, is the unexplained and ungrounded slide from the sublime to the holy. Granted that the existence of the world is indeed 'astonishing', 'mystical', a matter for 'wonder', it in no way *follows* that it is a 'wonderful' – in the sense of supremely pleasing – place in which to find oneself, that it is 'God' who reveals himself in existence. Schopenhauer, too, recognized cosmic 'astonishment' as the beginning of true philosophy. But for him, it is astonishment coloured by dismay, even horror. True philosophy, he claims, begins, like Mozart's *Don Giovanni*, with a minor chord (*The World as Will and Representation*, II, p. 171).

It seems, then, that we cannot take the mere fact *that* we exist – the mere fact of, in Heideggerian language, 'the clearing', of 'light' – as establishing the 'gracious' character of the sublime. Something about the *nature* of the clearing, the *how* of existence, needs to be brought into consideration. Though, in the ecstatic moment, it may *seem* that only the world's thatness is under consideration, it is hard to escape the conclusion that aspects of its howness are also, at least implicitly, present.

This, certainly, as Heidegger makes clear in the 'Holiday' discussion, is the character of Hölderlin's ecstasy. The reason the 'mighty', 'all-creating' one is gracious, its power concealed beneath a 'mildness', is that its 'creation', nature, is a thing of 'divine' or 'god-like' beauty (*göttlichschön*) (see p.101 above). It is beautiful because it embodies the 'thought' which is 'spirit'. (Influenced by his friend Hegel, one of the names for the holy that Hölderlin uses in 'Holiday' is 'communal spirit (*Geist*)' (*GA* 4, p. 50).)

The 'thought', explains Heidegger, is the 'unifying unity' that 'sets everything into the well-separated limits and structures of its presence' (*GA* 4, p. 60). It holds together 'mountain' and 'valley', 'the highest heaven and the deepest abyss', within a unity or fundamental 'peace'. This peace, however, is by no means a matter of 'flat sameness'. Rather, it is the unity of 'well-distinguished opposites', a unity which constitutes the essence 'beauty' (*GA* 4, pp. 53–4). Beauty is, then, sharply distinguished 'opposites' resting in the 'connectedness' (*ibid.*) of harmonious unity. (Think, by way of illustration, of a face. On the one hand there must be harmony and balance between, for example, its two sides. But, on the other, there must be sharply defined differences between its constituent elements. In the beautiful face there can be nothing nose-like about the ear or ear-like about the nose.)

For Hölderlin, then, and for Heidegger *qua* Hölderlinian thinker, cosmic 'thankfulness' is the *right* stance towards the world as a whole because that world is a beautiful place in which to find oneself. Being is holy because nature is beautiful. Here, I think, we find ourselves on familiar territory: what Hölderlin–Heidegger offer with respect to the howness of creation is an aesthetic analogue of the 'argument from design'. Whether this offering might not be vulnerable to the very same objection as was raised against the *Grundstimmung* of cosmic gratitude – that it is nothing more interesting than one man's (or rather two men's) *Gestalt* on beings-as-a-whole – is a question to which I shall return shortly.

From Nikeism to waiting

22. Let us, however, for a moment, suppose ourselves to be convinced that we really should accept that the sublime is also the holy. Given this assumption, let us now ask what difference it makes. What difference does understanding one's world to be a holy place make to one's life and thought? How does thinking (and living) that is based on the '*Ereignis*-experience' differ from thinking which is not? What, in short, *is* '*Ereignis*-thinking'?

Heidegger says that those who have not made the transition to *Ereignis*-thinking are incapable of *patience*, of 'the long patient waiting for the gift'. For them, patience is merely 'weakness'. What they demand instead is tough, instant and, where necessary, violent action – 'hardness (*die Härte*)' (*GA* 52, p. 181). They are, as we might call them, 'Nikeists'; they demand that we 'just do it'.

As thinkers of this ilk Heidegger identifies Ernst Jünger and his mentor Nietzsche (*GA* 52, p. 180): thinkers who understand the destitution or, in Nietzsche's language, 'nihilism' of modernity and respond to this insight with the demand for salvation now, for an immediate leading of the benighted many by the enlightened few into a 'revaluation of all values'. But he also says that when 'tough' (i.e. undemocratic) action fails to produce the desired result the Nikeist (my word, not Heidegger's) takes refuge in some kind of 'intoxication (*Rausch*)' which may easily turn out to be the 'intoxication of blood (*Blutrausch*)' (*GA* 52, p. 181).

This 1941 remark is, unmistakably, a reference to Nazism: a presentation of Nazism at war as the failure of Nazism as attempted social revolution. But given that reference there is also, surely, a reference to Heidegger's own former Nikeism – his own former commitment to immediate, tough action contained in the call for an alliance of poet, thinker, and state-founder, for the institution *now* of a 'politics in the highest and most authentic sense'.[22] *Inter alia*, Heidegger's critique of Nikeism is a critique of his own former self.

In contrast to the Nikeists, those who have made the transition to *Ereignis*-thinking enter into 'the long, slow patience (*Langmut*)' (*GA* 52, p. 181). To be noticed here is the emergence of one of the most central, and controversial, themes of Heidegger's postwar philosophy, the assertion that 'man's essence is to be the one who waits', one who, rather than trying to *make* history happen, 'attends upon the coming to presence of Being' (*QCT* p. 42).

23.   Why should the transition to '*Ereignis*-thinking' be a transition from Nikeism to waiting? For, I think, two reasons. The first concerns the futility, the second the superfluity of Nikeism.

Nikeists are, says Heidegger, locked into 'metaphysics' (*GA* 52, p. 180) – of which a great deal more in chapter 4. One inhabits 'the essential realm of metaphysics', he says, in an already quoted remark, when one fails to ascend from the 'space of beings' to its 'other side' (*GA* 52, p. 178). (Call to mind here, the Rilkean comparison between Being and the moon.) Since, for the Nikeist, i.e. 'metaphysician', there is nothing beyond beings, beings and beings alone are responsible for the way that beings are. Less abstractly, the levers of history lie entirely in human hands, man is the maker and master of history. For the *Ereignis*-thinker, however, for one who *has* ascended from beings to their 'other side', it is immediately clear that every attempt to 'make history happen', to create, through

---

[22] Contained, too, in what, in *HPN* (chapter 1 sections 14 and 21), I call Heidegger's 'Pol-Potism'. In the speeches made as rector of Freiburg University, as, that is, a Nazi official, in 1933–4, Heidegger called for an overcoming of the nihilism of modernity through deindustrialization. The dehumanized workers of German industry are to recover their spirituality through becoming subsistence farmers (becoming close to 'earth') on land conquered (reclaimed, Heidegger would have said) in the East. (How a deindustrialized state is supposed to *retain* the fruits of war in the face of industrially armed enemies Heidegger, caught up in the intoxication of the moment, does not mention. Given the craziness of his 1933 position it is not surprising that he soon recovered from it.)

human endeavour alone, a new historical epoch, a culture-wide 'revaluation of all values', is *futile*. For having understood that world is 'destined'
by, is the self-disclosure of, the awesomely self-concealing, one knows
immediately that 'Being has no equal' (*QCT* p. 44), that it 'will never allow
itself to be mastered, either positively or negatively, by a human doing
founded merely on itself' (*QCT* p. 38). Just as believing oneself the master
of God would show one to have no god, so to believe oneself the master
of Being would reveal, precisely, one's 'forgetfulness' of Being.

The second, and, in the Hölderlin texts, much more prominent, reason
given for rejecting Nikeism in favour of 'waiting' is that, having made the
transition to *Ereignis*-thinking, one sees that the attempt to overcome the
'destitution' of the present by precipitate action is *unnecessary*. Given that
we live in a world that is 'destined' to us by a graciousness, it follows that
our lives are, as it were, in gift-giving hands. More specifically, the attempt
to force the 'return of the gods', of 'the festival', is an attempt to force the
coming of that which is *already* 'coming'.

Modernity, we know, is a time of 'night'. In the early (pre-*Ereignis*)
texts Heidegger reads Hölderlin's image always as an absolute and unre-
deemed blackness. The 'darkening of the world, the flight of the gods'
(*IM* p. 38) stands for 'the demonic', absolute 'evil' (*IM* p. 46). With the
deepening of Heidegger's understanding of Hölderlin in the later texts,
however, night undergoes a radical reappraisal. Heidegger notices, as we
have seen, that in 'Bread and Wine' the 'wine-god's priests' journey
through '*holy* night'. Through 'Homecoming', he experiences night as
'serenely cheerful', 'joyful'. The reason for this, Hölderlin teaches him,
is that though our age is indeed the time of 'God's default', that default
is no mere absence but is, rather, a matter of the age's being the time of
the 'stored-up treasure (*gesparter Fund*)'. 'Therefore', Heidegger concludes, 'God's default is no deficiency (*Mangel*)'. And it follows he says,
expanding on Hölderlin's rejection, in 'Poet's Calling', of 'artifice
(*Listen*)', that

the citizens are not to strive, through artifice, to make their own god and so, by force,
to do away with the supposed deficiency. (*GA* 4, p. 28)

This prohibition on Nikeism reappears a decade later in 'Building
Dwelling Thinking'. Those with insight into that which is do not, says
Heidegger,

make their gods for themselves and do not worship idols. In the very depths of misfortune they wait for the weal that has been withdrawn. (*PLT* p. 150)

Of this passage, presented in a public lecture in 1951, Karsten Harries comments correctly that few in the audience could have missed the reference to Hitler.[23] But the same must have been true when the remark was first made – also in a public lecture, in Freiburg, in the far less secure circumstances of 1943. Heidegger's comment is directed against the Nikeism of Nazism and again, therefore, against his own earlier entanglement in it.

Why, however, is the future festival already present, in 'stored up' form, in the present age? Why is it already in the process of 'coming'?

Being's 'graciousness', we have seen, is manifested in the beauty of the world's 'design', a design that embraces 'opposites'. Heidegger's examples, in the discussion of 'Holiday', are of synchronic 'opposites' – mountain and valley (see p. 110 above). But the thought of a beautiful unity of opposites embraces, too, for Heidegger, diachronic opposites: the diurnal rotation, for example, and the cycle of the seasons. Heidegger suggests, under Hölderlin's influence, that human history, too, is cyclical, 'seasonal'. The default of God, we know, is 'night' time. Typically, says Heidegger (as, for example, in his early Hölderlin readings) night is regarded as absolutely 'negative' – nothing more than the absence of day. In fact, however, it only appears so when we forget the dusk and the dawn. In reality night, too, is something 'positive' (*GA* 52, pp. 86–8), the 'mother of the day', the holy place in which the 'past (*vergangene*)' and the 'coming gods' are concealed, 'its rest the still preparation of a Coming (*eines Kommenden*)' (*GA* 4, pp. 109–10).

In 'Holiday' the point is put, perhaps more perspicuously, in terms of a seasonal metaphor. The time of the default of God is, says Hölderlin, the 'winter' time of human history. To the undiscerning it seems that everything lies in frozen sleep. Initiates, however, know that nature never sleeps, that the winter rest is her 'self-collection for [the] . . . coming'. They, says Hölderlin, 'intimate always (*ahnen sie immer*)' the coming summer (*GA* 4, pp. 54–5).

Given this perspective, it becomes clear that the age of God's default is no more an age of 'deficiency' than winter is a season of 'deficiency'. Rather, like winter, it takes its place in the cyclical rhythm of 'opposites' that constitutes the diachronic beauty of Being's self-revelation.

[23] 'Lessons of a Dream', *Chora*, vol. II, eds. A. Pérez-Gomez and S. Parcell (Montreal and Kingston: McGill and Queen's University Press, 1998), pp. 91–108, at p. 104.

Knowledge or faith?

24. Cyclical thinking of the above sort permeates not just the later Hölderlin texts but also Heidegger's postwar philosophy. 'The Question Concerning Technology', for example, says that we are to 'foster the growth of the saving power in its increase' (*QCT* p. 33) (not, notice, *in the hope of* its increase), while 'The Turning' affirms Hölderlin's version of 'dawn begins at the darkest hour':

> But where the danger is, grows
> The saving power also. (*QCT* p. 42)

No one knows, it continues, when 'the turning' to a postmodern, post-nihilistic age will occur (*QCT* p. 41). But *that* it will occur seems never to be doubted.

What, however, is the status of this cyclical, 'season', view of history in Heidegger's philosophy? Are we really intended to accept it as, somehow, a metaphysically guaranteed *fact* that the future 'festival' really is 'coming', somehow guaranteed as, for example, in Hegel or Marx, the inexorably progressive character of *Geist*'s self-disclosure is guaranteed by the dialectical laws of history? If so, the appropriate response consists in the observation that we are offered no ground at all to believe the cyclical view of history. Solid, common-sense induction (not to mention scientific theory) tells us that winter will indeed be followed by summer but (particularly if, as 'The Origin' suggests, there have only ever been three Western epochs, the ancient, medieval and modern) we have no inductive grounds at all for being confident that there will be any 'glorious summer' to banish our present 'winter of discontent'. Offered as metaphysical fact, the seasonal view of history is just a bad joke: a mere *Gestalt* dressed up with an authority it in no way possesses.[24]

---

[24] Could one not, perhaps, extrapolate to the 'seasonal' view of history, the diachronic 'beauty' of the world, from the unity of opposites that is its synchronic beauty? Possibly, except for the fact that synchronic beauty is itself merely a *Gestalt*. Schopenhauer claims that the so-called 'design' of the world, far from proving it to be the work of a benevolent creator, is no more than the *minimum* condition of existence, *of there being any world at all*. An evil genius, bent on creating a torture chamber for his own entertainment, would be compelled to construct the same degree of unity-between-opposites. This, it has to be admitted, is a point of view.

But, in reality, Heidegger cannot possibly intend the cyclical *Gestalt* to be taken as metaphysical fact. For he says, in the Nietzsche lectures, that for all we know, the age of *Gestell* may be indefinitely 'self-perpetuating' (*N* III, p. 6) (as some have suggested of the American 'Goldilocks' economy that began with the 1990s). In (perhaps surprisingly) 'The Turning', Heidegger generalizes the point to cover all attempts to discover a shape to world history: 'All attempts to reckon existing reality morphologically', he says, 'are truthless and without foundation' (*QCT* p. 48). Yet there is nothing, surely, more 'morphological' than the 'seasonal' view of history elevated to the status of metaphysical fact.

The fundamental reason Heidegger must reject all such attempts is clear. Any attempt to delimit – and so limit – Being's character, to impose pattern, and hence *laws*, upon the process of its self-disclosure as world, is an attempt to force upon Being a particular (human-friendly) nature and hence an infringement of its inscrutability. Instead of 'earth', 'the mystery', 'the ungraspable', the 'other side' of beings becomes just another being (albeit, as I shall discuss in the next chapter, a being of a 'higher' type than manifest beings). Failing, therefore, to rise above the 'space of beings', the attempt falls squarely into the category of 'metaphysics'. With special reference to his doctrine of 'the eternal return of the same', Heidegger calls Nietzsche 'the last metaphysician', and portrays himself as the first post-metaphysical thinker. But the cyclical view of history is, surely, simply a vaguer, less specific version of Nietzsche's idea of history as the 'eternal recurrence' of everything that happens down to the very last detail. Offered as metaphysical fact, the cyclical view is, therefore, inescapably – 'metaphysical'.

There is, then, good reason to suppose that Heidegger does not offer the cyclical view of history as deep knowledge about the way reality actually is. Though 'The Turning' only says that 'when and how' 'the turning', the return of 'the festival', will happen is unknown, Heidegger must, in truth, also maintain that *whether* it will 'come to pass . . . no one knows' (*QCT* p. 41). (One might be tempted here by the thought that 'all possibilities are realized over infinite time' but that, of course, is metaphysics of, in Kant's language, the most 'dogmatic' kind.)

But why, then, *does* Heidegger omit the 'whether' of the turning, continue, into the 1950s, to speak as if the only uncertainty is its 'when'?

Following Hölderlin, as we have seen, Heidegger says the poets of wintertime 'intimate always' the oncoming spring and summer (*GA* 4, pp. 54–5). This, read *à la* de Man, might be a presentation of the view that those who stand above ordinary mortals – '*between* men and gods' (HE p. 312) – have occult knowledge of the future. But another reading is, not that they know, but rather that they are *always on the lookout for* signs of a return of the festival. Such signs are always present since, as Heidegger regularly insists, cultural epochs are always complex phenomena. Beneath their dominant and defining character they are always, too, 'a passing by and simultaneity of early and late' (*PLT* p. 185), a mixture of remnants of a past epoch and signs, hints, 'intimations', of a future one. These latter are, on the proposed reading, what the poets of wintertime, and those influenced by them, are on the lookout for. They 'wait for intimations of [the gods'] . . .coming' (*PLT* p. 150). Such waiting, however, as we have seen (section 9 above), is no merely passive *waiting for* but is, rather, an active *waiting on,* a 'foster[ing] the growth of the saving power' 'here and now in little things' (*QCT* p. 33). It is, in other words, an exercise of the human 'essence' of 'guardianship', of being 'the one who attends upon the coming to presence of Being in that he guards it' (*QCT* p. 42).

This, I suggest, is the proper reading of 'intimation'. It is a matter, not of occult knowledge but of, rather, cultivating those seeds which are the possibility of a *hoped-for* future.

It is, however, plausibly a feature of human action that unless one has faith in the *eventual* achievement of the goal at which it is aimed one will be unable to conduct the pursuit of the goal in, in Heidegger's language, a 'resolute' manner. Kant saw this in the final formulation, in the *Critique of Judgment*, of the 'moral argument' for the existence of God, a god conceived at this late stage in his thinking as, in essence, history. Unless, Kant says, the virtuous man has faith that the underlying tide of history is moving in the same direction as his own efforts to make the world a better place, he will succumb, in the end, to moral despair. Heidegger, I suggest, may be read as possessing a similar thought: unless the cultivator of the intimations of the return of the gods has faith that they will, in the end, return, unless he believes that, ultimately, history is 'on his side', he will be unable to practise that cultivation in a convinced and committed manner.

This, I believe, is why Heidegger continues, in his postwar philosophy, to speak not of the 'possible' or 'hoped for' but rather of the 'coming' festival, not of 'fostering the saving power' in the hope of its increase but in, simply, 'its increase'. The cyclical view of history, the Hölderlinian *Grundstimmung* of cosmic gratitude, is exemplary not because it corresponds to known metaphysical truth but rather because it is the faith that is the precondition of 'resoluteness' in one's fostering of the 'saving power'.

25. While Being's sublimity is, then, something that can be known, its holiness is a matter of faith, a faith Heidegger himself was infected with by Hölderlin. At the very end of 'The Turning' Heidegger, so to speak, steps, for a moment, outside his own faith to make clear that that, indeed, is its status. No longer, that is to say, does he speak, as he has done throughout the rest of the essay, as if only the 'when' of the turning is unknown but allows, now, that so, too, is the 'whether'. 'Will', he now asks, the turning happen?

Will insight into that which is bring itself disclosingly to pass? Will we . . . be . . . brought home into the essential glance of Being . . .? Will we dwell as those at home in nearness, so that we will belong primordially within the fourfold of sky, earth, mortals and divinities? Will insight into that which is bring itself disclosingly to pass . . .?

And he responds to this catechism, not with an affirmation, but with, rather, a prayer:

May world in its worlding be the nearest of all nearing that nears, as it brings the truth of Being near to man's essence and so gives man to belong to the disclosing bringing-to-pass that is a bringing into its own. (*QCT* p. 49)

And it is, in part, perhaps, this element of faith contained in the turn to *Ereignis*-thinking to which Heidegger refers in his 'Letter to a Young Student' when he says that he can 'provide no credentials' for what he has said, no 'checks' that it 'agrees with "reality"' (*PLT* p. 186).

Does this, then, mean – to return to the issue left unresolved at the end of section 21 – that there is no sense at all in which the Hölderlinian *Gestalt* of cosmic 'thankfulness' can be said to represent the *right* stance towards life and the world? One point to notice is that while the 'seasonal' view of history is only a *Gestalt*, it is also *at least* a *Gestalt*. It is perfectly *possible* that history is 'seasonal', that we do indeed inhabit the time of the 'coming' festival, of, as we might also call it, the 'New Age'. Given this, and given that the *Gestalt* is the precondition of redemptive action, why, one might well ask, should anyone want to *resist* its adoption, to prefer, for example, the Schopenhauerian stance of cosmic despair? Given, therefore, that the Hölderlinian stance is both possible and productive there is, it seems to me, a good sense in which it is also the 'right' one to adopt.

4   Modern art

1. The beginning of Heidegger's path of thinking about art was, we saw, permeated by thoughts of the death of art. Surprisingly, sepulchral thoughts persist, even intensify, in the postwar writings to which I now turn. Here we discover the discussion of art to be peppered by a regular litany of apparently exceptionless generalizations pronouncing the total absence of art (as a non-trivial phenomenon) from the world of Western modernity. Once again, it seems, not merely the gods but art, too, has deserted us.

So, for example, modern art is said to be nothing more than a fully integrated part of 'the sphere of the techno-scientific world-construction' (*SvG* p. 41), its works 'the steering-steered (*gesteuert-steuernden*) instruments of the cybernetic language of information-exchange' (*ZSD* p. 64). Since it 'arises no longer from the shaping boundaries of an ethnic or national world but is, rather, projected and led, in its construction and constitution, by scientific technology', 'the universality of [our] . . . world civilization', modern (so-called) art is a farewell to everything that art once was (*D* p. 140). Turning to the particular arts, we find that poetry has become absorbed into the industrial system, has become mere 'literary production' (*D* p. 153), while film is, as such, an integral part of 'the Europeanization of man and the earth [which] attacks at the source everything of an essential nature' (*OWL* p. 16). And so far as the reception of art, so far as modern humanity's capacity to respond in a significant manner to art is concerned, what we find, Heidegger claims, is that art occurs in 'empty space' since 'we no longer possess an essential relation to art' (*KuT* p. xiii).

If we think about modern art, about the place of art in modernity, from the point of view of 'The Origin', these sweeping condemnations are

120

completely unsurprising. For it is, as already observed, perfectly obvious
that there is nothing in Western modernity which plays the role played, in
Greece, by temple and amphitheatre, and, in the Middle Ages, by church
and cathedral. Moreover, if we think about the globalized, yet atomized,
character of modernity, about the absence of public, communal space,
and about the trivialization – 'aestheticization' – of modernity's expecta-
tions of art, it might well seem obvious that not only is there no Greek-
paradigm artwork in modernity, but also that there could be none. Short
of a world-historical sea change in our culture, the social preconditions
of such an artwork do not exist.

What renders postwar Heidegger's stance to the art of his own times
manifestly problematic, however, is – in apparently total contradiction to
the 'death of art' generalizations – first, the high esteem he expresses for
what turns out to be actually a considerable number of individual artists,
and, second, the facts of his own biography. Heidegger expressed, *inter
alia*, great esteem for, in music, Stravinsky and Carl Orff, in poetry, Georg
Trakl, Paul Celan, Réne Char, Stefan George and Rainer Maria Rilke, in
architecture, for le Cobusier, in sculpture, Bernhard Heiliger and Eduado
Chillida, and, in painting, Van Gogh, Braque, Klee and Cézanne. And in
the officially despised 'art business' (*KuT* p. xiii) of modernity he had, in
fact, a considerable number of friends and acquaintances: *inter alios*,
Georg Schmit, the Basel gallery director and friend of Paul Klee, the art
collector Ernst Beyeler, and the art historians Hans Jantzen and Heinrich
Petzet. (The latter he encouraged to publish Rilke's *Letters on Cézanne*
and to pursue book projects concerned with both Cézanne and Klee.) In
the mid-1950s he made a special excursion to Holland to see the Van
Goghs in the newly opened Kröller-Müller museum outside Arnhem and
was in frequent contact with the Erker Gallery in the Swiss town of St
Gallen for which he wrote (or rather engraved on lithographer's stone) the
essay on sculpture, 'Art and Space'.[1] Not least significant is the fact that

---

[1] The chief source for these, and other, biographical details is Heinrich Petzet's *Encounters
and Dialogues* (Chicago: University of Chicago Press, 1993). Also important are the contributions by Hartmut Buchner, Francois Fedier and Dieter Jähnig in *Erinnerung an Martin
Heidegger*, ed. G. Neske (Pfullingen: Neske, 1977) and Jähnig's contribution to *Kunst und
Technik (KuT)*. *Denkerfahrungen (D)* is an important source for many of Heidegger's published, as opposed to reported, observations on individual artists. 'Art and Space' appears
in *Man and World* 6, 1973, pp. 3–8.

Heidegger continued, as he had done all his life, to write poetry – sometimes of considerable quality. The late Heidegger was, then, in a word, up to his elbows in the 'art business' of his times. His life, his relationships, and his judgments on individual artists are completely at odds with his generalized pronouncements on the character of modern art as such.

Having completed our study of the Hölderlin texts we know, of course, what it was that opened up the possibility of his esteem for individual artists of modernity, opened up, at least, the possibility of combining that esteem with a clear theoretical conscience. The self-liberation from the tyranny of the Greek paradigm carried out in the later Hölderlin texts, which rendered his theorizing about art consistent with his esteem for Hölderlin as a poet, opened up, too, a place in his thinking for the esteem of other artists of modernity; for 'artists of modernity' not only in the broad sense that includes Hölderlin, but also in the narrower, and more familiar, sense in which the term means, simply, 'contemporary artists'. What is clear, that is to say, is that the coming into being of, as I called it, 'the modern paradigm' allows Heidegger consistently to acknowledge that modernity contains not merely the art of 'pastry cooks' but also 'great', or at the very least 'valid', art. But why, then, the continuation of the generalized pronouncements of the death of art?

These pronouncements, evidently, have to be regarded as rhetorical exaggerations. Heidegger's real position is the (less dramatic, less eye-catching, less slogan-like) assertion that *most* modern art is trivial[2] (or else, as we shall see, positively pernicious). The effect of the generalizations is thus to establish a duality between the general character of modern art, on the one hand, and the few, but significant, exceptions to the rule, on the other. The main point of the generalizations is thus, I suggest, to present the artists in whom Heidegger is interested as, not the mountain peaks of a generally thriving world of art, but rather something quite different: the, in Nietzsche's sense, 'untimely' exceptions to the rule, artists at the margins, out of step with, and in opposition to, the prevailing aesthetic order. This raises the question of what the principle of selection is which determines the exceptions as the exceptions.

[2] At an interesting moment in the *Spiegel* interview the interviewer, Rudolf Augustein, simply by gently repeating it, persuades Heidegger to 'cross out' the claim that modern art, *überhaupt*, is 'destructive' (*HC* p. 115). Heidegger was by no means insensible to the profile-raising value of sepulchral soundbites and knew when he had been caught out.

Anti-metaphysical art

2. Modernity, we know, is a time of extreme 'destitution', the nature of which lies in the 'extinction of the divine radiance', modernity's disenchantment, its failure to live any longer in the light of 'the holy'. The cause of this is described, in the first instance, as 'enframing', the reduction of everything to 'resource'. But the world-historical take-over by 'enframing', the fact that it has become the disclosure of Being which *defines* the modern epoch, is, according to Heidegger, only made possible by the completion of a long and gradual, historical process in terms of which Western humanity has lost what I called the 'festive' mode of disclosure (see chapter 3 section 3). The cause of this is what Heidegger calls 'metaphysics'.

There are two questions to be asked about that which, in a decidedly idiosyncratic use of the term, Heidegger designated with the word 'metaphysics': what is it? and how does it come about?

The answer to the first question has already been given. Metaphysics – which may occur either as explicit philosophical doctrine or implicitly in the layman's intuitive stance to reality – is the failure to 'ascend' from the 'space of beings' to its 'other side', ignorance, that is to say, of that 'other side'. Since Being is beings *together with* their 'other side', the lighted side of the 'globe of Being' *together with* its dark side, 'world'[3] *together with* 'earth', Heidegger's most fundamental characterization of metaphysics is to call it 'oblivion of Being' (*P* p. 318).

What oblivion of Being entails we also already know: oblivion to the 'awesomeness' of truth, to the sublimity of world. To enter that condition is for the world to 'obtrude and accumulate in a dry, monotonous, and therefore oppressive way' (*QCT* p. 17), for it to become the dis-enchanted, unsacred place that is the world of modernity.

Concerning the second question, Heidegger's answer, in brief (I shall have considerably more to say about it in section 20 below), is that one enters the wasteland of metaphysics through a (explicit or implicit) misunderstanding of truth (*P* p. 280). The fundamental mistake that creates metaphysics is the failure to see the dependence of truth (as

---

[3] 'World' in the sense, here, not of horizon of intelligibility, structure of disclosure, but meaning, rather, the totality of beings. Heidegger oscillates between these, in the language of *Being and Time*, 'ontological' and 'ontic' senses of 'world'.

correspondence) upon the world-disclosure that happens in, and only in, human 'linguistic' practices, in human beings' 'forms of life' (see chapter 1 section 18). Because, that is, one fails to see the *projected* character of one's horizon of disclosure – of, in the language of *Being and Time*, the 'meaning of being' or 'fundamental ontology' that one inhabits – one takes its articulation to be *the* – uniquely correct – articulation of the fundamental structure of reality itself, an understanding which, as Heidegger puts it, 'drives out every other possibility of revealing' (*QCT* p. 27). When this, as one might put it 'absolutizing' of a horizon of disclosure takes place, the insight that truth depends on a disclosure which is always also a concealment disappears. The result is that oblivion to the occluded possibilities of disclosure sets in, oblivion to the 'other side' of beings and hence to the majesty of Being.   .

Since the root of the problem of modernity is metaphysics, the principle by which Heidegger selects the exceptional artists he considers to be genuinely significant is the overcoming of metaphysics. The art which is important to our 'needy' times is art which provides an antidote to metaphysics, reappropriates for us the sublimity, the holiness of our world. That, we already know, is what artists are 'for' in needy times. Yet why, exactly, is the overcoming of metaphysics, the re-enchantment of the world, of such vital importance? What is it that sets the art of the modern paradigm apart from the triviality of 'aesthetics' as something corresponding to a genuine 'need'? Let us reconsider this question.

Another 'turn'

3. With one answer to the question we are already well acquainted. Our times are destitute because of the absence of the gods, because 'no god gathers men and things unto himself' and so 'disposes the world's history'. Because, in other words, there is no Greek-paradigm artwork. The importance of art which helps cure us of metaphysics is that it keeps alive and cultivates the possibility of a return of the gods by preserving and cultivating an 'abode' in which, one day, they might once more be found to be present. Only in the poet's preservation of the holy 'aether' is the danger of its complete extinction – the arrival of an age of endless godslessness – averted. Only in his infection of others with a renewed sense of the holy

can there be a 'fostering of the saving power in its increase'. Only, less metaphorically, in the poet's 'poeticizing' of 'earth' is the possibility preserved of the foundational values of Western culture becoming, once more, sacred to it, becoming once more authoritative, 'history'-disposing values.

This answer to the question of the importance of the overcoming of metaphysics Heidegger never abandons. Nonetheless, what seems to me distinctive about the postwar texts is that, unlike their predecessors, they provide a second, additional, answer to the question.

4. This second answer begins with, at least ostensibly, a new analysis of 'our destitution'. The fundamental destitution of modernity is, says the 'Letter on Humanism', 'homelessness'(*BW* pp. 217–18). Our plight, says 'Building Dwelling Thinking' is a 'plight of dwelling' (*PLT* p. 161).

What is this 'dwelling', this 'at-homeness', which we, in modernity, are said to lack? Postwar Heidegger identifies dwelling as the human essence: 'To be a human being means . . . to dwell', as is indicated by the fact that the '*bin*' of '*ich bin*' (I am) comes from the Middle High German and Anglo-Saxon '*buan*', to dwell (*PLT* p. 147). Dwelling, says Heidegger, is not an occasional or isolated achievement. Rather it belongs to 'every man and all of the time' (*PLT* p. 213).

How can 'man' dwell 'all of the time' yet 'homelessness' be the condition of 'contemporary man' (*BW* pp. 217–18)? Clearly Heidegger must be operating with two different senses of 'dwelling'. Let us refer to the dwelling which is the human essence as '*essential dwelling*' and that which is missing from modernity as '*ordinary* dwelling'. (Sometimes I shall drop the 'ordinary' and just say 'dwelling'.)

Essential dwelling, according to Heidegger, is 'nearness to Being', man's 'ex-sistence', that is – attending to the Latin derivation of the word – his 'standing-out' (*BW* p. 217) – standing out of the clearing of world and into its 'other side', the 'Other' (*GA* 15, p. 363; Heidegger's capitalization) of beings. I shall call this 'transcendence'.

That transcendence is something we all possess is a simple consequence of the understanding of truth as disclosive concealment. Since this world is just *one* of an unlimited number of potential disclosures of Being, it follows that I, along with every other being, have a being, am a 'plenitude' of 'facets', which transcends this 'clearing'.

Homelessness, lack, that is, of (ordinary) dwelling, is, says Heidegger, failure 'properly to experience and take over our [essential] dwelling' (*BW* p. 217). In other words, the cause of homelessness is simply 'metaphysics'. Because we are imprisoned, encaged, by it, because we are victims of 'oblivion of Being', we fail to understand and appropriate our own, and every other being's, transcendence. We fail to understand, as one might put it, the world's transcendence of itself.

Anti-metaphysical art is, therefore, important, according to this second answer, because, in releasing us from metaphysics it allows us to *dwell*. 'Poetically man dwells' is the Hölderlin quotation[4] that occurs more frequently than any other in the post-war texts. By being released from the domain of metaphysics and out into 'the poetic' (*PLT* p. 228) – that is, since this is what the poets of needy times found, 'the holy' – we achieve dwelling.

5. The crucial task, here, is obviously that of explicating the connection between overcoming metaphysics, on the one hand, and dwelling on the other. The crucial question, that is to say, is why an appropriation of one's 'essential dwelling' should produce anything which merits being described as dwelling in the ordinary sense, at-homeness in the world. Before addressing this issue, however, I should like to draw attention to the following point. Overcoming metaphysics is something you and I (provided it is granted to us to come under the power of anti-metaphysical thought and art) can achieve *here and now*. So, therefore, is dwelling. If, aided by the art of the modern paradigm, we do not merely affirm intellectually, but come to 'experience and take over', to inhabit, 'the poetic', to make the experience of our own and everything else's transcendence an integral part of our lives, then, if Heidegger is right, we dwell. Even, therefore, in the age of the absence of the gods dwelling is possible: '*as soon as* man gives thought to his homelessness' 'it is a misery no longer', since such thinking '*calls* mortals into their dwelling' (*PLT* p. 161; first emphasis mine).

---

[4] The quotation – in full, 'full of merit, yet poetically man dwells upon this earth' – is from a poem which begins 'In lovely blueness'. That the poem is authentic Hölderlin has been challenged by some scholars on the grounds that it appears in no surviving handwritten manuscript. Heidegger rebuts the challenge in '*Das Wohnen des Menschen*' ('Man's Dwelling') of 1970 (*D* pp. 153–60) with a masterly display of literary scholarship.

These reflections yield a new perspective on the art of the modern paradigm. In 'The Question Concerning Technology' Heidegger says that 'by looking into the constellation of truth' – by, in other words, understanding that truth is disclosive concealment and world merely the intelligible 'side' of the unfathomable 'mystery' – 'we are not yet saved' (*PLT* p. 33). He says this because he is thinking, here, of 'salvation' as a world-historical phenomenon – the arrival of a new 'God', a new Greek-paradigm artwork, which will, once again, 'dispose the world's history'. Salvation, here, and in the title of the *Spiegel* interview ('Only a God can save us'), is conceived as what one may call a '*world*-turning', the turning of Western culture as a whole to a new, postmodern, post-destitute age.

In fact, however, there is another – and more prominent – conception of salvation in the postwar texts consisting in, not a collective, but rather an individual or, as we may call it, '*personal* turning'. Salvation, from this perspective, consists in, and is completed by, an individual's breaking out of the cage of metaphysics, out into, as Rilke calls it, 'the open' (*PLT* p. 128) region of transcendence and holiness.

In *Being and Time* Heidegger's primary (though not exclusive) focus is the individual – individual 'Dasein'. Authenticity, anxiety in the face of death, mortality itself, its key concepts, are all, in their primary application, individual attributes. During the 1930s and the first half of the 1940s, however, his focus shifts strongly away from individual and on to collective Dasein. What concerns him during this period is, above all, the health or otherwise of the culture as a whole.

Now, however, in the postwar texts, first of all in the 1946 'What Are Poets For?', with the focus on dwelling, we return to an attribute which individuals either possess or do not possess. (It makes little, if any, sense to speak of a culture as dwelling or not dwelling.) It is not that the concern for the health of Western culture as a whole disappears. It surfaces, for example, in the prayer for the return of the Greek-paradigm artwork at the end of 'The Turning' (see chapter 3 section 25) and in the title of the *Spiegel* interview. Rather, it withdraws into the background. In the postwar texts the focal question is not, it seems to me, 'What must we do to promote the end of the nihilism of our world-historical epoch?' but, rather, 'How are you and I to live, without alienation, here and now, in this age of the absence of the gods?' (The centrality of *Gelassenheit*, 'equa-

nimity' or 'releasement', to Heidegger's postwar thinking is another manifestation of this turn (or return) from the collective to the individual.)

It is not, as I say, that late Heidegger ignores the earlier concern for collective salvation. The reason for this is that once the project of world-historical social engineering has been abandoned, the answer to 'What must
I do to achieve dwelling?' becomes identical with the answer to 'What
must I do to promote the revival of the culture as a whole?' In each case
the answer is: 'overcome metaphysics'. What is rather the case is that what
occurs in postwar Heidegger is a further pluralization of values. The individual 'turning' becomes valued as an end in itself and not merely as a
means to the world 'turning'. It is this return to the individual which, to
my mind, makes the postwar thinking more attractive than much of the,
one might feel, too strongly (though never exclusively) collectivist thinking which precedes it.

This pluralization of concern seems to me to mark yet another significant 'turn' in Heidegger's thinking, a turn that has implications for art.
As long, that is, as Heidegger looks at things solely from the world-historical perspective, the artist of the modern paradigm can never count as
being of the highest rank since his sole value consists in his preparing of
the ground for a goal that can only be achieved by an artist of a quite
different type: in terms of the distinction deployed towards the end of the
previous chapter, by the 'epic' rather than the 'lyrical' artist. With,
however, the introduction of individual salvation as a value in its own
right, a perspective comes into being that involves no invidious comparison between the artist of the modern paradigm and another, 'highest
essence'-embodying, type of art. The artist of the modern paradigm can
now be unreservedly acknowledged as 'great' – which, as we will shortly
see, is precisely how Heidegger wants to think of, at least, Cézanne and
Klee.

What is dwelling?

6. Why, to return, now, to the question of the connection between overcoming metaphysics and dwelling left dangling at the beginning of
section 5, does anti-metaphysical art facilitate dwelling? What, in the
'ordinary' sense, *is* dwelling?

In 'Building Dwelling Thinking' Heidegger says that '*the fundamental character of dwelling is . . . sparing and preserving (Schonen)*' (*PLT* p. 149; Heidegger's emphasis). But he also indicates, in a subtle passage requiring careful reading, that this 'sparing and preserving' – or, as one might also translate '*Schonen*', 'caring for' – is double-aspected. On the one hand dwelling is being in what old German calls '*das Frye*', the 'free' place, the place where one is 'at peace', 'preserved from harm and danger . . . safeguarded' (*ibid.*). Here the dweller is the *patient* of 'sparing and preserving'. On the other hand, however, the dweller is the *agent* of 'sparing and preserving'. Dwelling, in this aspect, is the dweller's 'safeguard[ing] each thing in its nature' (*ibid.*). 'Mortals dwell' in that they 'care for the fourfold' of earth, sky, mortals and divinities (*PLT* pp. 150–1), postwar Heidegger's preferred term for 'world' (*PLT* p. 179).[5] Dwelling is, then, first, a kind of fundamental security – the dweller experiences herself as cared for by her world, free from danger within it – and, second, the care and conservation of her world by the dweller. Dwelling is, in brief, both caring for and being cared for. This analysis seems to reflect intuitive notions about dwelling. To be at home somewhere, to experience one's place as a *Frye* or *Heimat* (homeland), *is*, as a matter of conceptual necessity, to experience there a security that is lacking in places in which one is an alien, and the 'homely' (in the sense of the German *heimisch*) *is* the to-be-cared-for in a way that the alien place is not. People do not litter their homes in the way they litter motorways.

7. What have these two aspects of dwelling got to do with the overcoming of metaphysics, with, that is, 'experiencing and taking over' one's

---

[5] In *Being and Time* Heidegger analyses human 'being-in-the-world' in terms of a number of its structural or necessary features, which he calls 'existentials'. In my 'What is Dwelling?' I argue that being 'before the divinities', 'on earth', 'beneath the sky' and 'among mortals' is postwar Heidegger's revised account of the existentials of human 'being-in-the-world'. When this four-part structure lights up poetically, when, that is, the fundamental values of one's culture light up *as* divinities, 'the beckoning messengers of the Godhead', our part of the planet *as* 'earth' ('the serving bearer blossoming and fruiting'), climate *as* 'sky' ('the vaulting path of the sun . . . the wandering glitter of the stars') and men *as* 'mortals' ('shrine[s] of the Nothing'), when all this happens then one is said to 'belong within the fourfold' (*PLT* pp. 150, 178), that is (*QCT* p. 47), to dwell.

dwelling in the essential sense? Why should doing this produce these results? Let us begin with the second aspect of dwelling.

To overcome metaphysics is, we know, to experience one's world as the self-disclosure of the self-concealing,[6] as, in the language of 'The Origin', transparent to 'earth'. It is to experience one's world as a sublime or 'holy' place. But the appropriate – conceptually speaking, the only possible – response to a world experienced as holy is care and conservation.[7] Overcoming metaphysics thus liberates us from the world-exploitation of 'enframing' and returns us to our 'essence' as the 'guardians' of Being – of, that is, Being's 'truth', its self-disclosure as world. Overcoming metaphysics, then, moves one to keep one's world 'safe', safe from exploitation and spoliation. Why, now, does it lead one to experience oneself as secure within it, to experience it as keeping one 'safe'?

Consider the question of what, from the perspective of one who is imprisoned by metaphysics, there is 'beyond', other than, beings. The answer is, of course, 'nothing'; an absolute, 'empty' (*ID* p. 28; *PLT* p. 151), 'negative' (*GA* 15, p. 363), 'abysmal' (*BT* 152; *PLT* p. 92), 'nihilistic' (*OWL* p. 19) and annihilating nothing. This means that entry into death is an entry into absolute nothingness. Death is annihilation. But death, we know, is inevitable. And it may, we also know, happen at any moment. (This is the spiritual side to the awfulness of pain: it is a reminder of mortality (compare *PLT* p. 96).) So, to the victim of metaphysics, world presents itself as a pinpoint of light surrounded by an infinite, eternal, final and absolute darkness – a darkness, moreover, that threatens to break into the 'clearing' and to claim one at any moment. It follows that to one suffering from metaphysics, the world is an *un*safe place, the opposite of

---

[6] *Self*-disclosure since an ultimate horizon of disclosure is never human 'handiwork' (*QCT* p. 18). It is always something we *receive*, something 'destined' to us by Being. This is no historical generalization but rather, it seems to me, a necessary truth. Since 'representational' thinking must always occur within a horizon of intelligibility, the notion of our planning and constructing our own ultimate horizon would have us thinking before we could think. At one, and I think, only one point during the period of his brief intoxication with Prometheanism, Heidegger lapses into this incoherence. The 'creators' of the world are, he says, '*apolis*, without city and place . . . without statute and limit, without structure and order, because they themselves must first create all this' (*IM* pp. 152–3). The impossibility of this task is obvious.

[7] Notice, to repeat, that the rise of *Gestell*, of the disclosure of reality as 'resource', the to-be-exploited, is only made possible by the loss of 'enchantment'. In chapter 3 (section 3) we saw how it was 'the festival' which kept enframing at bay. The decline, therefore, of the festival, of the 'festive mood' as I called it, is the precondition of the rise of *Gestell*.

the *Frye*. The most fundamental character of the metaphysical life – its *Grundstimmung*, in Hölderlin's language – is anxiety. If we look death in the face we experience terror, the horror of the void.[8] It is with reason, therefore, that most of the time (as *Being and Time* points out in telling detail) we evade such a direct confrontation. Because we cover death over with euphemism or with Woody Allenish humour, because we think of it as something that happens to others rather than oneself (and even then only when something extraordinary and unexpected, some accident or 'failure in the health system' happens), because we think of death as that which happens always tomorrow, never today, the terror of death is modulated into disquiet, unease, anxiety. But in anxiety one's world is experienced as a threatening, unsafe place and as such cannot constitute a 'home'.

Thus described the world is, I would suggest, the world of *Being and Time*, the key words of which are 'thrownness', 'abandonment', 'being delivered over', 'care', 'anxiety', 'death' and 'the nothing'. (Notice that this list, just by itself, constitutes a kind of (very) short story, a story with a tripartite plot and unmistakable tone.) There, too, Heidegger recognizes the incompatibility of anxiety and dwelling, identifying *Unheimlichkeit* – 'uncanniness' but also, he emphasizes, 'not-being-at-homeness (*Un-heim-lichkeit*)' – as an inescapable – 'existential' – feature of the human condition (*BT* 188–9). It is true that *Being and Time* tries to mark out a conception of the flourishing life, the life lived in the light of an 'authentic' facing up to death and commitment to communal 'destiny', but this is a life, I suggest, lived *in spite of* and in the face of homelessness, not its overcoming.

As many have argued, in other words, *Being and Time* is, I suggest, a

---

[8] Hubert Dreyfus has suggested to me that Michel Foucault was both nihilistic and non-evasive about death, yet experienced no terror. Twenty thousand years of human religion, however, calls this into question. For, as Schopenhauer points out, the fundamental point of religion has always been to provide us with an assurance of the non-finality of death. Were it to be somehow proved that our immortality is independent of, perhaps even incompatible with, the existence of gods, he points out sardonically, everyone would quickly plump for atheism (*The World as Will and Representation*, II, pp. 161–2). Perhaps Foucault was a genuinely 'post-religious' human being. But why, then, did he write so many books? Under Rilke's influence, as we will see, Heidegger suggests that the life of 'self-assertion' is a 'constant negation of death'. We invest our being in non-mortal things such as progeny, property, reputation – and books – very often, in order to assure ourselves that our egos, our selves as we know them, are, after all, immortal. (See, further, section 17 below.)

work of 'heroic nihilism'. It is heroic because it advocates 'living in the truth' about death, nihilistic because the 'truth' it discovers is that beyond the intelligible world of beings, is the absolute nothing, 'the abyss' (*BT* 152). In spite of containing, in section 44, the account of truth as disclosure that is the ground of all of Heidegger's later thinking, and in spite of *setting out* to overcome 'forgetfulness of Being', *Being and Time* is, therefore, in my view, a 'metaphysical' work, a work in which Heidegger has not yet liberated himself from metaphysics. This, it may be noted, is his own retrospective judgment. The work is, he says, one in which 'metaphysics . . . is still dominant' (*P* p. 256).

8. In metaphysics, then, one lives in anxiety, and in anxiety one cannot dwell. What, however, happens if one breaks out of the cage of metaphysics, 'breaks through to the Origin', as Heidegger puts it in his discussion of Zen art (see section 18 below)?

Late Heidegger, no less than early, insists that the 'beyond' of beings is 'nothing'. Having liberated himself from metaphysics, however, the character of this nothing undergoes a radical reassessment. No longer is it to be thought of as the 'abysmal', 'empty' or 'negative' nothing. Rather, it is to be understood 'positively' as the nothing of 'plenitude', the nothing that is, to be sure 'something completely and utterly Other (*Anderes*) than beings', but, for all that, undoubtedly 'something (*etwas*)' (*GA* 15, p. 363). Overcoming metaphysics is understanding, as Schopenhauer succinctly put it, that the 'Other' of beings is not an 'absolute' but only a 'relative' nothingness. Otherwise put, it is understanding that it is not an ontological but rather an epistemological nothing, 'nothing' in, but only in, the sense of being beyond our ultimate standards of intelligibility; 'nothing (comprehensible) to us', the mystical.

Why does the transition from the nothing of emptiness to the nothing of 'plenitude' allow one to experience one's world as a place of safety? Because in recognizing that, like every other being, one 'stands out' beyond the clearing, one understands the difference between the 'ego' and 'the self', that one's self transcends the individual that is the everyday referent of the 'I' (see *GA* 39, pp. 86–8; *GA* 4, pp. 102, 174). Understanding one's (in Kantian language) 'membership' of the mystical realm of 'plenitude' abolishes anxiety, establishes one as ultimately secure in one's world because one understands, now, that that which surrounds the clearing is no longer abysmal but is, rather, the richness of all those concealed (and unintelligible) possibilities of disclosure which, in addition to one's ego, one is. One feels safe, that is dwells, in one's mortality because, knowing that one belongs also to the realm of immortality, one can, in the words of Rilke that Heidegger quotes, 'face . . . death without negation' (*PLT* p. 125). Dwelling, that is to say, has a gently paradoxical character to it: one can dwell as an ordinary mortal, as a 'being-in-the-world', only because, simultaneously, one dwells beyond the world. Understanding one's transcendence transforms one's world into an unconditionally 'safe' place because one knows that nothing that happens in it can annihilate one's essential self.

Heidegger sums all this up in 'Building Dwelling Thinking' and 'The Thing'. 'Mortals dwell', he says, insofar as they 'initiate (*geleiten*)' themselves into 'their own nature . . . so that there may be a good death' (*PLT* p. 151). Doing this, however, is not 'staring' at an 'empty nothing'. Rather, being capable of 'the good death', being unterrified and unanxious about death, (being capable, where necessary, of the ultimate 'sacrifice' (*GA* 9, pp. 309–10; *GA* 54, pp. 249–50)), is a matter of grasping that death, as 'the shrine of the nothing' of plenitude, is 'the presenc[ing]' of 'the mystery [the mystical depth] of Being itself' (*PLT* p. 178). (See, further, the discussion of Rilke in section 17 below.)

9. To sum up, then, what Heidegger is looking for when he surveys the panorama of modern art is an art which, by overcoming 'metaphysics', by 'founding', 'bringing to presence', 'thematizing', 'the holy', discloses our world as a holy place, a place in which, first, we are absolutely (unconditionally) 'safe', and, second, in which the things in the midst of which we find ourselves are disclosed as holy things, things to be adored and cared for.[9] What Heidegger seeks is an art which makes 'dwelling' – the personal 'turning' away from metaphysics and out towards the holy – possible. What he is looking for is art which allows us, as individuals, to dwell

---

[9] Heidegger's description of the *Ereignis*, we saw (chapter 3 section 19), is double-aspected: the *Ereignis*-experience is a matter of '*Entrückung und Berückung*', transport and enchantment. These two aspects match, I believe, the two aspects of dwelling: 'transport' is the transcendence that makes one 'safe', 'enchantment' is the spell cast over one by things that are holy. Dwelling and living within the *Ereignis*-experience are, I suggest, one and the same.

– and, simultaneously, of course, helps prepare an 'abode' for the return
of the gods, for the possibility of a world-turning.

Supernaturalism

10. Dwelling, therefore, requires an art that has overcome metaphysics.
Who, then, are the artists that have achieved this?

Having raised our hopes with respect to at least some of the art of modernity, Heidegger appears immediately to dash them. 'Metaphysics', he
says, is 'the essential realm of Western art' (*Ister* p. 18). Western art, 'as
such', he writes in the Klee notes (see section 22 below), is metaphysical.
Since modern Western art falls, of course, within the scope of 'Western
art' this seems to preclude the possibility that we should ever learn,
through art, a non-metaphysical experience of the world.

Of course, just like the anti-modern art generalizations with which we
began this chapter, these generalizations are rhetorical exaggerations
intended only to identify the rule so as to focus more sharply on the character of the exceptions for which we are looking. They are, I shall suggest,
best construed as foils and filters, 'questions even if they are uttered in the
form of assertions', as Heidegger says, in 'Art and Space' (p. 3) of its
remarks about art.

Heidegger offers two arguments for the (ostensible or formal) conclusion that all Western art is metaphysical. He manages, however, to
confuse the situation by presenting them as if they were the same argument – which they cannot possibly be since their premises are incompatible with each other. The situation is further confused by the fact that he
presents two versions of the first argument, again without making clear
that two versions are involved.

What these arguments in fact do is to identify two quite distinct kinds
of art as the kind of art that is incompatible with dwelling. I shall call
them 'supernaturalistic' and 'naturalistic' art. These two kinds of art, I
shall suggest, act as Scylla and Charybdis with respect to the art for which
Heidegger is looking. The kind of art he seeks is art which avoids 'supernaturalism' without thereby lapsing into 'naturalism'.

11. The first of Heidegger's arguments, the 'symbolism' argument I shall
call it, claims that all Western art is metaphysical in that, far from over-

coming or challenging metaphysics it presupposes and confirms it. The reason it does this is that it is 'symbolic'. This connecting together of 'symbolism' and 'metaphysics' appears in various places but at length in section 3 of the 1942 *Ister* lectures, which is entitled 'The Metaphysical Interpretation of Art', and in '*Denken und Kunst* (Thought and Art)' (*DK*), the authorized protocol of a colloquium that took place on 18 May 1958 between Heidegger and the Japanese philosopher Höseki Shindichi Hisamatsu.

My word 'symbolic' is taken from Heidegger's '*Sinnbild*' – 'symbol', 'symbolic image' or, most literally, 'symbolic picture'. In the *Ister* discussion he says that the term includes legends, fairytales, allegory, myth, metaphor and simile (p. 16). Heidegger argues that Western art in general, and poetry in particular, has always been understood, and has understood itself, as essentially concerned with *Sinnbilder*, concerned, that is, with 'a proclamation of something else by way of something, namely, by way of something familiar that can be experienced sensuously' (*ibid*.). The point, that is, of an 'image' – something intrinsically sensuous – is to present indirectly something, in itself, 'non-sensuous' (p. 17). (Were it itself to be 'sensuous', the thought must be, there would be no purpose to such indirection: one might as well present, directly, the thing itself.)

That at least a great deal of Western art has this character is beyond doubt. What is puzzling, however, is the question of what connection there could possibly be between 'symbolism' and 'metaphysics'. Even more puzzling is the idea that an authentically non-metaphysical artwork would have to be symbol-free. How, one might well wonder, could, for example, poetry survive without symbols, without, that is, given Heidegger's all-embracing use of the term, the use of any imagistic language at all? It seems obvious, for example, that Hölderlin, whom, in the *Ister* discussion, Heidegger explicitly identifies as standing 'outside metaphysics . . . and thus outside of the essential realm of Western art' (*Ister* p. 18), uses the River Ister (Danube) as an image of the poet's journey to 'the Source' where he is to rediscover the 'fire from the heavens'. Yet according to Heidegger, 'Hölderlin's hymnal poetry is not concerned with symbols at all' (*ibid*.).

It turns out, however, that in defining the symbol as that which stands for the 'non-sensuous' Heidegger really means the 'suprasensuous', in other words, the supernatural. In all Western art, his argument claims, 'what is sensuous about the artwork . . . exists for the . . . suprasensuous, for that which is also named the spiritual' (*Ister* p. 17). So the real claim is that the mainstream of Western art is not just symbolic but, more specifically, symbolic of a supernatural realm.

Once this is understood it becomes clear that the real target of the symbolism argument is not symbolism in general – one may, after all, symbolize perfectly natural phenomena such as human faith, hope, charity and love – but the supernaturalist art of traditional Christianity, which Heidegger takes to be simply the form in which Platonism became the dominant outlook of medieval Europe: the 'framework' within which the symbols of Western art 'have their ground', says Heidegger, is the distinction between the sensuous and suprasensuous realms the 'decisive drawing' of which was carried out by Plato (*Ister* p. 17).

12. Leaving aside, for the moment, the dubiousness of the claim that *all* (post-classical) Western art has been Christian art, the question that now needs to be answered is why the fact that an artwork is concerned to symbolize (and thereby 'thematize') a supernatural domain, why the fact that its *raison d'être* is the exposition and reinforcement of the 'simple and essential' truths of traditional Christianity, should render it a 'metaphysical' artwork.

Here we confront one of Heidegger's extremely unhelpful ambiguities with respect to crucial terminology. For the fact is that he uses the term 'metaphysics' in at least two[10] quite different senses. In the later critique of 'symbolic' art in 'Art and Thought', he uses the term 'metaphysics' in his own, as already remarked, highly idiosyncratic sense. But in the earlier *Ister* critique, in spite of the fact that he has already forged and deployed his own idiosyncratic meaning (*GA* 52, pp. 178–80), he reverts to using the term in the (or at least a) thoroughly traditional, non-idiosyncratic way.

The ground, that is to say, given for the 'metaphysical' character of symbolic art in the *Ister* discussion is that its topic is the suprasensuous, *in other words*, the 'metaphysical': 'since Plato, all Western conceptions and interpretations of the world [e.g. by art] have been metaphysical' because 'in

---

[10] Actually at least three, since, as we found out in chapter 1 (section 7), he also uses 'metaphysics' to mean 'enlightenment'; rationalism, positivism, scientism.

relation to the physical the suprasensuous realm is the metaphysical' (*Ister* p. 17). This is the use of 'metaphysical' that is standard among the nineteenth-century German Idealists – 'metaphysics', at them, is the study of the meta-physical – and is quite different from his own idiosyncratic use.

Hölderlin says, to quote his line more fully, that 'poetically man dwells *on this earth*' (my emphasis). For Heidegger dwelling is the *human* essence, something which, if we live properly, we realize here and now, in *this* – natural – world. Given this it is easy to see why he looks unfavourably on the 'meta-physical' character of Christian art. Since it is art which interprets the 'earthly realm' of human life as 'a transitory, preliminary stage to the eternal' and therefore 'something to be surpassed, given up and thereby "lost"' (*Ister* p. 30), it represents dwelling not as a human, but only as a post-human possibility. Dwelling as understood by Heidegger–Hölderlin, dwelling as a human being 'on this earth', is impossible from within the meta-physical interpretation of world.

Heidegger has, then, good grounds for rejecting the art of Christian meta-physics. As formulated in the *Ister* discussion, his objection is *not*, however, that such art is 'metaphysical' in the sense of the term in which he identifies 'metaphysics', as the ground of its 'destitution', as *the* problem of modernity, its 'supreme danger' (*QCT* p. 26). Since we live in a post-Christian age our art has *already* overcome the meta-physical so that we do not need to search for a new and exceptional kind of art in order to do so. The problem of modernity is not meta-physics but rather 'metaphysics' in the unique sense that is defined in terms of Heidegger's philosophy of Being and truth. It follows that, from the point of view of understanding, by way of a contrast, the kind of art we need now, the *Ister* critique of supernaturalist art is uninteresting.

13. Not so, however, Heidegger's later critique, which is of a very different character. According to this, the reason that the art of *Sinnbilder* is something 'metaphysical' which needs to be 'overcome' is that, as 'symbolic', it is concerned to 'bring forth' something 'objectual (*gegenständlich*)' (*DK* pp. 213–14). Not then the meta-physical but rather the 'objectual' character of that which it thematizes is, it seems, the focus of the later objection to Christian art. What is the connection between 'objectification' and 'metaphysics'?

Heidegger claims that since early Greek times philosophy has always been what he calls 'onto-theology' (*ID* pp. 31ff., *P* pp. 287ff., p. 300ff.). Its concern has always been to establish the overall character of the manifest world, of the 'being of beings' ('ontology'), not, however, as an end in itself but rather as the basis for an inference to a being of a different onto-logical order, a 'highest being' understood as being of such a nature as to provide the ultimate explanation for the manifest character of beings ('theology'). (So, for example, the 'wonderful adaptation of ends to means', the organic character of the 'being of beings' observed through-out the natural order might serve to ground the inference to a powerful and benevolent God as nature's ultimate ground.)

Christian theology, Heidegger claims, acquired the character it did because it 't[ook] possession of Greek philosophy' (*P* p. 288). The God of Christian theology became assimilated to the 'God' of Greek onto-the-ology. Given this understanding of medieval Christianity, the thought presents itself that in his later critique of symbolic art Heidegger thinks of it as, essentially, propaganda on behalf of the worldview of medieval theology, and that his objections to it are identical with his objections to onto-theology.

What are these objections? Heidegger says that (at least in the religious context) onto-theology arises out of a 'quail[ing]' before the phenomenon of 'unconcealment', out of a 'misinterpret[ation]' of disclosure (*QCT* p. 26). One senses that disclosure is also concealment, senses the awesome-ness of 'truth'. Then, however, seeking to give voice to that sense yet lacking the capacity (or spiritual courage) for 'poetic thinking', one attempts to capture it in terms of a 'representational thinking' which pre-sents everything in terms of a 'cause-effect coherence'. The result is that the concealed ground of the world becomes thought of as its very pow-erful 'efficient cause'. In this way the relation between the 'concealed and the unconcealed' becomes 'define[d] . . . in terms of the causality of making'. When, however, this conceptual vulgarity comes into play, when God becomes 'the God of the [onto-theologically minded Greek] philosophers', he loses the 'mysteriousness of distance', ceases to be located beyond the limits of intelligibility, ceases to be 'the ungraspable' and becomes instead, the grasped and conceptually tamed solution to an intellectual problem. Since mystery is the element in which alone the holy is to be found, the consequence of this is that 'God . . . for representational thinking, lose[s] all that is exalted and holy' (*QCT* p. 26).

In short, by trying to capture, to represent, to conceptually picture 'the mystery', by turning it into something 'objectual', representational thinking destroys what it seeks to honour. By misinterpreting the Other of beings as another being, as the hidden, supernatural cause of natural beings, by reaching for Greek philosophy to articulate its sense of the awesomeness of truth, medieval theology effects the *abolition* of the Other of beings and hence becomes, not merely meta-physics, but 'metaphysics', in Heidegger's own unique sense. The result is the disenchantment of the cosmos. World, as grasped in medieval theology, ceases to be a holy place, ceases to be a place of dwelling.

14. When the world ceases to be holy the 'festive mood', as I call it, disappears. 'Before the *causa sui*', the God of onto-theology, as Heidegger puts it, 'man can neither fall on his knees in reverence, nor play music nor dance' (*ID* p. 26). But in the Middle Ages one *did* pray, play music and dance. To represent the God of Christian onto-theology as the God of the Middle Ages as a whole is a travesty of the epoch. Equally it is a travesty to represent medieval art as mere propaganda on behalf of onto-theology. For as remarked in chapter 1 (section 25), medieval art (and so medieval life) is full of the golden mystery of the divinely Other. And when inhabiting another line of thinking, Heidegger himself is perfectly well aware of this, since otherwise he could not have represented the art of the cathedral as 'great' art in the sense established by the Greek paradigm. (Without such a light it would have to be accounted as failing to satisfy the 'earth' condition.)

Nonetheless, viewed in the light of my working hypothesis that Heidegger's characterizations of supernaturalistic and naturalistic art are really intended, not as serious art-historical theses but as, rather, caricatures designed to make it easier to identify, by contrast, the character of the authentically non-metaphysical art for which he is looking, something of importance emerges from his later discussion of 'symbolic' art. What emerges is that the art for which we are looking will thematize the 'other side' of world *without* turning it into a 'highest' member of the world, will thematize the Other of manifest beings *without* falling into the self-defeating trap of turning it into another, occult being. The art for which we are looking will be art which allows 'the enigma' to come to presence *'as the enigma'* (*Ister* p. 35) and will not transform the unknown and unknowable into the natured and the known. What this means is that the art which overcomes metaphysics will be a thematizing that is not a representing. For as soon as 'representational thinking' comes into play – thinking that is limited to and confined within a horizon that articulates reality into an intelligible world of beings – that which is thematized becomes 'reified' into a being (*DT* p. 67). How this difficult idea of a bringing to presence that is not a representing is to be understood we will see Heidegger trying to elucidate in his discussion of the individual artists of modernity he believes to be authentic 'founders of the holy'.

Naturalism

15. Treated as a serious account of Western art, the claim that its 'symbolic' character renders it 'metaphysical', 'Other-excluding' is, I observed, a travesty of that of Western art which really is 'symbolic'. An even more glaring fault, however, is that whatever the merits or otherwise of its critique of supernaturalism, the symbolism argument is completely irrelevant to Western art created after the 'death' of the world of Christian supernaturalism. It is irrelevant to that art in which, though the externals of Christian symbolism are retained, supernatural meaning has been replaced by humanistic content – most of the art of the Italian Renaissance – and to art in which those externals are not even nominally present – nearly all the art of the twentieth century.

Given these historical limitations to its scope, it is not surprising that Heidegger, without making clear that this is what he is doing, buttresses his critique of Western art with a second, quite different line of reasoning which I shall call the 'representation' argument. The premise of this argument – diametrically opposed to the premise of the symbolism argument – is that all Western art is 'representational'. It is, in its 'essence', 'realism' (*OWL* p. 17), *'mimesis'*, 'representation (*Darstellung*)' (*DK* p. 213). Hence, Heidegger concludes, it is essentially metaphysical, an oblivion of the Other of beings and hence of Being.

Before trying to grasp whatever plausibility there might be here, it is important to notice that the horizon of beings beyond which, if Heidegger is right about it, 'representational' art acknowledges no Other, is a horizon, exclusively, of natural beings. Since *mimesis* can only be of perceptible, 'sensuous', beings, if an artwork is essentially *mimesis* it cannot be about a supernatural world. The effective scope of the 'representation' argument is thus quite different from that of the 'symbolism' argument. It applies to post-Christian, post-supernaturalist art, the art, as I shall say, of pure 'naturalism'. Though Heidegger gives no help in sorting things this way, the two arguments are thus best seen as historically complementary. The 'symbolism' argument is supposed to bear on traditional, authentically Christian art, the 'representation' argument on post- or non-Christian art.

Heidegger recognizes, of course, that representational Western art is not exactly the same as (mundane) photography, that it does not *simply* hold a mirror up to nature (see *GA* 52, p. 178; *GA* 4, pp. 134–44). Theorists of Western art, conspicuously Schopenhauer and Nietzsche, have traditionally accounted for the difference by saying that art *perfects* objects: it essentializes, transfigures, beautifies, *idealizes* them. In the tradition this is generally put, as it is put by Heidegger, by saying that what art represents is the (Platonic) *eidos*, the 'idea' or 'form' of objects. This refinement of the idea that Western art is pure *mimesis*, Heidegger believes, accurately captures its nature: 'European art is in its essence distinguished by the character of representation (*Darstellung*). Representation, *eidos*, making visible' (*DK* p. 213).[11] But whether art takes its essential task to be the

---

[11] In 'The Origin', *en route* to his own account of the artwork as disclosing a world, Heidegger needs to dispose of the idea that great art is great in virtue of accuracy of representation. He dismisses as obviously absurd the idea that the greatness of the Van Gogh shoes consists in 'successfully' depicting 'a pair of actually existing peasant shoes'. But he recognizes that the defender of the view that the point of art is representation, can make the move to 'ideas'. Perhaps, he muses, the Van Gogh is a 'reproduction of the thing's general essence'. It is in order to demolish such Schopenhauerian Platonism – as at least a *universal* account of the nature of art – that he makes the move from the Van Gogh to the Greek temple: 'where and how', he asks sardonically, 'is this general essence, so that artworks are able to agree with [i.e. represent] it? With what nature of what thing, should a Greek temple agree? Who could maintain the impossible view that the Idea of Temple is represented in the building?' (*PLT* p. 37). Of course, that architecture is a pretty good counter-example to Schopenhauerianism makes it an equally good counter-example to his own later claim about the 'essence' of 'European art'. But we know already that the latter claim is not really intended as a universal truth.

representation of idealized or non-idealized objects makes no essential difference. In either case the art in question, rather than challenging, accepts and reinforces that understanding of reality which is the metaphysics of naturalism.[12]

16. As a seriously intended account of the universal character of post-Christian art the representation argument is, clearly, no more successful than the symbolism argument's account of Christian art. The idea that all modern Western art is either a slavish imitation of nature or else an air-brushed version of such imitation designed to produce pleasant, 'aesthetic' sensations is no more plausible than the idea that all medieval art is mere propaganda on behalf of the claustrophobic outlook of scholastic theology. As I suggested, however, like the symbolism argument, the representation argument is best understood as a contrast or foil designed, in tandem with its partner, to highlight the character of the anti-metaphysical art for which Heidegger is looking. Putting the two foils together, therefore, what we learn is the following. Unlike 'representational' art, the art of the modern paradigm will be art in which something other than natural beings comes to presence, is thematized, *without* its being the case, as happens in 'symbolic' art, that this Other of natural beings is transformed into another, supernatural being. The art of the modern paradigm will be art which steers between the Scylla of naturalism and the Charybdis of supernaturalism.

I proceed now to four, as it were, case studies: cases where Heidegger believes himself to have discovered genuine examples of the modern paradigm, examples of an art which is neither 'symbolic' nor 'representational'. The case studies I shall discuss concern the art of Rilke, East Asia, Cézanne and of Klee. There are others – the studies of Hebel, Trakl and Stefan George, for example – but these are the ones which strike me as the most significant.

---

[12] Notice that the account of Western art as essentially concerned with the *eidos* of objects, with objects 'as we would like them to be' as he quotes Klee as saying (see section 22 below) dovetails together with the earlier analysis of Western art as having been progressively taken over by 'aesthetics'. As Heidegger sees it, presumably, the motive for the straightening out of imperfections of harmony, balance, economy, organic unity, and so on, the motive for making everyone look like Julia Roberts, is to produce, in the beholder, pleasant feelings, 'experiences of the beautiful'.

Rilke

17. Heidegger had always been interested in Rilke. He is the only artist to receive a more than passing reference during the period of *Being and Time* and, as we have seen (chapter 1 section 17), had an important influence on 'The Origin'. Though well-disposed to Rilke during that period, Heidegger had, by 1942, become sharply critical, complaining in the *Ister* lectures about the 'thoughtless lumping together of my thinking with Rilke's [which] has already become a cliché'. In fact, he claims, his own and Rilke's modes of thinking, in particular their use of the phrase 'the open', are 'completely opposite'. Rilke's 'open' is really that 'fateful modern and metaphysical concept of "the unconscious"' which is simply a kind of waste bag for whatever will not fit into 'consciousness (*ratio*)'. It is 'the irrational', 'a domain [which] remains the preserve of feeling and instinct' (*Ister* pp. 91–2).

People posit the unconscious, Heidegger's critique seems to suggest, in the grips of the idea that Being (reality) is disclosed to, and only to, 'reason'. They are, in other words, gripped by the metaphysics of naturalism, by the idea that the (one and only) way reality is, is the way that is revealed by science and by sound common sense. They understand, however, that human beings often experience reality in other, 'irrational', ways. There is, for example, not just the 'nature' of science and common sense, but, as *Being and Time* puts it, 'the nature which 'stirs and strives', which assails us and enthralls us as landscape' (*BT* p. 70). To accommodate this, the 'rationalist', as part of a human pathology, posits 'the unconscious' as the 'domain of feeling and instinct' and views the poet's nature as the unconscious projection of 'subjective colouring' on to what is really there.

Rilke, as Heidegger understands him, rightly rejects the metaphysics of scientific naturalism. Yet by simply elevating the 'irrational' ('unconscious') over the 'rational' ('conscious') he goes about the revolt against scientism in the wrong way. Irrationalism, Heidegger stresses in many places, is simply the obverse of rationalism, tarred with the same faults. The irrationalist does not escape the metaphysical character of scientific naturalism but simply replaces it with his own metaphysics, a metaphysics according to which *the* way the world is, is disclosed, not by reason, but by 'feeling and instinct'. (In practice, as we are about to see, this leads to a metaphysics in which the key term is no longer 'matter' but rather 'will'.)

By 1946, however, by the time he came to write 'What Are Poets For?' to commemorate the twentieth anniversary of the poet's death, Heidegger had considerably moderated his dismissal of Rilke as someone hopelessly ensnared by metaphysics. Though the poet indeed stands, he says, in the 'shadow' of German metaphysics, the Leibnizian-Nietzschean metaphysics of 'will', his entanglement in metaphysics is a 'tempered' one (*PLT* p. 108). In spite, that is, of the use of sometimes inappropriate language, different, non-metaphysical currents are present in Rilke's 'valid' (*PLT* p. 96) poetry. In his best work, Rilke achieves, or at least points the way towards, a non-metaphysical experience of Being and is, therefore, a poet of great significance 'for needy times'.

For Rilke, as Heidegger expounds him, the '*Urgrund*', the 'primordial ground' of beings, that is to say, 'Being', is, at least officially, the 'will' (*PLT* pp. 101–2) out of which 'truth' appears (*PLT* p. 60). In his best work, however, Rilke calls the *Urgrund*, not 'the will', but rather 'the venture' and, even better, 'the Open'. Though this is indeed, as Heidegger said in 1942, the opposite of his own use of 'the open' as a synonym for 'the clearing', he now sees the merit of Rilke's usage, sees that since what 'Open' most naturally means is 'the unbounded' (*PLT* p. 105) (the Dionysian), the expression points towards a non-metaphysical experience of Being. Since a 'bounding' is when a being '*begins its presencing*' (*PLT* p. 154), the *sine qua non*[13] of beinghood, that Rilke thinks of Being as unbounded suggests that it is conceived in a non-entifying way.

'The venture', says Rilke, offering a poetic metaphor of his experience of Being, flings us 'ventured ones' out into existence yet at the same time holds us in a 'gravitational pull' towards itself as the 'centre' (*PLT* p. 104).

The 'danger' to human beings is that they will become completely insensible to 'the Open' and its 'pull', cut off by the metaphysics of naturalism. The seeds of the danger lie in the fact that (unlike the animals) we 'represent', conceptualize the world into objects (*PLT* pp. 115–16). 'Objectification' as such, however (in other words, our gift for the

---

[13] 'A boundary is not that at which something stops [as if a thing could be recognized as the thing it is independently of establishing its boundary] but, as the Greeks recognized, the boundary is that from which something *begins its presencing.*' In a slogan (which says the same as W. V. Quine's 'no entity without identity'), 'no being without a boundary'.

'Apollonian'), is not itself the danger. For so long as we retain the 'festive' mode of disclosure objects remain, for us, capable of being 'transparent' to the Open, to, in other language, 'earth' (see chapter 3 section 4.) When, however, the festive mood finally and completely abandons us, as happens in the age in which things show up as and only as resource, then objects become completely 'opaque' (*PLT* p. 108), an impenetrable curtain between us and the Open. This is the condition of the present age. In our enframed world the Open has become completely 'invisible'. Modern humanity thus exists in the 'destitution' of oblivion to the gravitational pull of the 'Other'. And it exists, too, in illusion. In its metaphysical insensibility to the 'other side' of the 'globe of Being' (*PLT* p. 124) it resembles the child who, oblivious of the dark side of the moon, thinks of it as a flat, illuminated disk.

Why, for Rilke–Heidegger, is the obstruction of the Open a condition of 'destitution'? Modern life is, as Rilke sees it, a constant 'negation of death' (*PLT* p. 127). Life is riddled with anxiety on account of our 'unshieldedness', our lack of 'securedness' (*PLT* p. 121) in the face of death. The covert (and, of course, irrational) motive of *all* action, says Rilke, is the quest for absolute security, the attempt to overcome death. We take out health insurance,[14] invest in non-mortal things like progeny, property and reputation, we engage in the death-evading strategies detailed in *Being and Time*, in the quest to escape anxiety, the quest for a final 'safety'. The quest is, of course, futile.[15] Security cannot be achieved by taking measures of 'protection' (*ibid.*). The absolute, unconditional

---

[14] It is worth noting that the master poet of anxiety, Rilke's contemporary and fellow native of Prague, Franz Kafka, was, in professional life, an insurance broker and theoretician of actuarial risk.

[15] Heidegger quotes and requotes Sophocles on this tragic point:

> And into the sounding of the word
> and swift understanding of all
> he has found his way, even into courageous
> governance of the towns.
> And he has pondered how to flee
> exposure to the arrows
> of unpropitious weather and its frosts.
> Everywhere venturing forth underway, experienceless without any way out
> he comes to nothing.
> The singular onslaught of death he can
> by no flight ever prevent,
> even if in the face of dire infirmity he achieves
> most skillful avoidance.   (*Ister* p. 59; *IM* p. 147).

security that we seek can only be achieved 'outside all caring' (*ibid.*), outside all practical calculation and measure-taking. As Hölderlin, too, sees, 'full of merit, *but* poetically man dwells': though man indeed deserves great credit for his practical achievements, when it comes to 'dwelling', to unconditional security, it is something entirely different, the 'poetic', which grants it to him.

The reason for our anxiety in the face of death, the reason we cannot 'read the word 'death' *without* negation' (*PLT* p. 125), as we know, is that, gripped by metaphysics, we think of the 'side of life that is averted from us' as something entirely 'negative', 'empty'. Rilke, however, who describes poets (*inter alios*, of course, himself) as 'bees of the invisible', bees which 'ceaselessly gather the honey of the visible, to store it up in the sweet golden beehive of the Invisible' (*PLT* p. 130), teaches us once more to see the unseen, to sense the dark side of the 'globe of Being'.[16] In this way he brings us to see that

within the widest orbit of the sphere of beings there are regions and places which seem to be negative but are nothing of the kind if we think of all things as being within the widest orbit of beings. (*PLT* pp. 124–5)

Understanding that, understanding the 'other side' of beings not as an emptiness but rather a 'plenitude' of all the, to us, unknowable 'facets' of beings (*ibid.*), allows us to face death without anxiety.

Rilke, then, by allowing us to become 'ecstatic', to stand out of the visible and into its 'other side', offers us the 'poetic' experience of Being which allows a genuine overcoming of anxiety about death, the first of the two conditions of 'dwelling'. But he facilitates, too, our satisfying the second condition, the condition that our world should become a world of sacred, to-be-cared-for, things. For by allowing us to experience it as, like the lighted side of the moon, the disclosure of an immense concealment, by allowing us to experience Being as, like an iceberg, possessed of both a visible and invisible 'dimension' (*PLT* p. 220) – the latter of 'unfathomable' proportions[17] – the poet is, as Rilke himself puts it, the 'angel'

---

[16] 'That is', Heidegger adds, 'the globe of all beings as a whole' (*PLT* p. 124).
[17] Heidegger quotes Rilke as suggesting that however vast the world of space and time may be,

it hardly bears comparison with the dimensions, with the depth dimensions of our inwardness, which does not even need the spaciousness of the universe to be within itself almost

(*PLT* p. 138) who sings into being the 'haleness' and 'wholeness' of the 'globe of Being' and thereby the 'holy' (*PLT* p. 141) (Heidegger puns here on the various meanings of '*Heil*'). As such he allows us to dwell in a 'safe' and holy place and is, truely, therefore (the question Heidegger poses at the beginning of the essay), 'a poet for needy times'.

East Asian art

18. In spite of the positive character of Heidegger's 1946 appraisal of Rilke, reservations, as we have seen, remain. Anti-metaphysical thought and experience is present but partially obscured by the language of metaphysics. Not just by the language but also by the imagery. For all its virtues, Rilke's image of Being as a 'globe' possessing a lit and unlit 'side' is not really all that appropriate to the unboundedness of 'the Open', for which reason Heidegger says that we must not 'press' it very far (*PLT* p. 124). None of these reservations, however, are present in his discussion of East Asian art. There is a sense here, I think, that what is encountered is art of a still higher order than is encountered in Rilke.

The primary records of Heidegger's encounter with Eastern art are the authorized protocol of the 1958 discussion between Heidegger and the Japanese philosopher and Zen-master Hoseki Hisamatsu, 'Thought and Art' (*DK*), and 'A Dialogue on Language', subtitled 'Between a Japanese and an Inquirer' (*OWL* pp. 1–54). This latter work, it seems, was loosely based on a visit paid to Heidegger in 1954 by the Japanese scholar of German literature, Tezuka Tomio.

According to Heidegger, as we have seen (section 15 above), according, at least, to *one* of his accounts, 'Western art', the Western art tradition, has, as its essence, *mimesis*. It takes the representation of (idealized) nature to be its central task. 'East Asian' art on the other hand, does not. While it is indeed representational – or, better, 'pictorial' (*bildhaft*) (*DK* p. 213) – it does not, as Heidegger understands it, take representation to be its central task.

unfathomable . . . To me it seems more and more as though our customary consciousness lives on the tip of a pyramid whose base within us (and in a certain way beneath us) widens out so fully that the farther we find ourselves able to descend into it, the more generally we seem to merge into those things, in their independence of space and time, which are given in our earthly, in the widest sense, *worldly* existence. (*PLT* pp. 128–9)

Heidegger's encounter with Eastern art is largely an encounter with Japanese and, in particular, Zen art. It is in this light that his account of the essence of Eastern art is to be understood. Rather than reporting on the state of nature the point of Eastern art is, he suggests, to facilitate, to be, a form of meditation. The aim of this meditation is to achieve a kind of freedom, 'freedom (*Ledigsein*) from all forms of bondage' (*ibid.*). According to the Japanese concept of *Gei-do*, 'art is a way (*Weg*) in which man breaks through to the Origin (*Ursprung*)' (*ibid.*), an origin understood as 'the Nothing' (*DK* p. 212); as, that is, 'the empty', 'the formless', 'the Open' (in *Rilke's* sense), as 'silence', 'stillness', 'peace' – Heidegger's various attempts to translate the Japanese word '*Ku*'. But this is not a 'negative nothing' (*DK* p. 213). There is nothing 'nihilistic' about it (*OWL* p. 19). Rather, it is the 'loftiest name' for what Heidegger 'means to say with the word "Being"'. In fact, '*Ku*' is almost certainly a better word than 'Being', since the latter term 'belongs, after all, to the patrimony of metaphysics' (*ibid.*).[18]

The point of a Zen artwork concerns, then, 'the Nothing', the Other of manifest beings. Its point, however, is not to symbolize an occult 'highest being': the artwork 'brings forth nothing objectual (*gegenständlich*)', is 'no symbol (*Symbol*), no symbolic image (*Sinnbild*)' (*DK* p. 213). Rather, in Hisamatsu's formulation,

The beauty of an artwork lies, for Zen, in the fact that, somehow, the formless comes to presence (*Anwesung*) in the pictorial. Without this presence of the formless itself in the formed, a Zen artwork is impossible. (*DK* p. 214)

How is this presence of 'the Nothing' in the pictorial possible? How is it possible to experience 'the Origin' as present in manifest things? (How, in the language of 'The Origin of the Work of Art', is it possible for 'earth' to 'rise up' through 'world'?) The pictorial is, says Hisamatsu, Janus-faced:

As long as man finds himself on the way to the Origin (*Ursprung*), art, as the presentation of the pictorial, is an impediment for him. But when he has broken through

---

[18] Traditional philosophy has aways taken 'Being' as its fundamental topic. But because the 'metaphysical' misunderstanding of Being is endemic in the tradition ideally, later Heidegger holds, one would abandon this fraught term completely for something free of metaphysical baggage. In 'The Question of Being' he performs this act of abandonment by writing '*Sein*' with a crossing-out through it – S̶e̶i̶n̶ (*P* p. 310) – though he does not, in fact, adhere to this self-denying ordinance.

to the Origin then the making visible of the eidetic (*des Eidetischen*) is no longer an impediment; it is then the appearing of the primary (*ursprünglich*) truth itself. (*DK* p. 213)

Attuned to Hisamatsu's thinking, Heidegger repeats the point in his own way and out of his own experience: 'The written, the drawn (*Gezeichnete*), is not only an impediment (*Hinderung*) but also a freeing-from-impediment (*Ent-hinderung*), an occasion for the movement of self to Origin' (*ibid.*).

The pictorial can, then, be an impediment to the 'breakthrough to the Origin'. But it can also be the opposite. What determines it to be one or the other?

Though many Westerners think to experience the charms of the Japanese world in Kurosawa's famous film *Rashomon*, the film, claims Heidegger, is, in fact, quite un-Japanese,[19] an example of the 'all-consuming Europeanization' or, 'if you will, American[ization]' (Hollywoodization), of the world. For the film is characterized by a pervasive 'realism', by naturalism: the 'massiveness of presentation' means that 'the Japanese world is captured and imprisoned . . . in the objectness of photography'. This is not peculiar to, or the fault of, Kurosawa. For the character of *Rashomon* is, in fact, the character of all film, indeed of all photography. Since *all* photography 'forces the world into the sphere of . . . objectification', 'the Eastern world and the technical-aesthetic product of the film-industry, are incompatible' (*OWL* pp. 16–17).

In a word – Rilke's word – Kurosawa's film, film and photography in general, is 'opaque'. It blocks thematization of anything other than beings, prevents objects becoming, as one might put it, windows on to the 'Other'. It is purely representational, metaphysical. The pictorial, in this case, is not merely a possible 'impediment to the breakthrough to the Origin' but an actual and absolute one. The Nothing never happens in Hollywood.

If one wishes to encounter authentic Japanese art, one should turn, not to Kurosawa's film, but rather to the traditional *Nô* play. What is of significance here is that the stage is entirely empty, a fact which demands

---

[19] Kurosawa, who had studied Western painting, literature, and political philosophy, based *Yojimbo* on a Dashiell Hammett novel, *Throne of Blood* on *Macbeth*, and *Ran* on *King Lear*. He never pretended otherwise than that his films were cultural hybrids.

'uncommon concentration' from the audience. Thanks to this, the slight-est gestures on the actor's part 'cause mighty things to appear out of a strange stillness'. For example, by slowly raising the open hand to eyebrow level the actor causes a mountain landscape to appear (*OWL* p. 18).

What, exactly, is the point here? What is the point of the contrast between film and *Nô* play? It seems to be a rather straightforward one. In the right conjunction of circumstances, the play allows 'the Nothing', 'the empty', to presence because emptiness is *literally* present: the stage is empty. Film, on the other hand, because it cannot avoid providing a denseness of naturalistic detail, cannot allow anything but objects to presence.

Something, I think, has fairly clearly gone wrong in these insightful[20] yet exaggerated dismissals of film as an art form, a matter to which I shall return shortly. The point to be noticed here, however, is that, in contrast to earlier dismissals of the value of Eastern art and thought to the West (*BT* 178), Heidegger is now prepared to allow authentic Japanese art to be an art for our (Western) needy times. We Westerners may be able, through acclimatizing ourselves to the reception of Japanese art, to expe-rience the presencing of the non-metaphysical 'Other' of world, and, through this experience, learn to dwell.

Cézanne

19. Heidegger was probably led to Cézanne thorough his reading of Rilke's *Letters on Cézanne*[21] during the preparation of the 1946 Rilke lecture 'What Are Poets For?' Shortly after that he saw several Cézannes in the Basel art gallery, including '*Mont Sainte-Victoire seen from the Colline des Larves*' (1904–6) (plate 3). The relationship became personal and intense when he began to visit Cézanne's homeland, the region around Aix-en-Provence, in the mid-1950s, a region, according to Francois Fèdier, he came to regard as his 'second homeland' (E p. 83).[22] Heidegger is reported to have said, *inter alia*, that Cézanne's path is 'the

---

[20] And prescient, since a marked trend in recent times has surely been what one might call the Spielbergization of film, the ever-increasing reverence for 'special effects' – and, corre-spondingly, the ever-increasing emptiness of mainstream film.

[21] Rilke had been Rodin's secretary in Paris and had viewed with wonder and astonishment the major 1904 exhibition of Cézanne's work.

[22] It is hard to resist the thought that Heidegger's love of Hölderlin and his 'Remembrance' of the Dordogne was a preparation for his later love of Provence and of Cézanne.

Plate 2   Paul Cézanne, *The Gardener Vallier*, c. 1906.

path to which, from beginning to end, my own path as a thinker responds (corresponds) in its own way'. And, at the end of one of his visits to Provence, 'These days in Cézanne's homeland are worth more than a whole library of philosophy books. If only one could think as directly as Cézanne painted.' These and other anecdotes[23] (half-remembering, perhaps, the title of Thomas Mann's *Magic Mountain*, Heidegger is reported to have described Mont Sainte-Victorie as Cézanne's 'wondrous

---

[23] These anecdotes are conveniently collected together in Christoph Jamme's excellent 'The Loss of Things: Cézanne-Rilke-Heidegger', *Kunst & Museumjournal* 2/1, 1990, pp. 33–44. Excellent work analysing the relation between Heidegger and Cézanne is carried out in this article and also in Gunter Seubold's 'Der Pfad ins Selbe', *Philosophisches Jahrbuch* 94, 1987, pp. 62–78 and in his important *Kunst als Enteignis* (Bonn: Bouvier, 1996); see especially pp. 103–18.

mountain') make it clear that Heidegger admired Cézanne greatly and regarded him as, somehow, a model for thinking. They do not, however, make it clear what it was about the painter that he valued so highly or how he took him to be a model for thinking.

Unlike the case of Rilke, Heidegger wrote no major essay articulating what it was he found to be of such significance in Cézanne. The sole text on the basis of which we must attempt to understand him is a poem (or, more exactly, '*Gedachte*', 'thing thought', as Heidegger called it) inspired by one of Cézanne's final works, a portrait of his gardener (plate 2).

The poem reads:

> Cézanne
>
> Das nachdenksam Gelassene, das inständig
> Stille der Gestalt des alten Gärtners
> Vallier, der Unscheinbares pflegte am
> chemin des Lauves.
>
> Im Spätwerk des Malers ist die Zwiefalt
> von Anwesendem und Anwesenheit einfältig
> geworden 'realisiert' und verwunden zugleich,
> verwandelt in eine geheimnisvolle Identität.
>
> Zeigt sich hier ein Pfad, der ein Zusammen-
> gehören des Dichtens und des Denkens führt?
>
> (The thoughtfully serene, the urgent
> stillness of the form of the old gardener
> Vallier, who tends the inconspicuous on the
> *Chemin des Lauves*.
>
> In the late work of the painter the twofoldness
> of what is present and of presence has become
> one, 'realized' and overcome at the same time,
> transformed into a mystery-filled identity.
>
> Is a path revealed here, which leads to
> a belonging-together of poetry and thought?) (*D* p. 163)

Various important late-Heideggerian themes are present here. First, the personal ideal of '*Gelassenheit*' – 'serenity', 'equanimity', 'release-ment' or, one might almost add, 'dwelling' – here explained as a 'stillness', which, however, is not apathy but rather an 'urgent' readiness for action. Second, the 'small-is-beautiful' theme, the importance of the 'inconspic-uous', of 'fostering the growth of the saving power', not by attempting grandiose, world-historical action, not by enlisting the aid of the 'state-founder' in the building of a 'temple of modernity', but in, rather, the intimate and personal sphere of action, in 'little things' (*QCT* p. 33). Third, the importance of gardening – of not mastering and exploiting the earth in the manner of *Gestell*, but rather preserving and enhancing, caring for, that on which we dwell.

The heart of the poem, however, is the second verse, the mysterious talk of 'realizing' and 'overcoming' the dualism between 'presence' and 'what is present'. This is the poem's heart, I suggest, since it is because he has realized and overcome the dualism that the gardener has achieved *Gelassenheit*, because he has overcome the dualism that he is a gardener rather than exploiter of the world, and because he has overcome the dualism that he embodies the unity of poetry and thought. As I read Heidegger's imaginative recreation of the painting, the gardener *is* the poet-thinker, is, one might say, Heidegger himself, the 'tender of the inconspicuous' at the hut in Todtnauberg.

The task, then, is to try to understand the dualism and its overcoming. In a so-called 'later version' of the poem produced in 1974,[24] Heidegger adds the following comment, by way of explaining this idea:

What Cézanne called '*la rélisation*' is the appearance of what is present (*des Anwesenden*) in the clearing of presence (*des Anwesens*) – in such a way, indeed, that the duality (*Zwiefalt*) of the two is overcome in the oneness (*Einfalt*) of the pure radiance of his paintings. For thinking, this is the question of overcoming the ontological difference between being and beings.

Taking these texts together, the second verse of the poem and the explanatory comment, confronts us with three central ideas. First, that in Cézanne's late works the duality of 'presence' and 'what is present' is 'realized', that is, made manifest, second, that it is simultaneously overcome, transformed into a 'radiant', mystery-filled, 'oneness', and, third, that these two features together constitute an overcoming of 'the ontological difference'. I shall begin by discussing the last of these ideas.

20. Why, first, of all, is 'the ontological difference between being and beings' something that *needs* to be 'overcome'?

That there is a radical *difference* between being – that is, 'presence' (see

---

[24] This was privately circulated as a Christmas gift to a few friends in 1975. The following quotation appears in Seubold's *Kunst als Enteignis*, p. 107.

also *BT* p. 2; *ID* p. 18) – and beings – 'what is present' (see also *P* p. 299) – is, of course, a fundamental Heideggerian insight: being is not a being. It is, rather, that 'truth' or horizon of disclosure which renders beings possible and 'legislates' (*P* p. 300) the kinds of beings they can be.

Heidegger compares the relation between being and beings to that between a visual field and its contents (*DT* p. 63). To deny the difference between being and beings would thus be as absurd as denying the difference between the visual field and its contents.

What is a serious mistake, however, is to construe the difference as an *ontological* difference, a difference between *entities* (beings). For this is precisely to deny the difference between beings, on the one hand, and something *other* than a being, on the other. It is to turn being into a being. Yet this, Heidegger asserts, is precisely what metaphysics does.

As we have seen (section 2 above), metaphysics mistakes what is, in fact, the humanity-dependent structure of disclosure for the humanity-independent structure of reality itself. Thus the beings–being relation which, properly thought, is a relation between beings and a *non-being*, becomes, says Heidegger, misconstrued into a relation between 'changeable beings' and 'an entity at rest' (*P* p. 300). What is in reality the horizon of disclosure in terms of which reality makes itself intelligible to us is transformed into the eternally fixed structure preserved by (other) beings in their coming and going.

The task, then, of overcoming metaphysics is the task of overcoming the *ontological* difference, of allowing it to become just 'the difference' (*ID* pp. 53–4). Only when we have achieved that do we understand truth as disclosive concealment, and only then does the world appear in its holy 'mystery'.

In *Identity and Difference* Heidegger says that what is needed for the overcoming of metaphysics is 'the step back', 'the step back out of metaphysics' (*ID* p. 41). This suggests that the source of metaphysics lies in being, somehow, 'too close up' to things.

'Metaphysics', we saw in section 2 above, misses the *projected* character of being, the fact of its dependence on those intelligibility-creating 'forms of life' in which human beings find themselves and become the human beings that they are. Imagine, then (to use an analogy that was already a cliché by the time Schopenhauer came to expound Kant but is nonetheless a useful one), that one wears, all the time, green-tinted sunglasses. The analogue of metaphysics is ignorance of this fact, an ignorance which will result in one taking the fact that everything shows up in shades of green to be one of the fundamental and 'universal traits' (*P* p. 287) of reality itself, absolutizing one's understanding of the structure of *a* disclosure into *the* one and only true account of the structure of reality.

Normally we cannot see the glasses we are wearing. (This is the analogue of the reason that, according to Heidegger, metaphysics is no mere philosopher's vice but rather the *natural* condition of human beings: our consciousness is so entirely object-directed that we have a natural disposition to focus exclusively on the project*ed* thereby missing, completely, the project*ing* (*BT* pp. 70–1).) Imagine now, however, that, with the glasses remaining where they are, one 'steps back' out of them. Then one sees not only the objects but also the source of their universal greenness. What one understands, that is, is the *projected* character of that greenness. Since Cézanne is said to facilitate an overcoming of the ontological difference and hence of metaphysics, this suggests that what Heidegger discovers in Cezanne's 'late works' – in the portrait of the gardener, but above all, I think, in the studies of the 'wondrous mountain' – is the 'step back'. Somehow, they allow us to experience the *projected* character of the being ('presence') of our world. Why should this be so?

The salient feature of Cézanne's late works is their progressively and evermore marked 'dematerialization' of objects (plate 3). Unlike the early works, objects falter and collapse, unable to sustain their integrity against the abstract patterns created by the *'plans'*, as Cézanne called his brush strokes, against the relative absence of modelling and of both geometrical and colour perspective. For a moment, the work confronts us as an entirely abstract, two-dimensional space. But then – miraculously – the objects reconstitute themselves and reappear. Their tenure remains, however, a fragile (and for that reason all the more precious) one: they threaten, always, to disappear again.

The experience of the Cézanne is thus, as Heidegger reads it, I suggest, a flickering alternation between two states: a state in which we experience an abstract, meaning-less space, and a state in which the abstract shapes have transformed themselves into a meaningful world of objects. What is,

Plate 3   Paul Cézanne, *Mont Sainte-Victoire seen from the Colline des Larves,* 1904–6.

however, I think, crucial is the transition from the first state to the second. For it is in this transition that we experience the happening, the *Ereignis* or 'worlding' of world.

In the last chapter we saw that, with Hölderlin, Heidegger calls the creative origin of the visible world – that which concealingly discloses itself as world – 'holy chaos' (see chapter 3 section 15, and especially footnote 16). As an origin, however, he says, meditating on the meaning of Hölderlin's phrase, the holy must be structured, for otherwise it could provide no 'footing' for the 'distinctions' which exist in the visible world. 'Chaos' cannot, therefore, mean 'wildness and confusion' but only unintelligibility, meaningless to us.

This, I suggest, is what Heidegger takes us to experience through Cézanne: the birth of the meaningful world of objects out of its numinously meaning-less, yet structured, ground; in Nietzsche's language, the birth of the Apollonian out of the Dionysian.

Two points need to be emphasized concerning this Cézanne-facilitated experience. The first is that were the 'universal traits' of objects to be, as metaphysics thinks, located in reality itself then those traits would *always* be there, would inescapably intrude into *every* encounter with reality. There could be no possibility of experiencing reality apart from them and hence no possibility of experiencing the *birth* or *Ereignis* of world. In Cézanne, however – this is what sets him apart from the metaphysical tradition of Western art – we do. This lets us understand the *projected* character of world, allows us to understand that this world of red earth, viridian pines, wondrous mountains, serene (and mortal) gardeners, is but the content of one of the uncountably many possible readings, 'interpretations' (*P* p. 245), of Being.

This is what Heidegger means in saying that Cézanne 'realizes' – thematizes, makes manifest – 'presence' as well as 'what presences'. In Cézanne we take the 'step back' so as to become aware not only of the project*ed* but also of the project*ing*. We become, as never happens in metaphysical art, aware of 'presence' itself, aware, as Heidegger equivalently (*P* p. 298) and more perspicuously says, of 'presencing', 'worlding'.

Having understood this it is only a short step to understanding the idea that the duality of presence and what presences is transformed into an 'identity'. Because they owe their birth to a worlding and endure only as long as it does, objects stand to worlding as a run stands to a running, a song to a singing, and thunder to a thundering. They are, as one might put it, *verbal* objects, and as such identical with the activity to which they owe their being. As a run *is* its running so our world of objects *is* its worlding.

The second point that needs to be emphasized in connection with the Heideggerian experience of Cézanne is that to experience the *Ereignis*, the happening of world, is necessarily to experience, as well, that *out of which* it happens. One cannot experience 'holy chaos' giving birth to world unless one experiences, along with worlding and world, holy chaos itself. Thus in thematizing the *Ereignis* of world Cézanne thematizes, too, world's 'other side'. As with the Zen experience of the genesis of world out of the 'Nothing', therefore, one achieves, through Cézanne, a 'breakthrough to the Origin', to, in the language of 'The Origin', 'earth', the 'originating region'[25] out of which 'truth' appears (*PLT* p. 60). In numerous places (for example, *P* pp. 254–5) Heidegger speaks of the 'It' (Heidegger's capitalization) which 'gives', 'destines' or 'sends' world to us, an 'It' that has not been thought by the West yet remains *the* 'matter of thinking'. Inaccessible to 'representational' thought the 'It' can be grasped, if at all, only in 'poetic' thinking. It is because, I think, Cézanne thematizes the 'It', enables us to 'grasp the ungraspable' in its ungraspability and hence the world as a holy place, that Heidegger calls him, at the end of the poem, a 'poet' – a poet for 'needy times'.

Klee

21. Heidegger began to discuss Klee with his art-historian friend, Heinrich Petzet some time during the 1950s, though it seems that the decisive encounter came with a visit to the home of Ernst Beyeler in Basel at the end of that decade. (Beyeler had purchased a large collection of Klees from the Pittsburgh industrialist, David Thompson, and before selling them on to the city of Düsseldorf he made them available to a Europe-wide circle of friends, acquaintances, and scholars at his home – 'the Klee house' as, for a time, it became known (see Petzet, *Encounters and Dialogues with Martin Heidegger* (pp. 146–7)).

We know from Otto Pöggeler that the discovery of both Klee's paintings and his writings on art made a deep impression on Heidegger. The painter's, in Heidegger's view only partially successful, attempts to gain theoretical understanding of the significance of his own work led Heidegger, as we have seen (chapter 1 section 35), to the idea of writing a 'pendant', a 'second part' to 'The Origin'.

Heidegger's actual written remarks on Klee were confined by his death to the *Nachlass* where they exist in an extremely sketchy and incomplete condition.[26] They consist in a combination of Heidegger's own thoughts

---

[25] *Herkunftsbereich*. Hofstadter obscures the generative character of earth by translating this as 'reservoir'.

[26] Since the *Nachlass* is not available to general inspection, the following remarks are based entirely on the valuable work of Gunter Seubold, who obtained permission to view the Klee notes and has published part of what he found. See 'Heidegger's nachgelassene Klee-Notizen' in *Heidegger Studies* 9, 1993, pp. 5–12, and the later *Kunst als Enteignis*. Since all the quotations I shall use appear in *Kunst als Enteignis* between pages 119 and 134, I shall not bother to give individual references.

about Klee and quotations from Klee's writings which strike him as being of particular importance. One of the remarks in the *Nachlass* is: 'What Cézanne prepares begins with Klee.' So we should expect the analysis of Klee's significance to be relatively similar to that of Cézanne's.

22. Klee sums up the task of art, or of modern art, in the slogan '*vom* (from the) *Vorbildlichen zum* (to the) *Urbildlichen*'. The *Vorbildliche* is, for Klee, 'visible things', things of the kind 'one used to portray' in Western art, that is, idealized versions of objects of the type which belong to the everyday world (see section 15 above). (Though Heidegger clearly hears the '*bildlich*', 'pictorial', in '*vorbildlich*', the central, everyday, meaning of '*vorbildlich*' is 'exemplary', 'to be taken as a model'.) Klee writes (and Heidegger copies):

previously one described things to be seen on the earth that one liked, or would have liked, to see. Now the relativity of visible things [Einstein?] makes clear that the visible in relation to the world [Being?] as a whole is only an isolated example [disclosure?].

Thus, for Klee, there exists the necessity for a 'deformation of the world of natural appearances' in order to disrupt the dominion of the *vorbildlich*, of the pictorial (and the 'aesthetic'). Such a disruption is necessary in order to make possible the historical transition from the aesthetic–representational tradition in Western art to an art that is concerned to reveal the *Urbildliche*.

Urbildliche, which in ordinary German means 'prototype' might, here, be translated as 'primarily pictorial'. A better translation, however, if we follow Seubold's helpful suggestion of hyphenating '*Ur-bildliche*' à la Heidegger, is 'origin of the pictorial'. Klee describes the *Urbildliche* as the 'forming powers' that generate the visible, 'the secret ground where the primordial laws (*Urgesetz*) of developments are stored up'. The task of art, he continues, is to make this hitherto invisible visible. Art (Heidegger quotes) 'does not repeat the visible but makes visible' (compare Rilke's 'bees of the invisible'). To do this the artist must no longer be content to remain, like, for example, the Impressionists, on the 'periphery'. He must go, rather, to 'the heart of creation'. This may sound like onto-theological metaphysics but since, apropros Klee, Heidegger writes 'art' with a crossing-out through it, as he writes 'being' with a crossing-out through it, to

Plate 4   Paul Klee, *Saint from a Window*, 1940.

indicate his own freedom from metaphysics (see footnote 18 above), he clearly takes Klee's experience of the 'Other' of manifest beings to be a non-entifying, non-metaphysical experience.

Like the art of Zen and Cézanne, then, Klee's art facilitates a 'breakthrough to the Origin', an 'Origin' which presences in a non-metaphysical way. How does this happen?

Klee's concern is with the normally 'invisible', in Heidegger's language, to make visible the 'other side' of beings. This does not, however, lead him to ignore the ordinarily visible, to become entirely 'abstract'. Rather, his art occupies, as the painter himself puts it, a 'region-between (*Zwischen-Reich*)', a region between 'representational (*gegendständlich*)' and non-representational art. It is this intermediate character which makes it appropriate to describe his work as 'semi-abstract'. Heidegger notes the 'semi' with approval: in Klee, he observes, 'objects . . . [do] not disappear'.

Like Cézanne, therefore, Klee thematizes both the visible and the (non-metaphysical) invisible. But, also like Cézanne, he thematizes something else too: the *Ereignis* or 'worlding' of the former out of the latter: in Klee, Heidegger observes, 'objects . . . [do] not disappear but step back . . . into a worlding which is to be thought out of the *Ereignis*'. As with Cézanne, Klee thematizes the '*her-vor-bringen*' of objects, their 'being-brought-forth-out-of-concealment', their emergence out of the meaning-less into the clearing of intelligibility. How is this achieved?

For worlding to happen in the work, says Heidegger, too much detail must be avoided. Focusing on *Saint from a Window* (*Heilige aus einem Fenster*) and *The Northern God*, he observes that 'the sparser the indica-tion of the object the more [it presents itself as an] appearing'. Too much detail blocks 'worlding'. Sparseness of detail, sketchiness, on the other hand, compels the viewer to 'read' the work, a temporal process in which abstract and meaning-less patterns transform themselves into the intelli-gibility of objects – before our very eyes. Thus Klee's works are not 'fin-ished' things, as the word 'picture (*Bild*)' implies. Rather, they are '*Zu-stände*', beings which 'stand-ready-before-one' as occasions for the experience of worlding.

Heidegger's idea, I think, is that, at first, if only for a split, subliminal, second, we respond to a Klee as an entirely non-figurative work. Then, slowly (or relatively slowly), fish, boats, faces and so on materialize before our eyes, are born out of the abstract shapes. The *Ereignis* of world out of 'holy chaos' happens as we watch.

Why does Heidegger say that Klee 'begins' what Cézanne only 'pre-pares'? Why has he moved further down the path of putting us in touch with the numinous 'It' that gives us world?

Cézanne's images are, I think, unambiguous. Though we may some-times struggle to read them figuratively rather than non-figuratively, there exists no ambiguity between different figurative 'readings'. Trees, when they appear, are undoubtedly trees, rocks are rocks, sky is sky, mountains are mountains. This means that though Cézanne presents us with the idea of world as a 'reading' of Being and hence with the possibility of other readings, other worlds, that possibility remains implicit rather than explicit in his 'poetic thinking'.

Klee, however, is different. As Heidegger reads them, the images in which he is especially interested[27] resemble, to a degree, *Gestalt* figures – the duck/rabbit, the ambiguous cube, the chalice/two faces in profile, and so on. Though it would be wrong to press the analogy too far (Klee's paintings are not, finally, ambiguous, if only because the title disambiguates them), Heidegger notes (on completing his own sketch of *Saint from a Window*) that if one narrows one's focus to part of the face (and forgets the title) it becomes questionable whether there are 'still facial features'. Other objectual associations suggest themselves: 'church, ship'. This means that whereas, like Cézanne, Klee thematizes the presencing of world, unlike Cézanne, the works explicitly present us with the presencing of other worlds as well. The possibility of other 'revealings' merely implicit in Cézanne becomes explicit in Klee, who thus makes us more alive to the character of the 'Other' of beings as a 'plenitude' of alternative 'facets', alternative possibilities of disclosure.

Be this as it may, both Klee and Cézanne remain 'poets for needy times'. For each of them, in his own way, allows a 'breakthrough' to the 'other side' of beings and thereby allows world to be experienced as a holy place, a place of dwelling.

Cubism

23. I want to conclude this study by constructing a number of critical questions concerning the material that has been discussed in this chapter. Sometimes these are critical in a merely formal way, the point being to illuminate, further, certain obscurities in Heidegger's thinking, but sometimes, too, they are raised with genuinely critical intent.

---

[27] In addition to the paintings already mentioned Heidegger notes down the following titles: *The God of the Northern Wood* (1922), *Little Town on Rocks* (1932), *Resting Sphinx* (1934), *Penitent* (1935), *Harmonized Strife* (1937), *Faces of a Region* (1938), *Serious Face* (1939), *Higher Guard* (1940), *Death and Fire* (1940).

We have observed, several times, that Heidegger's fundamental strat-
egy, in discussing modern art, is to begin with an apparently sweeping
condemnation and then to discover, grudgingly, as it were, a few shining
exceptions. The first of my critical questions asks why, in the entire field
of the visual art of Western modernity, only two artists, Klee and
Cézanne, emerge as exceptions to the dispiriting rule. Surely, one might
suggest, this must be regarded as insupportably arbitrary, all the more so
since the quality Heidegger admires in Klee and Cézanne is, in fact,
common to a great deal of modern art. What he admires, that is to say, is
'semi-abstraction', the fact that while objects do not dominate the scene,
neither do they 'disappear'. But semi-abstraction is the salient feature of
a very great deal of (at least early) modern art, in particular the art of
cubism and of those influenced by it. Having admired semi-abstraction
in Cézanne and Klee, the criticism concludes, Heidegger ought therefore
to have felt compelled to admire it in a great number of other artists. In
particular, in Picasso.

The first part of this criticism is easily dealt with. Though Heidegger
only wrote about Klee and Cézanne (and *en passant*, in 'The Origin',
about Van Gogh) the scope of his admiration for, and involvement with,
modern plastic artists was very much wider, as the biographical detail
supplied in section 1 of this chapter makes clear. The second part of the
criticism is, however, more interesting. For what it assumes is that a
certain *technical* feature of artworks – what we might call the deconstruction–reconstruction of objects – is a necessary and sufficient condition of
a work's being a work in which the 'breakthrough to the Origin' occurs
(in which 'earth' 'rises up' through 'world'), its being a work, in other
words, which facilitates dwelling. It is important to see, I believe, that both
parts of this presupposition are, in fact, false, that deconstruction–reconstruction is neither a sufficient nor a necessary condition for the kind of
'greatness' which, in modern art, Heidegger is trying to discover.

24. The experience of figurative images emerging from seemingly abstract
shapes of which Heidegger makes so much in his discussions of Klee and
Cézanne is actually quite commonplace. Everyone has had the experience
of discovering the face in the clouds, most people have from time to time
discovered the landscape in the wood grain of the door, in the wallpaper,
or in the linoleum on the bathroom floor. A certain amusement, pleasure

even, may be derived from such experiences and they may sometimes – as in the ink-blot test – be useful revelations of aspects of personality and may be helpful stimuli to the creative imagination. Yet none of these experiences counts as what Heidegger calls an '*Ereignis*-experience'. Heidegger says, as we have seen, that the *Ereignis*-experience is accompanied by a feeling of 'transport and enchantment' (*GA* 65, p. 70). Yet this, clearly, would be far too purple a description of the pleasure of discovering a figure in the bathroom linoleum.

The reason such a discovery is not an *Ereignis*-experience is that the ground out of which the figure emerges fails to be 'holy' ground. The artist of the modern paradigm is, we know (from chapter 3 section 13), one who 'founds', thematizes, 'the holy', brings it to presence. This is the reason why, in the final verse of the poem, Cézanne is accounted a 'poet'. It is being, in this sense, a poet that is crucial, for, as we know, it is only in the poetic, the holy, that one dwells.

In the case of both Klee and Cézanne it seems a true and important observation that the world-ground out of which objects are born is a numinous ground. Their works possess, as Heidegger puts it in the explanatory comment on 'Cézanne', a 'pure radiance'. (In the case of Klee it has, perhaps, something to do with their tiny, icon-like character, in the case of Cézanne something to do with his unique and omnipresent blue,[28] present not just in sky, but in tree, field and earth as well. Blue, as Heidegger says, is the colour of the holy, the 'blue depth of the aether' (*PLT* p. 149) being the region inhabited by the gods (*PLT* p. 94).) But what reflection on figures in the bathroom linoleum reveals, is that deconstruction–reconstruction is not, of itself, a sufficient condition of an artwork's being, in Heidegger's sense, 'poetic'.

Heidegger had an equivocal relationship to Picasso. Though in no doubt at all as to Picasso's titanic genius, and deeply moved by some of his earlier works, he doubted, as Petzet reports, that his art occupied, in the end, an 'essential' place. And to the (surely pretentious) suggestion made to him by an enthusiastic former student that he 'does the same

---

[28] Cézanne knew that blue had a special significance for him. Poeticizing the history of art as a 'chain of colour' to which each great artist added a new 'link', he referred to his own contribution as 'my own blue link'. (Quoted on the penultimate page of Theodore Rousseau's *Paul Cézanne* (London: Collins, 1954).)

thing as Picasso in the dismantling of the object – when he speaks [in the introduction to *Being and Time*] of the necessary 'destruction' in philosophy' Heidegger responded, Petzet reports, with a smiling 'silence' (Petzet, *Encounters and Dialogues*, pp. 144–5). The reason for Heidegger's final lack of interest in the later Picasso is that he does not take him to be – and he is surely correct in this – in his sense a 'poet'. Picasso indeed 'dismantles' objects. But deconstruction–reconstruction is not a sufficient condition of 'poetry'.

And neither is it a necessary condition. Heidegger himself seems to me to lapse into the error of supposing that it is in his remarks on film and photography (see section 18 above). (Though it is possible to take these remarks as deliberately provocative over-generalizations, I am more inclined to take them as simply displaying an ignorance of the diversity of possibilities inherent in the medium.) Whatever the validity of Heidegger's remarks on Kurosawa's *Rashomon*, a reasonable acquaintance with the films of, say, Bergman, Visconti or Wenders reveals as clearly absurd the claim that film can provide nothing but densely naturalistic representation of the mundane world, that film, as such, cannot be 'poetic'. And so far as still photography is concerned one need go no further than the extraordinarily evocative photographs of Heidegger himself taken in and around the hut in Todtnauberg by Digne Mellor Marcovicz at the time of the 1966 interview with the journal *Der Spiegel*,[29] to realize that, of course, photography, too, can rise to the 'poetic'. (Since, in spite of his deep suspicion of the 'media', Heidegger invited Marcovicz to his home in Freiburg for a second session of photographs, he may well have, eventually, realized something of this himself.)

The mistake behind this attempt to make deconstruction–reconstruction a necessary condition of 'poetic' art, and behind the attempt to make it a sufficient condition, too, is to suppose that it is possible to specify a *technique*, or even part of a technique, for the production of 'poetic' art. Though, as already remarked, art criticism of a technical character is, of

[29] See *Martin Heidegger: Photos 23 September 1966/16. und 17. Juni 1968* (Frankfurt-on-Main: Klostermann, 1985). What is remarkable about the nearly 200 photographs in this collection is that although they nearly all portray Heidegger in a poetic, deeply sympathetic light, Marcovicz, as indicated to me in private correspondence, seems to have had no personal, and certainly no political, liking for Heidegger at all. Yet another proof, perhaps, of the often noted divorce between artist and person.

course, possible – it is possible *post facto* tentatively to identify particular technical features as contributing to a poetic effect – no a priori specification of poetic technique is possible. Art, as Kant observed, cannot be reduced to a rule. It cannot be discovered in a 'creative writing class'. The task – Heidegger at times seems to forget his own (Kantian) wisdom – is to 'see the enigma', not to 'solve' it (*PLT* p. 79).

Abstract art

25. My second critical question concerns not 'semi-abstract' but rather abstract art proper. Is it not the case, I want now to ask, that Heidegger's attitude to it has to be adjudged a mixture of arbitrary neglect and unjust denigration?

The one thing that is clear about Heidegger's attitude to 'non-representational (*gegenstandlos*)' or abstract art is that he sees it as failing to constitute a genuine break with the metaphysical character of the Western tradition. Abstract art does not liberate us to the holy, to dwelling. The grounds for this judgment, however, vary. In the 1955–6 *Principle of Reason*, for example, he says that 'that to which one gives the inappropriate title "abstract art" finds its legitimate function' in 'the region of the technical-scientific world-construction' (*SvG* p. 41). 'Non-representational art', he continues, stands at the peak of the contemporary experience of things as *Bestand*, resource (*SvG* p. 66). However, in a 1964 letter to R. Krämer-Badoni, who had criticized 'The Origin' for overlooking the age of abstract art, while continuing to insist that abstract art does not figure in a redemptive way in his thinking, Heidegger concedes that 'this does not imply that abstract art is a branch (*Ableger*) of modern technology'.[30]

How are we to explain these different assessments? Reasonably clearly, I think, Heidegger thinks of two different kinds of art as generally embraced by the vague titles 'abstract' and 'non-representational'. Hence his attitude to 'abstract art' really divides into two attitudes directed towards these two different kinds of art.

---

[30] Quoted in R. Krämer-Badoni's *Zwischen allen Stühlen* (Munich/Berlin: Herbig, 1985), p. 182.

In the first of the above quotations, Heidegger suggests that the title 'non-representational' is *misleadingly* applied to the kind of art he had in mind. It is not hard to think of the kind of art this might be. Consider Mondrian's famous *Broadway Boogie Woogie*. Though composed entirely of strips of brightly coloured squares, the picture can be read as a busy street seen from the top of a very tall skyscraper. Indeed Mondrian's title invites us so to read it. (The same is true of his famous series of apple-tree studies. By locating the final study, composed entirely of lines and dashes in a sequence through which a naturalistically represented tree is progressively 'dematerialized', Mondrian invites us to view the final version as remaining figurative.)

Heidegger nowhere discusses Mondrian. But let us, for the sake of explicating his position, make the (relatively improbable) assumption that, *inter alios*, he has Mondrian in mind. We know that Heidegger often associates globalization, uniformity (uni-formity) with *Gestell*. In enframing, everything is reduced to a unit, or collection of equi-sized units, of resource. It would, then, be possible (in no way do I wish to *defend* this reading of Mondrian's wonderful painting) to read *Broadway Boogie Woogie* as a *celebration*, an idealization or, as Nietzsche would say, 'transfiguration' of *Gestell*. The work would then fall into the same category as Ernst Jünger's *Der Arbeiter* and much of the work of the fascist wing of Italian Futurism in being a celebration of the disappearance of everything that was once considered essential to human dignity, distinctive of the human mode of being. I suggest, then, that (whether or not Heidegger had Mondrian, in particular, in mind) it is art of this type which he rejects as simply a 'branch' – a branch with the important 'function' of self-glorification – of *Gestell*.

One way of describing the, contrary to appearances, not-fully-abstract quality of Mondrian's work would be to apply to it the term used in connection with Klee: 'semi-abstract'. The second type of art Heidegger has in mind, I suggest, is that which is fully and genuinely abstract: Kasimir Malevich's famous *Black Square*, for example. It is art of this kind, I believe, of which Heidegger concedes, to Krämer-Badoni, that cannot be regarded as a mere 'branch of modern technology'. If it genuinely does not represent then it cannot represent the world of *Gestell* and *a fortiori*, cannot glorify it. So it is innocuous.

At the same time, however, Heidegger claims, it cannot be considered redemptive with respect to the 'destitution' of modernity created by metaphysics. Why not? Fairly clearly, from Heidegger's perspective, for the very same reason that it is innocuous. If an artwork fails to represent the world then it cannot represent it as holy. Art cannot represent the world, allow it to presence, as a dwelling place except on the condition that it – represents the world. This is why, as we saw, Heidegger selects for special approval the fact that, in Klee, 'objects do not disappear but step back, as objects, into a worlding'. If an artwork is to allow dwelling objects *must not* disappear.

Music

26. This claim about (genuinely) abstract painting leads directly to the question of the absence, in Heidegger, of any sustained discussion of music. The third of my critical questions asks: does not Heidegger unjustly – or, perhaps better, unphilosophically – neglect music? Does he not, to his detriment as a philosopher, evince a certain blindness in this direction?

The foundations of Heidegger's stance to music go back to his critique of Wagner in the mid-thirties, in volume I of the Nietzsche study. Like Nietzsche (after breaking off his friendship with Wagner in 1876), Heidegger criticizes the unarticulated, structure-less, 'sea'-like quality of Wagner's music. Unlike Nietzsche, however, he identifies this quality with the character of music *as such*. What Wagner sought in the idea of opera as *Gesamtkunstwerk* (collective artwork) was indeed, he says, a collecting together of all the individual arts. But it was by no means a collecting that granted equal rights to each. Rather, he claims (glossing over the difference between Wagner's earlier (pre-*Tristan*) and later musical theory and practice), what Wagner wants

is the domination of art as music, and *thereby* the dominance of the pure state of feeling – the tumult, and delirium of the senses, tremendous contraction, the felicitous distress that swoons in enjoyment, absorption in 'the bottomless sea of harmonies', the plunge into frenzy and the disintegration of sheer feeling as redemptive. (*N* I, p. 86; my emphasis)

In 1936, then, Heidegger's fundamental objection to Wagner is that since what he writes is, in effect, purely instrumental – in Wagner's own language 'absolute' – music, he cannot 'set forth' a world – in the rich, onto-ethical sense of 'world' deployed by the Greek paradigm.

By the postwar period Heidegger has ceased to require such a grandiose function of art. Yet the selection of musical works for which he expresses particular esteem – Carl Orff's *Carmina Burana* as well as his music for *Antigone* (Petzet, *Encounters and Dialogues*, pp. 80, 161), and Stravinsky's *Symphony of Psalms* and *Persephone* (*D* p. 113) – includes no examples of absolute music. What this strongly suggests is that, insofar as he thought about music at all, he continued to insist that in 'valid' musical artworks, music must always be subordinate to a linguistic text, subordinate, as 'The Origin' maintained, to 'poetry'.

Given his concern for dwelling it is easy to discern the line of thinking that must underlie this insistence. Art cannot facilitate dwelling in the world, cannot present one's world as a holy place, unless it represents, or in some other way brings that world to presence. But this is something (absolute) music cannot do. Hence music, pleasant though it undoubtedly is, cannot be an essential art form. What are we to make of this line of thought?

This is no place to become deeply involved in precisely that which is almost entirely missing in Heidegger; the philosophy of music. I shall content myself, therefore, with a few brief and, I fear, dogmatic remarks.

Theorists of music, by and large, seem to agree with Schopenhauer's assertion that, with the deviant exception of 'programme' music, music does not represent the 'outer', visible world. Apart from formalists who hold that music is connected to nothing but music, they tend to conclude from this that the domain of music is the 'inner' world of feeling. The significance of music, it is frequently suggested, is that it 'expresses' emotion or at least something closely related to emotion. Thinking about music is dominated by the 'inner–outer' contrast together with the notion that the domain of music is confined to the 'inner'.

Insofar as he thinks about music at all, *Heidegger's* thinking about music, too, is dominated by this contrast – in spite of the fact that his general philosophy is devoted to demolishing it. Left to itself, his remarks on Wagner affirm, music brings to presence a 'pure state of feeling'; the inner, subjective response to worldly things and events severed, however, from their usual objective complement. The effect is no doubt relaxing and 'aesthetically' pleasing, but it does not help make our world a place of dwelling.

Nietzsche did not make the mistake of supposing music to be confined to a supposed 'inner' world of feeling. (Though his own music, as Hans von Bülow told him, is entirely without merit, he did, at least, write music and understood it in a way that Heidegger could not.) The full title of his first book is: *The Birth of Tragedy out of the Spirit of Music*. What Nietzsche understood in this title is that it is not the case that music's only route to the bringing of a world to presence is by accommodating itself to a pre-existent text. Music does not have to take second place to drama because it can itself give 'birth' to drama, to action, to a world – as painters, like Mondrian, who have derived inspiration from musical sound and mood, have always known. Another fact which points in the same direction is the disposition of listeners to give titles, *Pastoral Symphony*, *Moonlight Sonata* (titles which may be more or less appropriate) to works of absolute music. Translated into Heidegger's language, what Nietzsche understood was that music possesses, in fact to a consummate degree, the power to be an *Ereignis*-experience. Heidegger's discounting of absolute music is thus, I believe, *in his own terms*, a serious error as perhaps, for similar reasons, is his blanket discounting of the (genuinely) abstract in painting.

Of Webern, Heidegger said, in a letter to the musicologist Martin Zenk,[31] that he could find 'no point of entry'. Though the remark, in this particular case, might well be forgiven, it actually applies, to a rather large degree, to Heidegger's relationship to music in general. Only someone afflicted by a certain musical deafness, or lack of musical education, could, even for a moment, be tempted to suppose Wagnerian 'structure-lessness' to be a quality of Western music in general.

To a degree, Heidegger's musical deafness diminishes his thinking about art. He was, however, gifted, to a consummate degree, with a sensitivity to the poetic word. It seems to be a rough kind of truth that those who are hypersensitive to one art form are typically afflicted by a compensatory blindness to another. The price we pay for Heidegger's – among philosophers, it seems to me unparalleled – insight into poetry is the comparatively low quality of his thinking about music.

---

[31] See Seubold, *Kunst als Enteignis,* p. 79 footnote 126.

A *philosophy* of art?

27. The final critical question I wish to discuss comes in two parts. The first arises from Heidegger's discussion of Eastern art. His interest in this, it will be remembered, is generated and sharpened by the sense that in authentically Eastern art he has discovered something that is an exception to, lies outside the margins of, an 'all-consuming Europeanization' (*OWL* p. 16). Yet he ends up discovering, as the essence of Zen art, precisely the presencing of that 'Other' of beings which he discovers, too, to be the essence of Rilke, Klee and Cézanne. In the end, therefore, the essence of great Eastern art turns out to be the same as the essence of great Western art. The first part of my critical question asks, therefore: does not Heidegger end up denying the difference between East and West, falling, in other words, into precisely the trap he sought to avoid?

The second part of the question observes that even though Heidegger thought deeply about those Western artists he admired, there remains much about them that he ignores. Thus with regard to Klee, for example, in spite of the undoubted insight of Heidegger's observations, what strikes one is how much that is salient in, and central to the distinctiveness of, Klee's art – his humour, his unchildish childishness, his immersion in dreams and the unconscious – is simply ignored. And with regard to Cézanne neither his overpowering sensuousness, his manifest concern to 'realize [his] sensations' of 'the magnificent richness of colour that animates nature' nor his neoclassical concern to 'treat nature by the cylinder, the sphere, the cone'[32] receives any mention at all. The question then arises, to put it in a slogan: does not Heidegger Heideggerize the art he admires? Putting the two parts of the question together, then: does not Heidegger Europeanize Eastern art and Heideggerize European art, and so end up Heideggerizing everything?

The first part of this question can be quickly dealt with. It is not the case that Heidegger denies the essential difference between Eastern and Western art since, as we have seen, he maintains that while the (post-supernaturalist) Western tradition is, *qua* tradition, mimetic, metaphysical, the Eastern tradition, though 'pictorial', is not. What Heidegger

---

[32] *Paul Cézanne: Letters*, ed. J. Rewald (London: Bruno Cassirer, 1941), pp. 262, 234.

rather does is to discover an affinity between particular Western artists and the Eastern tradition. Does he obliterate the difference between those particular artists and their Eastern counterparts? Surely not. That different artists may have the same *ultimate* concern no more obliterates their uniqueness and difference than the fact that different religions are concerned with 'the divine', or that different languages are concerned to 'talk about reality', obliterates theirs.

The second part of the question is, however, more interesting. Does Heidegger 'Heideggerize' the Western art, the art in general, which interests him? The answer is, I think, that, on a certain understanding of 'Heideggerize', he does. For what is quite clearly the case is that both what he talks about and the way he talks about it are determined by his own unique way of thinking and writing. But why should this be problematic? Because, so the subtext to the question suggests, such an approach to art is inconsistent with the kind of impartiality and objectivity that allows an approach to art to count as properly *philosophical*.

One reply to this criticism, one that is offered by Gunter Seubold, is to suggest that since Heidegger's discussion of art is 'integrated' so completely into the structure and vocabulary of his late philosophy – the vocabulary of 'Being', 'clearing', '*Ereignis*', and so on – it is, 'therefore', quite evidently, *not intended* to possess 'the character of a philosophy of art' (*Kunst als Enteignis*, p. 98). Heidegger, the thought presumably runs, was concerned above all with his own *Seinsphilosophie*, with understanding the standing of beings to being and being to Being. From time to time he found insight and assistance in the works of individual artists, and when he did he would approach them on an opportunistic basis, appropriating what he found to be useful and ignoring the rest. Pursuing this line of thought, one might be inclined to quote Georges Braque's inscription on the back of a lithograph he sent to Heidegger as a seventieth birthday present: 'Echo begets echo / everything reflects back / for Martin Heidegger' (quoted in Petzet, *Encounters and Dialogues*, p. 46). As Braque saw, one might suggest, on the occasions that their paths come close to convergence, art 'echoes' in Heidegger's thinking. An echo of art is not, however, a philosophy of art.

Though Heidegger himself was often disposed to a 'post-philosophical' view of his thinking, this seems to me the wrong response to the critical question. For three reasons.

First, it is, in fact, not the case that Heidegger's discussion of art is con-fined to opportunistic forays into the works of individual artists. For as we have seen, though they are usually polemically overstated, sometimes unclear, and occasionally, as in the case of film, based on ignorance, Heidegger offers seriously intended, and seriously interesting, views about the character of Western art *in general*. And he offers too, a seri-ously important view about the role of art in modernity – that it is to facil-itate dwelling – and in postmodernity – that it is to recreate authentic community. There is thus no lack of generality in Heidegger's discussion of art. (In fact, there is too much. If his generalizations had been more restricted his meaning would have often been clearer.)

The second error that is embodied, it seems to me, in the Heidegger-attempts-no-philosophy-of-art position, is an unreasonable expecta-tion of comprehensiveness. It is true that his treatment of the individual arts is uneven. The discussion of music is thin and weak, of novels, (post-Greek) theatre, and dance, non-existent. And with regard to indi-vidual artists of modernity, rather than dutifully and impartially attending to those figures agreed by common consent to be 'great', Heidegger attends to those and only those who speak, especially strongly to him and about whom he has something special to say. I fail to see, however, any obligation on the philosopher of art to give arts and artists 'equal rights'.

At the beginning of the Enlightenment there was, it is true, a close asso-ciation between philosophers and encyclopaedists, and it is true that phi-losophers of art have traditionally felt obligated to climb methodically through the 'hierarchy' of the arts. (Witness, for example, Schopenhauer's dutiful attention to landscape gardening and animal painting, art forms in which he actually has relatively little interest and consequently about which he has relatively little of interest to say.) But the philosopher is no encyclopaedist and it is a mistake to impose on the former duties that properly belong to the latter.

The third, and most important reason Seubold's attempted 'defence' of Heidegger's discussion of art seems to me in error is that it *accepts*, without question, the requirement that the philosopher of art should be 'objective', should *not* approach art from the perspective of his own thought structure and vocabulary.

Seubold wishes to read Heidegger's discussion as art interpretation of a non-'art philosophical' character. Considered as such, it appears, he has no quarrel with its general approach and style. This suggests that he has little general difficulty with Heidegger's view (later elaborated by his pupil, Hans-Georg Gadamer) that, first, there is no point in interpreting an artwork unless that interpreting is also an appropriating, and, second, that appropriation is always a 'translation' of the work into one's own frame of reference, one's own 'horizon' of understanding (*Ister* pp. 61–3). The view, in other words, that all (non-pointless) interpretation is perspectival. I see no reason to suppose that, in this respect, philosophical interpretation should be different from interpretation of any other sort. The inclination to demand, of the philosopher, the 'view from nowhere' can only be explained, I suspect, as the unconscious by-product of the ancient, but erroneous, disposition to elevate the (true) philosopher to the status of an omniscient, or semi-omniscient, being.

Index

absolute, the, 7, 60
abstraction, 10, 170
action, 11, 26, 35, 111, 113
aesthetics, 8, 9, 10, 12–14, 16, 18, 21, 49, 62,
    67–9, 91, 121, 124, 142, 159
aether, 95, 99, 124, 164
agitation, 62, 63
aletheia, 22, 39, 63
alienation, 57, 59, 74
anxiety, 10, 11, 127, 131, 145, 146
Apollo, 40, 85 n. 1, 88 n. 6, 145, 156
appearance, 3, 42
art
    aesthetic conception of, 9, 11
    anti-metaphysical, 126, 128, 142
    Christian, 136, 137
    East Asian, 142, 147–50, 171
    fine (*die schönen Künste*), 9, 18
    great, 6, 8, 14–15, 94
    industry, 11, 18
    modern, 69, 70
    naturalistic, 134, 139
    non-representational, 166, 167
    post-Christian, 141, 142
    receiver of, 7, 16
    supernaturalistic, 134, 139
    symbolic, 138, 139
    Western, 9, 15, 134–41, 147, 157, 159,
        171, 173
artwork, 7, 15–20, 29–30, 33–8, 41–2,
    44–52, 54, 55, 57–9, 61, 62, 66, 76, 77,
    88, 89, 91, 92, 95, 97, 121, 124, 127, 141
    collective (*Gesamtkunstwerk*), 60, 168
astonishment *see* wonder
at-homeness, 125, 126, 131
authenticity, 54, 59, 73, 79, 127
authority, 25, 45, 46, 90
awe, 42, 44, 62
awesomeness, 43–5, 47, 50, 90, 108, 123,
    139

Bamberg, 19, 52, 59
beauty, 9, 10, 49, 110, 114
Beethoven, Ludwig van, 31, 51
beginning, 53, 81
being, 25, 29, 32, 36, 40, 42, 43, 64, 81, 104,
    108, 109, 111–14, 116–18, 123, 124–5,
    130, 133, 137, 140, 143, 144, 146–8,
    154, 157, 161, 172
    forgetfulness of (*Seinsvergessenheit*), 41,
        113, 123, 126, 132
beings, 161, 172
    being of, 23, 24, 76, 106, 138
    horizon of, 140
    space of, 112, 116, 123
Beyeler, Ernst, 121, 158
Braque, Georges, 1, 48, 65, 121, 172

care, 10, 86, 130, 131
cathedral, medieval, 7, 19, 44, 48, 50, 51, 52,
    59, 61, 67, 69, 82, 121, 139
Cézanne, Paul, 1, 2, 31, 49, 50, 65–8, 121,
    128, 142, 150–8, 159–61, 163, 164, 171
chaos, 156, 157, 161
charisma, 17, 90
Christ *see* Jesus
Christendom, 19, 46, 52, 81
Christianity, 32, 38, 81–3, 106, 136, 140
clarity, 65, 97
    of presentation (*Klarheit der Darstellung*),
        40, 45, 96, 97, 104
clearing, 45, 106, 110, 125, 133, 144, 172
commitment, 55, 56, 74
community (*Gemeinschaft*), 54, 55, 60, 73,
    74, 77, 85, 89, 92, 99, 173
concealment, 39, 41, 64, 108
conditions
    communal, 65, 89, 91
    earth, 65, 66, 91, 139
    truth, 65, 66
    world, 90, 91

consciousness, 143, 155
conservation, 18–19, 130
contrast (*Auseinandersetzung*), 63, 64
creation, 58, 74, 111
cubism, 162–6
culture, 22, 59, 106, 127, 128
cyclicality, 114, 115, 118

Dasein, 32, 55
  collective, 54, 59, 127
  inauthentic, 53
  individual, 54, 59, 127
  see also existence
death, 54, 127, 130, 131–3, 145, 146
  of art, 1, 6, 12, 14, 120, 121, 122
decisions, 28, 81
deconstruction-reconstruction, 163, 164, 165
decontextualization, 9, 10
definitions, 16, 17
despair, 109, 119
destinings, 67, 99
destiny, 55, 56, 73, 75, 89, 96, 131
destitution, 18, 85, 89, 90, 93, 94, 95, 98, 111, 113, 123, 125, 137, 145, 168
Dionysus, 40, 82, 85, n. 1, 88 n. 6, 99, 144, 156
disclosure, 64, 75, 86, 107, 125, 133, 138, 145, 154, 155, 162
  horizon of, 23, 39, 104, 106, 124, 154
disinterestedness, 9, 10
drama, 18, 170
Dreyfus, Hubert, 17, 18, 30
dwelling, 125, 127, 128–34, 137, 139, 146, 150, 162, 163, 166, 168–70, 173

earth, 38–50, 52, 62, 72, 89, 91, 99, 100, 106, 108, 116, 118, 123, 129–30, 145, 148, 157, 163
education, 12, 105, 107
endowment (*Mitgegebene*), 7, 51, 53–5, 75, 96
enframing, 54, 123, 130, 167
enlightenment, 13, 78
Enlightenment, 13, 173
equanimity (*Gelassenheit*), 127–8, 152
Ereignis-thinking/experience, 3, 106–7, 111–13, 118, 164, 170
essence, 71–3, 86–9, 91, 94, 96, 98, 112, 117, 118, 130, 137, 140
ethics, 8, 24, 25–9, 73, 81, 83
ethos, 24, 45, 53, 66, 81, 85, 95
everydayness, 37–8, 59, 86, 87, 89, 104, 108
existence (*Dasein*), 32, 76, 86, 108, 110, 125

facts, 23, 25
fear, 10, 11
feeling, 13, 60, 169
festival, 83, 84–90, 92, 93, 113–19, 139, 145
film, 120, 150, 173
fire (holy) from heaven, 40, 96, 97, 135
firstness, 29, 31, 32, 33
founding (*stiften*), 57–8, 66, 72–3, 76–7, 81–2, 89–91, 99, 100, 102, 133, 164
  idea (*Grundegedanke*), 16, 38
fundamental mood (*Grundstimmung*), 74, 105, 107, 111, 118, 131
future, 74, 77, 79, 80, 92, 94, 100–1, 117

George, Stefan, 1, 22, 69, 121, 142
Germans, 56, 75, 98
  poet of, 79
Gestell, 86–7, 90, 97, 116, 167
God, 17, 47, 109, 110, 113, 117, 127, 138, 139
  default of, 85, 90, 95, 113, 114
gods, 66, 72, 73, 75, 80–3, 88, 89–93, 95, 98, 99, 105, 113, 114, 117, 118, 129, 164
  absence of, 90, 99, 105, 124, 126
  death of, 80
  return of, 117, 124, 134
graciousness, 113, 114
Graecocentricism, 80–3
gratitude, 105–8, 111, 118
greatness, 6, 8, 12, 20, 50, 52, 65, 66, 68, 70, 81, 97, 105, 122, 139, 163
Greece, 1, 15, 52, 60, 80, 81, 85, 87, 90, 92, 95
Greek art, 8, 11, 27
Greeks, the, 18, 19, 22, 26, 54, 80, 87, 90, 96

happening (*Ereignis*), 64, 88, 102, 105–7, 111, 156, 157, 161, 172
harmony, 10, 62
Hegel, Georg, 1, 6, 7–8, 12, 14, 16, 18, 23, 51, 61, 96, 110, 115
Heidegger, Martin:
  'Art and Space', 121, 134
  The Basic Problems of Phenomenology, 32
  Being and Time, 4, 22, 24, 29, 30, 32, 33, 35, 37, 47, 53–5, 59, 65, 67, 74, 79, 86, 94, 124, 127, 131, 132, 143, 145, 165
  'Building Dwelling Thinking', 113, 125, 129, 133
  Contributions to Philosophy, 106
  '*Denken und Kunst* (Thought and Art)', 135, 147
  'A Dialogue on Language', 147
  'Essence of Truth', 22

'Germania Lectures, 34, 75, 79
'Hölderlin and the Essence of Poetry', 5,
    11, 34, 35, 58, 71, 72, 73, 75, 80, 92
'Hölderlin's Earth and Sky', 84
Hölderlin's Hymn 'The Ister', 13, 27, 41,
    78, 135, 143
Identität und Differenz, 154
An Introduction to Metaphysics, 5, 24, 26,
    30, 63, 71
'Letter on Humanism', 24, 25, 125
'Letter to a Young Student', 118
'The Nature of Language', 69
Nietzsche, 5, 18, 116; *The Will to Power as
    Art*, 5, 6, 8, 9, 11, 52, 60, 67, 168
'The Origin of the Work of Art', 1, 2,
    5–7, 15, 16, 19, 22, 23, 27, 29, 30, 32,
    33, 35, 37, 38, 40, 49, 50, 53–6, 58, 60,
    61–6, 68, 70, 72, 73, 75, 79, 81, 88, 89,
    94, 96, 98, 103, 106, 108, 115, 120, 130,
    132, 143, 148, 157, 158, 163, 166, 169
Poetry, Language, Thought, 84, 93
Principle of Reason, 166
*The Question Concerning Technology and
    Other Essays*, 93, 115, 127
'Rectoral Address', 56, 62–3
'Rhine' lectures, 75
'The Saying of Anaximander', 42
'What are Poets for?', 3, 95, 98, 127, 144,
    150
'What is Metaphysics?', 109
Heraclitus, 59, 63
Herakles, 82, 85
heritage, 53, 54, 55, 56, 59, 80, 81, 90
history, 7, 14, 23, 27, 51, 52, 53, 54, 55, 61,
    100, 112, 114, 115, 116, 117, 118, 119
Hitler, Adolf, 17, 29, 55, 76, 78, 114
Hölderlin, Friedrich, 2, 3, 22, 44, 47, 66,
    69–119, 122, 131, 135, 137, 146, 156
'As when on holiday', 101, 102, 107, 108,
    110, 114
'Bread and Wine', 113
'Germania', 5, 71, 80
'Homecoming', 100, 101, 108, 113
hymns, 69, 102
'The Ister', 98
'Poet's Calling', 113
'Remembrance', 58, 72, 85, 87, 92, 98,
    103, 104
'The Rhine', 5, 40, 71
'The Turning', 115, 116, 118, 127
'The Voice of the People', 35
holiday (*Feiertag*), 86, 87
holiness/holy, the, 2, 24, 27, 31, 38, 41–4, 46,
    47, 52, 60, 65, 88, 89, 91, 95, 96, 99,

102, 104, 106–8, 110, 111, 118, 123,
    124, 126, 127, 133, 138–40, 147, 156,
    164, 166
homelessness, 125, 126, 131
Homer, 2, 12, 31, 34, 69, 77, 81, 82
hope, 10, 11
horizon, 39, 74

iceberg, 43, 45, 146
inauthenticity, 74, 90
inconspicuousness, 32, 33, 36–8, 52, 65, 96
ineffability, 40, 47
insight, 109, 124
integration, 57, 59
intelligibility, 4, 48, 106, 161
invisible, the, 159–61

Jesus, 54, 82, 83, 85, 90
Judaism, 54, 83, 90
Jünger, Ernst, 111, 167

Kant, Immanuel, 9, 16, 25, 34, 35, 39, 42,
    44, 45, 50, 116, 117, 154, 166
Klee, Paul, 1, 2, 49, 50, 64–8, 70, 71, 121,
    128, 134, 142, 158–64, 167, 168, 171
knowledge, 10, 26, 33, 45
Krämer-Badoni, R., 166, 167
Kurosawa, Akira, 149, 165

language, 23, 28, 34–6, 39, 57, 90, 103, 106,
    172
    eindeutig/vieldeutig, 103–4
    poetic, 104
Le Corbusier (Charles Edouard Jeanneret),
    1, 121
light, 63, 110

Man, Paul de, 109, 117
materials, 47, 48, 49
meaning, 57, 59, 85, 103
meaninglessness, 57, 74, 156, 161
measure, 88, 93
meditation, 48, 148
metaphysics, 13, 104, 112, 116, 123–4,
    126–30, 132, 133, 134–40, 142, 143,
    144, 146, 147–9, 154, 155, 157, 159–60,
    168, 171
metapoet, 79, 91, 94, 102
Middle Ages, 1, 7, 8
mimesis, 140, 141, 147, 171
modernity, 11, 54, 66, 67, 73, 74, 86, 89, 90,
    91, 95, 99, 111, 113, 120–1, 123–5, 137,
    153, 168, 173
Mondrian, Piet, 167

moon, 40–3, 48, 112, 145, 146
moral intuitionists, 25, 26
mortality, 127, 130, 132
mortals, 72, 118, 129
mourning, holy (*heilige Trauer*), 74, 75, 105,
    107
music, 168–70
mystery, 50, 116, 139, 154
mythology, Greek, 30, 61, 83

nature, 16, 47, 100, 110, 111
naturalism, 140–2, 143, 149
Nazism, 17, 30, 64, 76, 77, 81, 112, 114
need, 73, 94–5, 101, 124, 126, 144
Nietzsche, Friedrich, 2, 16, 34, 36, 38–40,
    42, 61, 74, 78, 80, 88, 91, 93, 94, 96,
    111, 116, 122, 141, 156, 167, 170
night, 113, 114
nihilism, 25, 56, 59, 74, 111, 127, 130, 132,
    148
Nikeism, 111–14
Nô plays, 49, 50, 149–50
nothing, the, 131, 132, 148, 150, 157
Nuremberg, 18, 29, 78

objectification, 137, 139, 144, 149
ontology, 24, 25–9, 124, 138, 153, 154
ontotheology, 138, 139
open, the, 143, 144, 145, 147, 148
openness, 37, 58, 63
order, 27, 28
Orff, Carl, 121, 169
origin (*Ursprung*) 15, 16, 29, 132, 160, 163
originality, 33–4
Other, the, 41, 123–5, 132, 139–42, 145, 149,
    150, 160, 162, 171

Paestum, 19, 52, 59
paradigm
    cultural, 18
    Greek, 1, 2, 65–72, 75–7, 79, 89–92, 94,
        95, 98–100, 105, 121, 122, 124, 127,
        139, 169
    modern, 2, 94–5, 99–102, 105, 122, 124,
        126–8, 142, 164
past, 74, 80, 100–1
pastry cooks, 69, 73, 101, 122
pathos, holy, 40, 96
patience, 111, 112
peace, 11, 110
people, 53–5, 57, 58, 61, 74, 76
Petzet, Heinrich, 65, 121, 158, 164–5
philosophy, 110, 138, 139
photography, 141, 149

Picasso, Pablo, 163, 164, 165
place, holy, 105–6, 108, 111, 130, 133, 139,
    147, 162, 169
Plato, 6, 9, 13, 15, 16, 25, 76, 136, 141
poesy, 17, 61
poet, 78, 82, 89, 91, 94, 98, 100, 105, 112,
    146, 164
    modern, 89–94
    of the poet(s), 79, 81, 94
    thinker, 78, 153
poeticizing, 78–9, 125
poetry (*Dichtung*), 17, 32, 34–5, 53, 61,
    71–3, 75–6, 79, 94, 103, 120, 126, 135,
    146, 169, 170
    epic, 100, 128
    Greek, 75
    lyric, 100, 128
Pöggeler, Otto, 64, 158
polemos, 26–7, 63–4
politics, 76, 92, 93
position, 26, 27, 28
positivism, 13, 14
postmodern epoch, 98, 115, 173
power, 26, 46, 51, 75, 95, 97, 110
presence, 3, 75, 90, 99, 105–7, 110, 112, 117,
    133, 142, 153–5, 157, 162, 164, 168, 169
present, 74, 94, 100–1
preservation, 51, 57–9, 64, 66, 91, 129
primal conflict (*Urstreit*), 61–4
projection, 33, 35, 48, 157
Prometheanism, 29–31, 32, 34, 36, 53, 58

radiance, 41, 45, 106, 123, 164
Raphael (Raffaello Sanzio), 20, 62
realism, 140, 149
reality, 36, 41, 43, 58, 123, 124, 140, 142,
    143, 154, 155, 157, 171
realization, 57, 153
reception, 50, 51, 52
religion, 7, 44, 60, 172
remembrance (*Andenken*), 74, 75, 77, 80, 83,
    85, 90, 92, 93
renaissance, 62, 82, 83, 92
representation (*Darstellung*), 10, 42, 138,
    140–2, 147, 149, 158, 159, 161, 167–9
resource, 54, 87, 88, 97, 123, 145, 166, 167
Rilke, Rainer Maria, 1, 2, 22, 32–3, 40, 42,
    45, 65, 69, 84, 112, 121, 127, 132, 142,
    143–7, 149–51, 159, 171

sacredness, 88, 90, 97
salience, 38, 42, 45, 47, 49, 52, 57, 88, 96
salvation/saving power, 111, 118, 124, 125,
    127, 128, 152

Schopenhauer, Arthur, 10, 11, 16, 44, 108–10, 119, 132, 141, 154, 169, 173
science, 7, 13, 14, 49, 56, 143
scientism, 13, 143
security, 129, 145, 146
Seinsphilosophie (philosophy of being), 3, 172
self-collection, 56, 76
self-conflict, 63, 64
self-disclosure, 44, 45, 108, 113, 115, 116, 130
self-secludingness, 47–9
semi-abstraction, 163, 167
sky, 72, 99, 100, 118, 129
Socrates, 13, 16
Sophocles, 2, 12, 22, 71, 77, 81
Spiegel, Der, 69, 72, 127, 165
state, 76, 82, 89, 93, 102
state-founder, 112, 153
Stravinsky, Igor, 1, 121, 169
stress, 10, 11, 12, 86
structure, 26, 29
sublime, the, 43, 108, 110, 111, 118, 123, 124, 130
supernatural, the, 134–40
suprasensuous *see* supernatural
symbol (*Sinnbild*), 134–41, 148

task, 75, 79, 80
    appointed (*Aufgegebene*), 53, 54
    of poetry, 71, 95, 98, 101
techne, 18, 52
technology, 120, 166
temple, Greek, 7, 18, 19, 29, 30, 31, 44, 47, 48, 51, 52, 56, 59, 61, 62, 65, 67, 91, 121
thankfulness *see* gratitude
thematizing, 33, 36, 133, 136, 139–40, 142, 149, 157, 161, 164
theology, 30, 138
    Greek, 30, 61
thinker/thinking, 25, 78, 79, 82, 89, 93, 102, 111, 112, 138, 140, 151, 158
thrownness, 32, 33, 131
tradition, 18, 19, 82
tragedy, Greek, 31, 35, 59, 60, 61, 65, 88
Trakl, Georg, 22, 104, 121, 142
transcendence, 125, 126, 127, 133
transparency, 45, 52
triviality, 12, 21, 67, 69, 122, 124
truth, 6, 7, 13, 14, 17, 20, 39, 41, 42, 44, 55, 61, 63, 64, 106, 118, 123, 124, 130, 132, 137, 139, 154, 158

as correspondence to facts, 22, 39, 41, 123–4
    disclosure, 7–9, 13, 18, 23, 39, 51, 62, 67, 108, 125, 127, 132, 154
    happening of, 16–17, 19, 38, 42, 44, 45, 49–51, 56, 64
    historical, 76
    inner, 81
    of beings, 22, 76
    projection of, 17
    poet's, 76
    theory of, 48, 61, 62, 64
turning, the, 118, 127, 128, 134

unconcealment, 41, 138
ungraspable, the, 41, 42, 49, 98, 116, 138, 158
unholy, the, 24, 27, 31, 60
unintelligibility, 4, 42–4, 49, 156
usefulness, 47, 86

validity, 2, 68, 122
values, 37, 48, 49, 53, 54, 125
    revaluation of, 113
Van Gogh, Vincent, 5, 22, 33, 47, 51, 65, 70, 121, 163
voice, 59, 80–1

Wagner, Richard, 60, 78, 168, 169
waiting, 112–13, 117
will, 10, 11, 26, 144
Wittgenstein, Ludwig, 35, 109
wonder, 86, 88, 107, 109, 110
words, 35, 100, 102–4
work, 11, 19–21, 58
work-world relationship, 34, 57
world, 21–4, 27, 29, 32–47, 50, 52, 57, 59, 61, 62, 65, 72, 86, 88, 97, 100, 106–9, 111, 113, 114, 116, 118, 123, 124, 129, 139, 148, 156–8, 161–3, 169, 170
    Greek, 30, 80
    happening of, 106, 157
    opening up of, 19, 29, 33, 38, 124
world-earth duality, 40, 62, 63
worlding, 161, 168
world-withdrawal, 19–21, 59
worship, 31–2, 38, 44, 52, 114

Zen Buddhism, 2, 21, 132, 157, 160, 171
Zenk, Martin, 170

Printed in Great Britain
by Amazon.co.uk, Ltd.,
Marston Gate.